AMERICAN POPULAR HISTORY AND CULTURE

edited by
JEROME NADELHAFT
UNIVERSITY OF MAINE

A Routledge Series

OTHER BOOKS IN THIS SERIES:

EARLY AMERICAN WOMEN DRAMATISTS
1775-1860
Zoe Detsi-Diamanti

THE LYRICS OF CIVILITY
Kenneth G. Bielen

WRITING THE PUBLIC IN CYBERSPACE
Redefining Inclusion on the Net
Ann Travers

HOLLYWOOD'S FRONTIER CAPTIVES
Cultural Anxiety and the Captivity Plot
in American Film
Barbara A. Mortimer

PUBLIC LIVES, PRIVATE VIRTUES
Images of American Revolutionary War
Heroes, 1782–1832
Christopher Harris

TALES OF LIBERATION, STRATEGIES OF
CONTAINMENT
Divorce and the Representation of
Womanhood in American Fiction,
1880–1920
Debra Ann MacComb

READING COMICS
Language, Culture, and the Concept of
the Superhero in Comic Books
Mila Bongco

THE CLUBWOMEN'S DAUGHTERS
Collectivist Impulses in Progressive-Era
Girls' Fiction
Gwen Athene Tarbox

THE FACTORY GIRL AND THE SEAMSTRESS
Imagining Gender and Class in
Nineteenth Century American Fiction
Amal Amireh

WRITING JAZZ
Race, Nationalism, and Modern
Culture in the 1920s
Nicholas M. Evans

AUTOMOBILITY
Social Changes in the American South,
1909–1939
Corey T. Lesseig

ACTORS AND ACTIVISTS
Politics, Performance, and Exchange
Among Social Worlds
David A. Schlossman

STUDIES IN THE LAND
The Northeast Corner
David C. Smith

FIRST DO NO HARM
Empathy and the Writing of Medical
Journal Articles
Mary E. Knatterud

PIETY AND POWER
Gender and Religious Culture in the
American Colonies, 1630-1700
Leslie Lindenauer

RACE-ING MASCULINITY
Identity in Contemporary U.S. Men's
Writing
John Christopher Cunningham

CRIME AND THE NATION
Prison Reform and Popular Fiction in
Philadelphia, 1786–1800
Peter Okun

FOOD IN FILM
A Culinary Performance of
Communication
Jane Ferry

DECONSTRUCTING POST-WWII NEW
YORK CITY
The Literature, Art, Jazz, and
Architecture of an Emerging Global
Capital
Robert Bennett

No Way of Knowing
Crime, Urban Legends,
and the Internet

Pamela Donovan

ROUTLEDGE
NEW YORK & LONDON

Published in 2004 by
Routledge
29 West 35th Street
New York, NY 10001

Published in Great Britain by
Routledge
11 New Fetter Lane
London EC4P 4EE

Routledge is an imprint of the Taylor & Francis Group.
Copyright © 2004 by Routledge.

10 9 8 7 6 5 4 3 2 1

Library of Congress Cataloging-in-Publication Data

Printed on acid-free, 250 year-life paper
Manufactured in the United States of America

Donovan, Pamela
No Way of Knowing: Crime, Urban Legends, and the Internet
   p.   cm. — (American popular history & culture)
Includes bibliographical references and index.
   ISBN 0-415-94787-1 (hardcover : alk. paper)
   1. Crime in popular culture—United States—Case studies. 2. Crime—United States—Folklore—Case Studies. 3. Crime—Electronic discussion groups—United States—Case studies. 4. Urban folkore—United States—Case Studies. 5. Fear of crime—United States—Case studies. I. Title. II. Series: American popular history and culture (Routledge (Firm)).
   HV6791.D64 2003
   364.1'0973—dc21

                                                              2003012738

Contents

Preface

Rumors seem like the sort of thing sociologists should have a lot to say about. This has unfortunately been far from the case. Psychology and social psychology have contributed most to the very limited social science canon on the subject; but, with the exception of a spate of research related to wartime rumor during World War II, the subject has continued to languish. Perhaps this is because there is no perfect method for studying rumor. One could stand around and wait for someone to pass one along, and write field notes about the interaction between the promulgator and his or her listeners. Or, as French polling agencies sometimes do, one might survey telephone respondents about their level of knowledge about particular rumors. Finally, there's the tried-and-true practice of pitching an existing rumor into a university class and seeing what the students make of it. Each of these approaches has its benefits and costs, as does the one that I developed that sought to take advantage of the Internet as a research tool.

I began this study in 1996, at a time when Internet usage began to grow exponentially. Despite the social changes wrought by the use of this new medium, social science also seemed to have very little to say about it. Only a few books and articles had been published at that time that reflected the understanding that cyberspace was an important place for social interaction. By and large, journalists did a much better job of observation and prediction of social changes related to new media than academicians did. I more or less developed my own methodology for investigating my slippery subject on the internet: modern rumors about crime or "crime legends." Few models for systematic qualitative research were available; the emergence of commercial search engines that accessed Usenet archives were a godsend. The Boolean search protocols attached to these engines enabled some level of rudimentary quantification and standardized selection of materials. Digital archiving enabled rumor research that was simply impossible on a wide scale before: watching the development and social interpretation of rumors unfold in more or less "real time" in the context of conversation.

I had been an early user of Usenet news groups, having had university access in the early 1990s. This time period converged with my interest in the contours of fear about crime, and the question that I began to ask myself was: why, in an age of instant and plentiful digital and media gratification, did the ancient genre of folklore and more specifically, rumor, continue to hold some "broader truth" and salience for many people? Furthermore, would the emergence of new media shape the crime legend, and if so, how?

What I unearthed in the process was something new: a picture of three distinct rumors as they developed over wide geographical areas, and as they were discussed in Internet news group encounters. Using the above methods and gathering information about each rumor fairly exhaustively, I then used the traditional approach of field note-taking and content analysis. Since I have a particular interest in how the use of information is socially and culturally shaped, the resulting study no doubt reflects this concern. I hope that in the process I have been able to provide some reasonable answers to the initial question: what do urban legends and rumors provide that mass media, on the one hand, and less formally narrative conversation, on the other, cannot?

Like other modern writers who examine rumor and legend, I have tended to examine fear-driven rumor in "normal" social contexts, rather than the "crisis-bound" contexts—such as war, captivity, and civil unrest—that inspired rumor scholarship in earlier decades. This has something to do with the timing of the study, from 1995 to 1999, a time of booming enthusiasm about on-line technology, coupled with declining crime rates and relatively low unemployment in the United States, and the expansion of media outlets.

What a difference a few years—or maybe just one horrible day—makes. Since the terrorist attacks of September 11, 2001 it seems, at least anecdotally, that many more people have thought about the role of rumors and urban legends in our daily lives. The United States now fluctuates between various versions of the "new normal" and periods of crisis (anthrax, orange alerts, wars in Afghanistan and Iraq, economic strain—just to name a few). Associated anxiety increases the need for rumors, and dependence on them, as tools of understanding and of social interaction, for better or worse. I believe that the need for a revived sociology of rumor has been vindicated now more than ever.

Rumors associated with 9/11, at least here in the United States, seem to share many continuities with some longstanding legends. In particular, what they share with legends about crime is the underlying idea that they carry information that may not be available elsewhere. Like crime legends, they cover different emotional and political terrain than both news coverage and official public discourse of the attacks have. It is in understanding this gap, and perhaps this synergy, between media forms, that I hope is most useful in this book.

Acknowledgments

I most of all wish to express gratitude to my dissertation committee members, Mark Fishman (the Chair), Rolf Meyersohn, Paul Attewell, Dean Savage, and Lynn Chancer, who each gave invaluable feedback and support. Mark helped to shepherd and encourage this project at a time when "new media" studies were unheard of, and the sociology of rumor was for most a distant fond memory. Through close attention to each stage of the research and writing process, Mark helped me finish a project that had few models to rely upon. Lynn, as both a mentor and a friend, spurred me to think about this project in a criminology context, and provided support and encouragement. Whatever weaknesses may remain are attributable to my exhaustion, not theirs.

I would like to gratefully acknowledge the support of the Robert Gilliece and Helena Rubenstein Fellowship Foundations at the City University of New York Graduate Center.

I also want to thank my family and friends, especially the unflagging confidence of Gregg Wirth, my husband, best critic, soon-to-be partner in the adventure of parenting, and confident knower of the important things.

CHAPTER ONE

Introduction

This project explores the contemporary social meanings and persistence of a word-of-mouth genre, which I term the "crime legend." Using a case study approach, I examine three crime legends with a considerable public debunking history: the market in snuff films, the theft of vital organs for black-market transplant, and the abduction of children from shopping mall and theme park restrooms. For each case study, I collected previous versions published in folklorists' accounts and current versions circulating in Internet news groups and via electronic mail networks such as "listservs."[1] I then examine discussions that have taken place in Internet news groups about these stories and interviewed twenty regular news group participants who had been party to these discussions. The purpose of the latter was to compare the symbolic themes apparent in the "folk texts" with the themes of discussion and debate which surrounded them. This inquiry revealed that styles of belief and disbelief are varied and mutually dependent; that is, that the resonance of each tale involves the consideration and rejection of skepticism. This inquiry also revealed that specific legends are deployed to adapt to increasingly generalized fear. By generalized fear, I mean that which exceed the bounds of specific fears for personal safety and results from a sense of "ontological insecurity" (Giddens, 1990). Following Giddens' formulation, this insecurity is intertwined with distrust stemming from an uncertain relationship between the individual and social protection or "guardianship" expected in the past from both formal state activities and informal routines which were seen to provide "safety in numbers." Crime legends, when they are understood as social practices as well as texts, tame, individualize, and normalize public safety threats.

Below, a brief analysis of another crime legend, "Lights Out" which describes a gang initiation ritual, is presented as a means to illustrate the nature of the problem of crime legends.

WHAT IS A CRIME LEGEND?

In the Autumn of 1993, terrifying tales of gang depredations began to circulate in earnest in the United States and Canada. Printed warnings appeared:

> This new initiation of murder is brought about by Gang members driving
> around at night with their lights off. When you flash your car lights to signal
> them that their car lights are out, the Gang Members take it literally as
> "LIGHTS OUT" so they follow you to your destination and kill you! That's
> their initiation. Two families have already fallen victim to this initiation
> ritual. Be aware and inform your family and friends. DO NOT FLASH
> YOUR CAR LIGHTS FOR ANYONE![2]

The main story had been circulating for several months before, but picked up
steam when it began to circulate via fax and electronic mail. (Mays, 1994)
Then, at the end of September, the initiation ritual took on a devious new
quality: gangs were actually preparing a week of random terror across the
nation in the service of gang initiation. The weekend of September 25–26,
1993 was to be "Lights Out" weekend. Was it the Black Gangster Disciple
Nation, as a teletype sent to the Chicago Police suggested? Or the Bloods, as
a xeroxed fax, appearing in the mailboxes of employees at the University of
California at Irvine warned, planning nationwide "Blood Initiation
Weekend?"(Mays, 1994)

Were the gangs planning other terrors as well? Schools in the Salt Lake
City area took precautions when rumors abounded about gangs sent to rape
cheerleaders as an initiation rite. Perhaps the real story was that sorority
members would be targeted, as tales circulating at the University of Oklahoma and University of Illinois suggested.

Or had the notorious reign of gang terror already taken place? Stuart D.,
a participant in the Internet news group *alt.folklore.urban* told the group
that he had received, via friends in the military, a badly photocopied flyer
claiming that the "Lights Out" killings had already taken place in several
cities, and that the flyer-maker's mother had witnessed such a ritual in July
1993 in Tulsa. Subsequently, he found no mention of this event among relatives and friends in Oklahoma, nor any media coverage there, when the
motorist behind her flashed his lights at another car and was shot to death
for the courtesy.[3] The common denominator in all of the disseminated warnings—those spread by word-of-mouth, those publicized through duplicated
leaflets, and those transmitted electronically—is that no evidence exists to
date that any of them described real threats or events, nor were they presented
as such in public forums such as law enforcement warnings or news media
accounts. Fictional police officers, security personnel, and news media references do often appear, however, in these photocopied and e-mail texts.

The same rumor, accompanied by similar, but not the same flyers appeared
weeks earlier in Queens and Long Island, New York. In the Fall of 1993, I
began to collect rumors, warnings, and stories about crime threats in North
America, and told my sociology class at Queens College about my interests.
The room of students argued excitedly over the veracity of the "Light Out"
tale. About one half of the students, who live in New York City's outer

boroughs and suburban Nassau County had heard some version of the warning and many believed it to be true. On December 7, 1993 someone at the Queens campus received a fax with such warnings. Photocopies of the warning went up on bulletin boards across the campus, including in the Sociology department. Purporting to rely on information from the Queens Borough commander of the NYPD, the "memo" whose subject was "Random Violence Directed Against Motorists" repeated the language of the Chicago warning nearly verbatim, including the explanation that flashing your headlights is interpreted by gang members "literally as 'lights out'." This version was modified somewhat from the September story—claiming just that gang members would "attempt to kill you" not that they had succeeded in murder yet. A student in the class found another flyer taped to her garage in New Hyde Park, with the original claim that two families had fallen victim to this rite. (See Queens bulletins in Appendix 1A.) In a small rural hospital in southern New Jersey, the weekly employees' bulletin carried the warning, with the disclaimer, "while we don't know if this rite is practiced in our area, it's better to be safe than sorry."

Woven into this imprecise chronology of the "Lights Out" story are, in fact, numerous unequivocal debunkings, from both major news sources and from law enforcement agencies. New York Newsday, published a short item on December 11, 1993 (p. 13) by William Murphy entitled "It's Lights Out for Hoax." Before, during, and after this article, the New York Police Department branch in Queens received more than 100 calls on the threat. The San Jose Mercury News, The Atlantic City Press and The Milwaukee Journal all ran hoax-debunking articles during the Fall of 1993. The rumor continued to gather steam, and to take on local details as it spread. In this case of a sensational tale of terror told as fact, the mass media was clearly not the principal culprit in spreading the story. Law enforcement agencies, whenever contacted by the public or news reporters, unequivocally debunked the story. In this and other similar "contemporary legends" the social impetus for the scare is extra-institutional: reliant upon anonymous tips, authorless texts, word-of-mouth, and ill-defined whisper campaigns about unspecified perpetrators and victims.

"Lights Out" is an example of what I have called a "crime legend": a subcategory of what have come to be known as "urban legends" in the terminology of contemporary folklorist J.H. Brunvand. (1981) These are apocryphal tales, more exactly about modernity than about urbanism alone. Because they are largely "false" in an empirical sense, lacking documentation, evidence, and direct testimony, they resemble myth or folklore. Yet because they make claims to be news, are contemporary, and generally do not involve supernatural themes or heroic historical figures, they operate somewhat distinctively. The term "legend" is conventional in folklore studies for this type of tale. Bennett and Smith (1994) summarize conventional genre distinctions in the following way:

a myth is defined in folkloristic parlance, not as a synonym for error or fallacy, but rather as a sacred narrative explaining how the world and mankind came to be.... Folktales are fictional narratives, their fictional nature often signaled by an introductory formulas such as 'once upon a time.'.... The third category, legend, consists of narratives believed and/or told as true set in the post-creation time period.

In the current study I have been interested primarily in the content of contemporary crime legends in the United States, rather than the formal aspects of transmission, as emphasized in early 20th-century rumor studies. There were two main areas of investigation. First, in a world where information about true crime is available twenty-four hours a day from a variety of sources, what specific function does the crime legend play in public consciousness about crime? Second, how do tellers, hearers, believers, and debunkers of crime legends engaged in exchanges over the "truth status" of a legend, and of related propositions, justify their arguments by making general and often competing claims about the social world, and about the "reality" of social problems in particular? How do believers and debunkers of a given tale (and those in between) relate the story and its travels by unofficial routes to their own ideas about danger in the world?

I concur with Brunvand, and most other researchers of rumor, that what makes a crime legend a crime legend is not so much its falsehood as its extra-institutional, word-of-mouth quality. Technically, then, a story based on true events which is nonetheless passed along informally may qualify as a crime legend. However, it is unlikely that a serious crime that many people have heard about would go uninvestigated and unreported. Such real events are mainly passed along through "formal" routes: news reports, police and hospital reports, although they may also be transmitted informally and transformed through this process.

On the surface, such tale-telling simply expresses commiseration over a world grown chaotic and confusing and testifies to the breadth and depth of fear about crime in society. It also acts as a catharsis for fears, and perhaps from a psychoanalytic perspective, aggressive impulses and wishes as well, while deploying an authorless text to do so in a familiar narrative form. There is also a notable thematic distinction, however, between the results of surveys about the fear of crime and the themes in crime legends, suggesting that the latter address a different dimension of fear. Survey respondents say that what they fear most is random violence from a stranger such as murder, mugging, rape, and assault. (Bureau of Justice Statistics, 1988; Hale 1998) Actual crimes of this sort, however, often lack themes and motifs appropriate to a crime legend: someone shoots a tourist, a man with a knife demands money, the perpetrator escapes or is caught—a story, but no legend. This is the "ordinary brutality" that captures headlines. The crime legend, on the other hand, often comes with elaborate plot construction. As in the "Lights

Out" legend, the crime is ritualized, conspiratorial, involves confidence and deception, and a quasi-omnipotence for the perpetrators.

Additionally, the crime in the crime legend conspicuously consigns law enforcement to a marginal role—at best, they appear as ersatz authorities on "warnings" as in the "Lights Out" legend. In many other legends they are absent altogether. Often in these stories, as we shall see well illustrated by the case studies, the outside social world recedes: no witnesses, no police, just a binary world of powerful, calculating perpetrators and would-be victims, thrown upon their own devices to protect themselves and their loved ones from harm. Legends also involve passing arcane safety information (don't flash your headlights) along personalized communication networks and through untraceable public notices. Here, again, the contrast with surveys of the fear of crime appears. In those surveys crime avoidance involves generalized knowledge and practices: avoiding high crime areas, not traveling at night, adding locks, and so forth. In the case of "Lights Out" the hapless victim is the one who is singled out for playing Good Samaritan and engaging in what would normally be regarded as a safety-promoting behavior. In other words, the advice is valuable because it is counterintuitive. These apocryphal crime legends are in some sense, collective representations of fear of an objective threat (crime) but depart from other "media" such as news reports and television crime drama, in thematic emphasis and symbolic resonance. Thus, one cannot regard crime legends as "mere reflections" of a serious social problem. (Hilgartner and Bosk, 1988) They instead lead us to tacit, perhaps less commonly expressed or conventionally framed, ideas about the dangers of crime. Thus, Best (1990: 147) aptly refers to such legends as "unconstructed social problems."

Basic Research Questions of the Project

Three main research questions have guided the study. First, how and why do crime legends persist as a mainly extra-institutional form in a mass-media saturated world? The persistence of folklore and rumor runs contrary to the predictions of many social scientists and folklorists at the onset of the television age. Here the work of Shibutani (1966), who understands the role of rumor as a collective transaction and a problem-solving activity in ambiguous situations, is key. The fact that the current study concerns, by contrast to Shibutani's study, a non-crisis situation, and therefore reflects everyday concerns, complicates the role of problem-solving and the nature of contemporary ambiguity in interesting ways. This complication will be taken up in the concluding chapters.

Second, how does the crime legend compare with more organized and institutionalized "claims-making" and information about crime?[4] Crime legends are authorless and varied in their interpretive frameworks. Formal claims-making instead relies (when successful) upon the standardization of interpretive frameworks rather than their multiplicity, as well as strong or fervent forms of belief. By contrast, the crime legend holds an appeal to hearers and retellers on a different basis: unstable and inconsistent interpretive frameworks are tolerated and perhaps even desired, and conditional and instrumental forms of belief are dominant rather than fervent. By this I mean that when believers engage in discussions about the truth status of the story, promoting the story as true, they often do so in ways that stray from the presentation of empirical evidence or even mere personal trust of a previous source for the information. Instead, they describe how they believe in the stories because they are a useful part of their understanding of how the world works. The stories could be true, so they are true, or, they "realistically" describe the kind of world in which we live, therefore they are true. Finally, since belief in the crime legend is often conditional or instrumental, how is the "truth status" of the legend negotiated when people discuss the legend? Here the roles of debunkers, issue-specific skeptics, and the unknown are key. In news group settings, in contemporary e-texts containing these crime legends, and in fictional film and television depictions of the crimes described in these legends, skepticism, the overcoming of skepticism, and "not knowing" certain things about the social world are central objects around which meaning is constructed.

DATA AND METHODS

Sources of Data

The study involves the analysis of primary sources: crime legends and discussions of them gathered from public Internet news group discussions in the years 1995 to 1999 inclusive, and twenty semi-structured electronic-mail interviews with regular news group users whose participation was solicited on the basis of their past involvement in these specific discussions. Keyword and related Boolean search technology enabled a search of over 40,000 news groups at once. Thus, discussions relevant to each of the case studies were found both within and outside *alt.folklore.urban.* Other news groups identified included ones devoted to parenting, feminism, and movies. Originally I identified 90 participants who had contributed substantially to discussion of these stories from a variety of news groups. Having solicited interviews with them, 23 agreed and ultimately 20 interviews were completed. News reports about these legends, fictional film and television depictions of the crimes in these legends were also sought out. Secondary analysis of both scholarly and popular literature on contemporary folklore was also done in the respective case study chapters. Multiple sources of data were sought in order to address the elusive and hard-to-document nature of rumors and urban legends, particularly those whose spread is national or international, in contrast to those which are local, subgroup-, or subculture-specific.

I chose these three crime legends because in my estimation, based on following *alt.folklore.urban* since the early 1990s, they are the most recur-

rent and consistently receive the most attention from news group participants. Each tale has had enough staying power in the last decade to have
generated an entry in the selective archive of the news group
alt.folklore.urban. This archive was built and is maintained by active group
members; urban folklore topics with a high volume of discussion within the
group are selected for an entry.[5] Each also has a considerable history of being
debunked in public settings such as newspapers. Like the "Lights Out"
legend, there was little evidence that media outlets had disseminated them
credulously. There is currently no more accurate nor practical way to reflect
with any precision the overall incidence of various legends circulating, a
point which will be addressed in more detail below. Each of the tales I chose
is different enough from the others to avoid repetitive commentary from
participants. Yet they all concern violent rather than property or statutory
crimes, so as to keep separate the issue of fear for one's physical safety from
fear regarding the loss of personal property, which research into the fear of
crime suggests are quite distinct in their effects and cognitive associations. I
chose to focus upon fear of violent crime rather than that of property crime
due to the difference in their perceived seriousness that previous research
into the fear of crime has noted consistently (Hale, 1998). Thereby the issues
of anger and resentment, on the one hand, and mortal fear, on the other,
could be more easily distinguished.

The groups of informants, as well as the conversations about these legends
in news group settings, reflect the different intensities of belief among individuals. Those who participated in past discussions about these case study
legends in various news groups received a query from me. Also, I solicited
their feelings about news group participation and specific discussions of these
legends or "stories." The neutral language of "story" was used to encourage
the response of believers in various legends; they would not, of course, think
of them as "legends" in the way that debunkers do.

The informants were asked standard demographic questions, with the
purpose of ensuring that they did not deviate as a whole, in this respect,
from the typical Internet user at the time, who was college educated and had
a "white-collar" or professional occupation (Brightman 1995; Dibbell 1995;
Edmondson 1997; Cyberatlas, 1999)[6] Hereafter these informants will be
described as "middle class" based on their parents' levels of educational
achievement and occupations. Although a standard schedule of questions
was used initially (see Appendix 2), follow-up interview components were
more open-ended. The unit of analysis is the tale, however, not individuals.
The interviews provided contrasts, further elaborations, and patterns which
will in sum describe a part of the meaning-formation process.

There were several advantages to using the Internet news group as a
primary site of study of the social life of these legends. First, conversations
about the meaning and truth-status of these legends could be observed and
documented unobtrusively. A corollary to this benefit is that skeptics and
believers, and those in between, are spontaneously self-defined. In the past,

research on urban legends could only be conducted by a researcher introducing the topic herself. It was difficult to do this without planting the seed of skepticism, or without the researcher provoking uncertainty and perhaps fear. (Ethical concerns about this last matter are discussed below.) University classes or other assembled groups would be asked, "did you hear the one about ... " in order to generate data. The need to generate data through provocation was a practical necessity, however. It would have been impractical for a researcher interested specifically in rumors or legends to wait around and hope that one was told spontaneously. After all, no discrete group of urban legend tellers exists such that a researcher could "sample" them. This dispersion of tellers is complicated even further by the cyclical quality of urban legend dissemination. Thus I felt that what I had given away in "representativeness" of middle-class mores and concerns by limiting myself to news group manifestations was more than made up for by the opportunity to search for, and find, archived conversations about these tales that had taken place outside my presence.[7]

Yet this approach also has its limitations. The main drawback to researching the legends among Internet users of this time (the years 1995 to 1999) was that they are relatively early users of the Internet. The demographic composition of Internet users has been tilted toward the more privileged segments of society. In 1995, 24 million people in the United States used the Internet; one-fourth of them made more than $80,000 per year and 64 percent had a college degree. By contrast, in the general population, only 10 percent had an income above $80,000 and only 28 percent a college degree (Nielsen Media Research, reported in Miller, 1995). According to a 1999 survey, Internet use was moving towards gender balance (dominated slightly by men, but projected to be evenly divided by 2001). More than half of those planning to use the Internet for the first time between 1999 and 2001 have incomes of less than $50,000. (Pew Research Center, reported in Cyberatlas, 1999a; 1999b)

Although news groups specifically existed before the World Wide Web did, early users of them tended to be drawn from universities and computer companies exclusively. As Internet users diversify, news group users are drawn from all backgrounds, but are still more privileged than the general population.[8] The ways in which the demographic profile of news group users differs from that of the Internet user in general is still unclear. Thus overall it is important to keep logically distinct the norms and values of news group users as reflected in this study and that of the white middle and upper-middle class generally.

Mass media accounts on television, in print, and on film, of crime legends in general and the case studies chosen here in particular, were also sought out. Both news and fiction references were found. In the case of news accounts of the legends, I used keyword searches to find references in the *Reader's Guide to Periodical Literature* for magazines and *Lexis-Nexis Academic Universe* for broadcast and newspaper references.[9] In the case of fictional treatments on television and film, the search was more informal; I relied both upon tips from participants in *alt.folklore.urban* and friends to find fictional references. In studying the film and television materials, I found that crime legends are woven into a specific dramatic narrative arc that is distinctive from references to crime legends in informal settings.

In the case of the news media, I found not a single instance of "credulous" crime legend telling; that is, every reference to these case studies was either a clear attempt to debunk the legend or a metaphorical use of terms, for example, calling video footage of an accident at a speedway a "snuff film" or disputes over organ donation contract terms as "stolen kidneys." Thus, the news media do not appear to be a significant source of intentional dissemination.[10] This is significant because it suggests that crime legends remain a largely word-of-mouth, and now e-mail based form which travels mainly through informal, personal networks of dissemination.

The goal in developing this multi-source, multi-method approach was to seek out all available data in each of the above outlined categories about each of the case study legends.

PERSPECTIVES GUIDING THE STUDY

Several prior theoretical commitments informed my choice of data and methods. Some of these were, in turn, generated by my previous participation in *alt.folklore.urban*, mostly as a "lurker" (observer) but occasionally as a contributor. The first commitment was the distinction between an urban legend folk text qua text, either in written or verbal-raconteur form, on the one hand, and the talk about the text which the telling of the tale generated, on the other. It is the former which gets the most attention and is most often the object of analysis in both folklore and the social sciences.

Folklorist Linda Dégh (1971) has proposed instead that folklore can be seen as part of a "public conversation" in which the tale in its various incarnations, the tellers, the believers and the skeptics, as well as institutional actors such as those in government, media, and civic organizations are all contributors. The idea that the meaning and truth status of a rumor or legend could be understood as a "collective transaction" which is constantly negotiated both broadly and in discrete social settings is also raised by Shibutani (1966). This basic perspective underlies the choices, and very likely, the analyses of the material contained in this project.

For instance, few who are interested in contemporary legends have included the activities of debunkers as an object of inquiry, nor have they fully considered debunkers as contributors to the overall meaning-producing process. In the main, researchers tend to play the part of debunkers themselves. For the case studies I have chosen, the debunking has adequately been done by others. My purpose here is to look at both belief and skepticism as forms of relationship to new information and, at least as far as Internet news group settings, and television and film depictions go, these forms of relationship to information are often players on the same terrain and mutually dependent in order to generate interpretive frameworks for all assembled.

I also see crime legends as occupying a unique niche as expressions of distrust, anger, fear, and resentment about crime. The assumption has been made from the inception of the project that contemporary folklore remains a vital, extra-institutional force because it fulfills a set of needs not fulfilled by institutional responses to crime. What are those needs?

Finally, this project is not a search for the specific origins of each crime legend. Most folklorists and social scientists who have studied contemporary folklore agree that most contemporary rumors and legends have vague, piecemeal origins. Since "originators," if there are any, and embellishers are invisible to researchers, we cannot know their true motivations. While it is possible that intentional hoaxing explains such behavior, it is the uniform suspicion of most researchers that these tales are spread, and embellished, credulously rather than maliciously or in bad faith (Best & Horiuchi 1985; Fine 1983; Koenig 1986; Brunvand; 1984). To use a psychoanalytic metaphor, these human vectors might be unconsciously disseminating untruths rather than consciously lying.

This bears reiterating here for several reasons. First, it is part of what informs my overall perspective which tends to emphasize the collective nature of the problem; that is, the "demand" for the material contained in the legend rather than the supplier. Second, the desire for someone to "blame" for rumormongering, evidenced in the mid-1960s (Pilat, 1965; Ridley 1967) by the desire to find individuals responsible for rumors implicated in racial strife, remains strong today as we shall see in the chapter on stolen body parts. Such origins are still elusive. Finally, the vagueness of the origins of most urban legends refocuses our attention, admittedly out of necessity, to the often conditional, partial, and instrumental nature of belief in them.

The analytical approach herein is distinct from that of the traditional folklorist, who is generally focused upon comparative analysis, either historical or cross-cultural. The problem of origins tends to be addressed by the search for narratives and motifs with characteristics similar to that of the story under scrutiny. Ben-Amos (1976: i-xlv) suggests that this approach is a corollary outcome of that discipline's focus upon genre, where an ideal-type text, developed from previous research, is compared with specific variations in time and place. The emphasis of a folkloric approach, then, to a story about abducted children would no doubt look to a well established "permanent form" such as changeling stories—which could be considered a universal classification in the sense that all cultures use folklore to manage parental fears of losing their children. A recent critique of this orientation from within folklore studies is discussed below in the section on the history of rumor research, but here my main task here is to reiterate the current study's interpretive-sociological emphasis. This study attempts to develop an analysis of the crime legend genre within two perhaps narrower and more local concerns, and also in contrast, does not make an assumption of genre permanence.[11] These are: first, how do cultural forces shape the way in which we believe or disbelieve things in the post-industrial West, with empirical concentration upon how news group users in Anglophone countries are influenced by these forces; and second, in what ways and to what extent do crime legends reflect and reshape fears associated with violent crime, socially structured vulnerability and feelings of being endangered, and the politics and ideology of crime control in the last thirty years?

Ethical Concerns

Mostly unobtrusive techniques were chosen for this study, not only to preserve the practice of legend telling and hearing in its original form, but also to avoid some ethical hazards raised in the past about rumor research. The concern is that introducing material which might cause needless fear or anger in people who have not heard such material before constitutes a form of social harm. For instance, Kapferer (1989: 476) and colleagues distributed 500 previously collected leaflets in Rennes that warned, often erroneously, of the danger to health posed by common food additives and certain brands of food. They then followed up with interviews to measure the prevalence of belief. While the researchers did not invent the flyer and knew it to be a widely-circulating item even without their intervention (49 percent of primary school teachers and 39 percent of physicians had either heard about or seen the leaflet before the Rennes experiment), they nonetheless likely disseminated it to people who had not seen it before (Kapferer 1989: 473). Smith (1990) and Koenig (1992) objected to this practice on ethical grounds in that even if all respondents in the Rennes experiment were debriefed as to the erroneous quality of much of the information on the leaflet (and only about 150 were), anxiety was nonetheless temporarily induced and informal secondary dissemination outside the initial target response group almost certainly had taken place (Smith 1990). The same concern could be raised about introducing fearful stories in a social setting to elicit responses. A sole qualitative researcher may also not be able to successfully debrief respondents in the way that Kapferer's researchers did, as the latter had behind them the institutional authority of a public opinion research institute. Using the methods that I did, the problem of fear-induction on my part was not an issue.

Thus the rise of Internet technology has aided not only the preservation of conversations around these crime legends, it has lessened the ethical hazards around rumor research in general, except perhaps in cases where the researcher is primarily concerned about measuring the prevalence of rumor penetration, or is doing rumor research in specific groups with low Internet usage or access. In these latter cases, the ethical dilemma necessarily persists.

LITERATURE REVIEW

The development of this study stemmed in part from the paucity of contemporary sociological research on modern folklore. Knopf (1975: 11) suggests that the difficulty in documenting rumor and related genres has likely discouraged social science research. The social science study of the urban legend seems larger than it really is, since the topic's quirkiness and perpetually timely quality attracts news reporters eager to understand why rumor, legend, and hoax cycles occur again and again after they have been debunked.[12] In other words, urban legends are an area that the outside world expects social scientists to know a great deal about. The few who do are sought out for brief quotes on social strain, fear, distrust, and gullibility—but in actuality, much more debunking than analysis takes place in legend scholarship. This tendency likely comes from several practical concerns. The first is a sense of social responsibility—the desire to set the record straight, and in the case of those legends which promote fear, to relieve some of that unfounded fear. Second, the universe of urban legends does not lend itself to sample description in any cogent manner. In a related matter, because such legends circulate through largely undocumented channels—widely, cyclically, and anonymously—their meaning cannot be easily linked to specific local strains and anxieties, nor can it be said that discrete groups develop and promulgate legends independently. Thus, sadly the matter, for want of a perfect method, languishes. Still, the study of rumor, legend, and related word-of-mouth genres has, in the past, yielded a number of key insights into how people believe them.

Rumor Research in the Twentieth Century

During the first half of the century, rumor research was dominated by the field of psychology. Many studies were concerned with proving that rumor acted as the children's game "Whisper Down the Lane" or the parlor game "Telephone" has always averred: that the process was largely linear and that distortion of originally truthful material was inevitable as it was passed along word-of-mouth lines. Small amounts of erosion occurred, it was suggested, as the information bit moved along the chain of communication, creating a cumulative effect of falsity. (Hösch-Ernst 1915; Gorphe 1927) However, the problem with such studies was not so much in their method or quality of observation, but conceptually in what the experiments showed. Did a bit of information "whispered down a lane" really stand in well for a rumor in a natural setting? What about rumors that would eventually be verified as fact—how was the correct information preserved so well in those cases if distortion was inevitable? Here, the focus upon falsity of information was misleading. Shibutani (1966: 7–10) further observes of this early transmission-distortion research that it assumes that an objective communication standard exists somewhere, which rumor or word-of-mouth transmission fails to achieve. Further, he notes, the emphasis upon psychological analysis of rumor tends to individualize the interpretation of it. Researchers, up through the mid-20th century, sought to link transformation of rumor material to demographic and cognitive characteristics of individuals, which provided perhaps interesting information about those persons or groups, but did little to explain why rumor so frequently disobeyed these boundaries to produce a "public" informal medium. In other words, the collective nature of rumor was obscured.

By mid-century, though, greater attention was paid to regularities in the distortion of information in word-of-mouth settings. The desire to control rumors in North America during World War II resulted in a spate of rumor clinics and hence systematic research. Allport and Lepkin's study (1945: 14) of rumors alleging waste and special privilege concludes that, compared with the actual hardship imposed by rationing, the lack of access to accurate information was much more direct a cause. "The more information he has, and the more carefully he thinks, the less chance that he will be led into believing by his inner, and often unrecognized, impulses." Opinion leaders in government, media, and civic organizations identified rumor as a possible source of morale erosion or even subversion. (Rosnow, 1976: 26–27) Knapp (1944) categorized the themes of different sorts of wartime rumors: there were "pipe dreams," "bogies," and "wedge drivers." Pipe dreams are wishes stated as fact. Bogies predict impending doom. Wedge drivers target certain social groups, typically alleging that they are "getting away with something." The latter, in Knapp's estimation were by far the most common, suggesting that rumor was able to speak to hostile and divisive impulses which could not be easily articulated in other ways, perhaps for fear of approbation.[13] Allport and Postman (1947) identified three characteristics of rumor as it passed along informal routes of communication. First, information was "leveled." The tendency was for accounts to be shorter, more concise, and simpler. Second, certain retained details were "sharpened." Choice of retained details was likely to be selective. Finally, rumor material was "assimilated," or adapted to pre-existing cognitive frameworks which were consistent with the presuppositions and interests of individual study participants. Peterson and Gist (1951), by contrast, found a great deal of "snowballing" or creative elaboration, rather than leveling or sharpening, in the circulation of rumors.

Shibutani (1966: 56 -58, 62) employed Allport and Postman's basic principles in his case study investigation of rumor among Japanese-Americans in internment camps in California during the war, but regarded the rumor process as a normal rather than pathological aspect of social life. It was understood a problem-solving activity by groups of people who are deprived of adequate information; thus, they produce "improvised news" through a "collective transaction." The process was collaborative and in some ways functional. What differed among scholars of this era was really how much this behavior could be controlled and whether it was really desirable to do so. (Klapp 1972: 252–253)

Allport and Postman also offered a basic formula for the formation of rumor which became widely accepted in rumor studies: that both the importance of the issue and an absence or ambiguity of information must be present for a rumor to take hold. That is:

Rumor = importance X ambiguity

To this basic formula, Chorus (1953) added:

Rumor = importance X ambiguity X 1/C

where C is a critical or skeptical sensibility. In other words, the specific absence of a critical mindset must also be in place for a rumor to thrive. Caplow (1947) had previously offered one qualification, however. Critical sensibility did not necessarily stop a rumor; rather the rumor was more likely to be more accurate as it passed through skeptical ears and was subject to sharpening stemming from verification, rather than along subjective lines. Buckner's (1965) review of rumor transmission literature leads the author to conclude that sharpening and elaboration are likely to be examples of different outcomes stemming from different contexts of transmission. At the same time, Rosnow's (1976: 51) review of rumor studies suggests that at least with regard to experimental method studies, Allport and Postman's focus upon the role of ambiguity in the formula has been largely supported, while the need for "importance" has been less strongly demonstrated. It may be that ambiguity was regarded as less subjective than importance and thus more easily established empirically. Details are lost inconsistently in experimental settings, most likely because the "importance" of the information is to some degree established by the experimental situation rather than naturally, according to the participants' own cognitive filtering.

However, Rosnow also questions the previous operationalization of the concept of ambiguity as one where mass media or other "official institution" reports are absent. Instead, the plentiful nature of news by the 1970s also meant that multiple perspectives had emerged about important events such as the Vietnam War, racial and gender relations, and economic crisis. "In a society with a free and divided press, different sources may contradict one another—which must inevitably add to the confusion and increase feelings of anxiety and fear." (1976: 116)

Knopf (1975) also observed certain regularities in crisis-related rumor, but rather than focusing upon ambiguity or immediate events as an explanatory etiology, Knopf focused upon the "total existential context" of racial conflict and urban riots and associated rumors from 1967 to 1969.

> [R]umor closes the gap between a hostile belief and its embodiment as 'fact'.... Thus, rumors are not only a refinement and crystallization of

hostile beliefs, but a realization of them—a confirmation by 'reality'—reality
as perceived by the group of people involved. (p.159)

Like earlier research on the subject, Knopf's work suggests that rumor
has built a niche as a symbolically condensing practice. Yet unlike previous
research, Knopf tempers the importance of ambiguity with the underlying
historical conflict which enables such constructions of reality. "Take away the
adversative aspects of an event and you take away much of its ambiguity."
(p. 163) Thus while the ongoing "collective transaction" may be built upon
ambiguity, this ambiguity in turn is inherently built upon existing conflict.

One of the persistent qualities that researchers of rumor have found is its
role in the reduction of anxiety through the reshaping of information into
acceptable forms. (Rosnow, 1976: 62) This quality in part explains why
word-of-mouth and informally circulated genres persist as sources of
meaning in a world which not only has high levels of information inputs but
also high diversity in the character of those inputs. Rumors and legends
remain as practices in which the teller and the hearer have some creative role
to play and direct; yet, as von Roretz (1915: 208) observed early in the line
of rumor research, the practitioners can at the same time avoid responsibility for what they are expressing by treating the information as factual
news.

In sum, sociological research into rumor and hoax between 1940 and
1975 focused heavily upon the role that such collective behavior plays in
times of crisis, whether due to natural disaster, war, or civil unrest. By the
mid-1970s, some basic assumptions about the nature of rumor were raised.
Some of this questioning came from the seemingly "atypical" character of
certain rumors of the late 1960s. However, a conceptual mismatch between
rumor theory and social conditions in the United States also provoked a reexamination of certain assumptions about rumor, such as in the work of
Rosnow and Fine (1976). These included the persistence of rumor outside
crisis situations and, as described above, a plethora of information inputs
that had to be waded through, sorted, and evaluated rather than a dearth of
information as the means to cause ambiguity. Shibutani's consensual or functional view of rumor was also questioned by Suczek (1972) and to some
extent Knopf as described above, but not widely elsewhere. Kapferer (1990:
103–4) also marks this period as one which moved from "rumor studies" to
"modern legend studies."

The years 1965 to 1975, roughly, saw a transitional phase in the concep-
tualization of the genre examined in this study. The years 1969 to 1970 in
particular were significant for three unrelated rumor cycles with three
different social effects of enduring interest in what is now termed contemporary legend study. In Orleans, France, rumors of young women
disappearing from dress boutiques provoked a crisis that just fell short of
violence directed at the town's mainly Jewish boutique owners. Morin (1970)

who investigated this incident using a community-study approach, describes it as an outburst of a medieval-type panic which was able to take hold due to the community's "civic immaturity." Thus we can regard this outcome of a rumor cycle as traditional or crowd-behavior related in the sense that it was directly implicated in an incipient panic and fed into it. It is also a conventional rumor in the sense that it is, in Knapp's words, a classic "wedge driver."

The second rumor cycle of interest here is the rumors that circulated around the real and widely publicized Tate-LaBianca murders in southern California. There was nothing atypical about the fact that the bizarre, ritualistic murders spawned a great deal of idle speculation. What was unusual that in the years to come, one particular allegation, that the Manson-family perpetrators had filmed their violence and that the tapes were being viewed for enjoyment among the Hollywood elite, apparently either led to or fueled what we now know as the "snuff film" legend. As we shall see in the case study chapter on that legend, filmmakers also became preoccupied with the idea of the snuff film. Here, we see a sharpening and leveling as in Allport and Postman's research, but on a collective rather than individual basis, and gradually so over time, supported by mass media amplification.

The third rumor cycle of those years with lasting impact upon the analysis of urban legends had not to do with crime at all, but with an alleged automobile accident. In the summer of 1969 a rumor began to circulate that Beatles member Paul McCartney had died in that accident in 1966 and was replaced secretly by a "look and sound alike" named William Campbell. Suczek (1972: 65) found that rather than conforming to Shibutani's collective problem solving model, the polarization between believers and skeptics was vivid, but non-engaged. "Rather than working dialectically to create explanations for new and ambiguous events … the publics in this instance seemed to withdrawal into fixed camps, facing each other as factional forces dedicated to the defense of separate positions." Suczek went on to note that debunking of the rumor had no discernable effect, perhaps, other than to fuel the part of the rumor which alleged a cover-up. Rather than information being absent, formal channels of communication were simply distrusted by "publics increasingly inclined to turn to folk communicational resources." (p. 69) In sum, idle antagonism characterized the rumor. It was disconnected not only from panic and information-seeking, but also from a sense that pooled resources could arrive at an acceptable truth about the matter.

Rosnow and Fine's (1976: 74—77) assessment of the McCartney rumor concurs with that of Suczek. They found no significant demographic or biographical differences between believers and skeptics. Rather they attribute the "idle" character of the rumor to an expanding market for contemporary folklore of this sort. Large numbers of people the right age to find the rumor "important" existed, due to the baby boom, in contrast perhaps to previous pop audiences. This interested public also had demonstrated skepticism about other "official stories" through popular protest. The McCartney rumor seemed to be a sort of new word-of-mouth form.

> It supposedly reported bad news, yet very little grief and fear was felt; no orientation toward action was associated with the report. It had the makings of a budding legend or literary invention, rather than the news item it supposedly was. (Rosnow and Fine: 19)

The second two legends characterize the typical behavior of such rumors now. Far from spawning collective panic, they are disseminated as "idle speculation" about the underworld, conspiracies, or individualized warnings. If Morin's Orleans episode was an example of the re-emergence of the pre-modern legend in a contemporary context, the latter two were in some ways the first post-modern ones. Neither leading to panic nor to truth-seeking or even information-enhancement, they became idle talk for individualized and heavily defended speculation.

A marked decline of interest in such research in the discipline of sociology is evident by the 1970s. The discipline of folklore in general became more oriented to the social life of contemporary legend at this time. Dundes (1980: viii) and others have argued that in the past folklorists were overly preoccupied with genre and structural relations between symbolic elements in folk texts, rather than social and cultural meaning, thus "treating 'lore' as though it were totally separate from 'folk.'" Dundes further suggests that folklore has a place in social science to be investigated as a vehicle "for the expression of what cannot be articulated in the more usual, direct way." Likewise Zipes' (1980) review of approaches to folklore concludes that even into the 1970s folklorists were reticent about connecting tales with developing social orders.

Criticizing a lack of disciplinary development in folklore studies, Dégh (1994: 1–11) cites mass communication, rapid technological shifts, population mobility, and cultural diversity and hybridization as the new context which contemporary folklore studies should regard as normal. She criticized certain earlier purely preservationist approaches which feared folklore would be supplanted by the onslaught of mass media as limited and static, suggesting instead that the folk speech and practice of the present is a part of the meaning of the folklore, and not a demeaning of it. [14] Contemporary folklorists like Campion-Vincent (1997) began to incorporate media images of folklore forms as well. Of course, the line at which a folk tale becomes predominately "mediated" rather than "passed along" informally will vary and sometimes be ambiguous.

It seems that where rumor left off, urban legends emerged as a category of analysis that has only recently attracted social scientists. Brunvand has collected urban legends for longer than twenty years and has published several books that catalog urban legends, with an emphasis on those circulating in the United States. The paradigm of "urban legend" or "contemporary legend" emerged with Brunvand's popularized works. He emphasized the recurrent nature of many such rumors and saw them as expressive reactions to the strictures of modernity.

Those who have taken an interest in urban legends debate the usefulness of the term. Some find Brunvand's terminology off-putting and confusing to the layperson, since not all, and in fact not even very many, contemporary tales of this sort take place solely in cities. Neither are they stories about cities per se, nor is the practice of urban legend sharing one that is limited to people in cities. Brunvand's intention was really to point to the stories' common themes as he saw them. Coursing through his collected tales of pets bursting in microwave ovens, celebrities rescued by hospital personnel from their bizarre sexual excesses, castration tales, and food contamination stories was Brunvand's observed unitary theme: these stories reflected anxiety about our transition to a fully modern life—urban in the sense of urbanized and urbane. In this theme Brunvand sees a kind of wistful regret about the loss of *gemeinschaft* charm and social familiarity that characterized much of the Western world up through even up through the 1920s. It is not necessary for people now to have actually lived more peaceful, simple, and solidaristic lives in the past, it is only necessary that they remember or imagine it that way for a whole repertoire of urban legends to emerge and evolve.

Popular urban legend books often offer up "sociological teasers" or brief suggestions to the reader that allude to the tales' latent expression of collective social anxiety. However, the few works by sociologists written for scholarly rather than popular audiences are often equally restrained analytically, attributing the diffusion and persistence of such stories to "social strain" and increased transience and anonymity. Nonetheless, the legend concept, taken up by the social sciences, has added a new sensibility to the study of rumor. It is now seen less an appendage to ephemeral crisis conditions than as a symptom, I think accurately, or collective expression, of more enduring social anxieties.

Contemporary Social Science and the Urban Legend

When those few sociologists who do study urban legends embark on specific investigations they usually select case studies by choosing a theme in advance related to the author's broader interests. This is a practical decision based upon the fact that hundreds if not thousands of legends circulate in the United States alone at any given time, judging from the archives of *alt.folk-lore.urban*, the books of Jan Harold Brunvand, and various web pages devoted to the topic.[15] Those works which mark recent social science approaches to urban legends are considered below; those that concern the snuff film, stolen body parts, and mall abduction legends will be considered in the respective case study chapters.

In English language literature the term "urban legend" or "contemporary legend" appears to have supplanted that of "rumor" to describe tales like those of the present study. This reflects the popularization of the term by Brunvand and other debunkers, as well as a paradigm shift in framing the urban legend as a genre.[16] Urban legends were previously confounded with rumors in research on the topic before the "breakout" of urban legend genre with the publication of Brunvand's first popular book, *The Vanishing Hitchhiker* (1980).

Best and Horiuchi (1985) studied legends about tainted Halloween treats because they were interested in the growth in public claims-making about threats to children and their social construction. Subsequently in a cumulative volume Best (1990) argues that urban legends concerning harm to children are a part of an intensified public focus upon threats to children beginning in the late 1970s. Although legends circulate outside official channels, the culture's larger preoccupation with "missing and exploited children" fueled by specific claims-making activities of social reform organizations and reported upon often unskeptically by the news media, created an atmosphere in which such legends flourished. Best describes child-threat legends as "unsuccessful" claims-making activities which spread "largely outside institutional channels." (Best 1990: 147) The author also describes Halloween sadism as a persistent legend which enabled parents to take individualized action (candy inspection) rather than act collectively for social reform as other more well-organized (for example, Mothers Against Drunk Drivers) claims-making activities would require.

Turner (1993) studied legends that circulate primarily among African-Americans about white enmity toward blacks, specifically against the black body. She argues that there is a congruity between some of these factually false legends and some more realistic concerns of African-Americans based on the historical record of white behavior toward blacks, as well as on present-day ambivalence about black consumption patterns. The rumor that an off-brand beverage popular in minority areas of cities causes sterility in black men, and others which allege Ku Klux Klan ownership of certain popular brands of fast-food fried chicken and expensive sneakers, employ condensing symbols of more long-standing alienation. The rumors also serve as a kind of incipient rejection of economic patterns that are perceived by more politicized members of the community as destructive, expensive, and dependent upon white-owned, non-local corporate chains. (Turner 1993: 174–179)

Fine (1992) chose several legends which seemed to capture American cultural ambivalence about sex and money. Along similar lines of cultural ambivalence about consumption, but perhaps broadly exercised in rumor among whites as well, Fine looks at these legends as an expression of alienation with both dissenting and conservative features. Licentiousness and consumer pleasure is at once enjoyed and guiltily repudiated. Another fast-food legend, "The Kentucky Fried Rat" is a cluster of stories about accidentally fried rodents ending up in buckets of take-out chicken. The legend simultaneously expresses distrust of corporations and discomfort with changing mores.

> The increased emphasis in American life on leisure and the changing roles of women make the fast food restaurant possible, and possibly necessary. Yet, these changes in value orientation did not occur without psychological effects, as individuals in transition have not completely reconciled themselves to the structural changes these new values imply. (Fine 1992: 133)

Such legends about corporations can affect their economic performance. Koenig (1985) is specifically concerned with the application of rumor studies to the combat of corporate-related rumors. Like Turner and Fine, and in continuity with the earlier rumor studies' emphasis upon importance, Koenig's study shows that "a primary requirement for rumor survival is that the message be relevant to the people involved." (Koenig 1985: 20) While this may be easy to discern in the case of allegations by Christian groups that certain corporations are run by avowed Satanists, relevance is not always so easily apparent. Hence the technique used by one accused corporation, the solicitation of "celebrity Christians" to denounce the rumor on its behalf, is not always available. Permanent financial damage is the norm regardless of efforts toward denial for two reasons. First, such rumors may resurface even after having been thoroughly debunked. Second, the consumer behavior of weak believers or even nonbelievers can nonetheless be affected. "Just the thought in the back of one's mind of worms in hamburgers was enough to steer one to a pizza parlor." (Koenig 1985: 15)

Kapferer's work (1990) is more wide-ranging; he seeks to understand the persistence of contemporary rumors of all sorts in France and elsewhere. He includes a number of different sorts of unofficial stories such as rumor panics, urban legends, and conspiracy theories. His work is most useful for general observations on rumor, which emphasizes its contrast with conscious social reality rather than their continuities. He argues that contrary to the linear "transmission-distortive" model of rumor, where an initial grain of truth is distorted as it is passed along, or where a structural reality is condensed into a simplistic narrative, rumors actually develop along separate lines from official reality to create a fairly autonomous popular reality which is often consciously antagonistic to that reality. (Kapferer 1990: 4, 263) Under the category "rumor," he includes some accounts of things which are based in fact, with the goal of showing that rumor does not cease to be rumor even if "facts" are eventually given an institutional imprimatur, or are shown to be "true." In a similar fashion to Brunvand, Kapferer defines rumor not by its falsehood, but primarily by its word-of-mouth character. Whether they are rationalized or modernized versions of ancient stories (which substitute, for example, foreigners for witches) or relatively new "exemplary tales,"

Kapferer argues that they are a form of unofficial cultural preservation and stasis amidst an "official" backdrop which champions progress and change.

> Even before knowing the exact answers, rumors try to reject innovation— the intruder, foreigner, or symbol of changing habits. Rumors are one of the defense mechanisms by which certain citizens try to preserve their old habits. They proffer up 'facts' that justify resistance to change and, more generally speaking, to our society governed by science and technology. (Kapferer 1990: 125)

Uniquely, Kapferer also takes up the issue of rumor-content denial and its effect on the career of the rumor. Here the flexible nature of rumor, in the face of denial, is emphasized. Implausible details are replaced with plausible ones and the story can then be believed. Denials of certain types can be absorbed.

> A rumor is not bothered by one or two details that seem somewhat abnormal. In many rumors, content takes precedence over form. The person who spreads the rumor generally does not try to stick to the precise message he has heard, but rather to persuade his public, and is willing to correct or improve the message in order to do so.... It is because rumors are supple and malleable throughout their construction that they are so at ease when faced with objection bearing on details. (Kapferer 1990: 244)

Rumor, then, is in constant dialogue with its barriers and foes.

In sum, the significant thread that is woven through these recent social science approaches to the urban legend is their placement of legend content within the framework of broader social conflict that is normalized rather than crisis-bound. Interlocutors are situated as consumers, minorities, or parents with the particular strains of those roles deeply implicated in the content of legends studied.

However, as the history of rumor research sketched above has suggested, I believe that some neglected ideas from older research should be brought forward into contemporary understandings of the problem. First, there is the consistently central role of ambiguity in the fueling of rumor behavior, emphasized in wartime research. In the analysis of this current study, I will argue that to some degree ambiguity is imputed by interlocutors themselves, rather than being situational. Second is the dialogic nature of the legend; whether the process is consensual or conflictual in various circumstances, it is still one that is very sensitive to objection and defense in the cauldron of interlocutory settings. This is true whether the setting is micro (local or small group, such as the news group) or macro (broad-based and mass, such as film depictions). Third, the ample evidence that rumor behavior has a tendency to transform overwhelming fears or aggressive feelings into "leveled" or "condensed" forms of dissatisfaction means that such behavior may be aimed at reducing anxiety and thus "fixing" a problem rather than merely expressing it. Anxiety may be reduced in two ways: (1) leveling is likely to take the form of simplification of problems and thus by implication, solutions and (2) the form enables the distanciation of the expressor from the intentions of the expression, by presenting the information as "fact" or "news." Finally, the work of Suczek (1972) and Rosnow and Fine (1976) suggests that the notion of ambiguity and the observed tendency of rumor believers to resist information-seeking needs to be understood in the dramatically changed ecology of information since World War II. The plentiful nature of information now, in the postwar era in general but especially in the last decade, means that ambiguity and absence of information in a rumor situation must be looked upon in a critically new light.

In the literature on the topic from all disciplines, speculations as to the cultural meaning of the legend are often based wholly on the narrative structure and symbolic elements of the texts themselves, even when they are collected in a specific time and place from informants. By contrast, as we shall see below, in the even smaller literature which examines informal talk about crime and safety, the role of rumor or legend is relatively marginal.

Informal Talk About Crime

The study of informal talk about crime is a relatively new field. However the small amount of work that exists on this topic suggests that informal talk differs systematically in its expressed themes from "formal" talk characterized by agenda-setting institutions such as law-enforcement and the news media.

Sasson (1995) compared the interpretive frameworks used to understand the causes of crime employed by people assembled in focus groups and that of print news editorials and op-eds in New England. These focus groups were drawn from different towns to include groups that were mostly white, ones that were racially mixed, and ones that were mostly black. The fact that the groups relied more heavily upon judicial "leniency" explanations of crime than did the op-eds suggested that in general a faulty adjudication system would be singled out for its failure to deter. However, this "faulty system" framework, while agreed upon across groups, was present in discussions mainly as a noncontested explanation than a fervently argued one. By contrast, approximately half of the print opinion articles used "faulty system" as a favored explanation.

By far more popular among the focus group participants was the framework of "social breakdown." This interpretive framework, which was wide-ranging and implicated a variety of social forces, was unanimously embraced by 60 percent of the focus group assemblies and provoked no dissent. Even in groups where "social breakdown" as a main cause was not unanimous, it was embraced by most. For 85 percent of the groups "social breakdown" was connected to a "general crisis of values or morality" which encouraged criminality and antisocial behavior. (Sasson 1995: 59–61) Part of the success of this framework was its ability to represent a consensus framework that incorporated political difference. Liberal and left-leaning versions describe social breakdown as the end result of capital flight, deindustrialization, and government neglect of urban neighborhoods. Conservative versions describe it as stemming from welfare dependency and the embrace of permissive social values since the 1960s. "Social breakdown" in general was a more robust impetus to discussion than were the other frameworks; people had more to say about it. Predominately black groups were most likely to embrace social breakdown in the specific form of "community breakdown" where past forms of informal social control and neighborhood solidarity had eroded. (Sasson 1995: 72, 84) The framework with the weakest support as an explanation was that of "blocked opportunity" where criminality is linked to the lack of legitimate alternatives. Where present, it was also the most contested, and even when gaining assent, it generated little discussion. Interestingly, the framework was even less popular with the black focus groups than the white. (Sasson 1995: 91–93)

The strength of the social breakdown framework, Sasson suggests, is due to the number of diverse and even contradictory concerns which can be interpreted through this lens. (p. 130) It also seems to address a sense of social disintegration which is less commonly reflected in a more "authorized" talk about crime such as op-eds. Sasson observes that the "experiential dimension" was much more often brought to bear upon the elaboration of social breakdown ideas than for other frameworks. Focus group members were more likely to relate anecdotes and personal experiences to illustrate the problem as framed in this manner. (Sasson 1995: 136, 154) In sum, Sasson found social breakdown to be the most popular and the least contested framework. It seemed to generate the most emotional investment.

Wachs' (1988) study also seems to uncover similar themes. Wachs gathered 150 "crime victim narratives" (first and second hand real stories, and also some likely legendary incidents) using a snowball sample drawn from women in New York City, both in individual interviews and small focus groups. The prominence of concern about judicial leniency is seen in Wachs' texts as related to urban incivility, and here the specific concern is leniency for juvenile offenders. Wachs makes a distinction between the crime narrative and the crime victim narrative, where the centrality of the victim, often portrayed as a hero or heroine, obscures or even obliterates the offender as a meaningful actor.

Wachs' informants did not distinguish between kinds of crimes, telling one story after another and making general observations about crime. "The depiction of urban life found in the crime-victim stories results in a common reporting technique, of which narrators are often unaware: the juxtaposition of narrative plots regardless of the severity of crimes mentioned." (Wachs 1988: 11–12) Wachs took note of the common use of humor and sarcasm, and the theme of ordinary settings shattered by extraordinary events. (p.5)

Part of the reason why the victim plays a heroic role in these narratives is the absence of justice-producing rescuers. "Most tellers present offenders who inflict harm and then escape unpunished, [whereas] in other folk narratives, punishment is meted out against the antagonist for violating a law or breaking some taboo, thus maintaining the social order." (Wachs 1988: 16) Victims are victims because of bad luck and bystander apathy in these stories, but they are nonetheless clever or perseverant. "Victims are quickly placed in subordinate roles once the attack by the offender is made apparent.... what is being praised, however, is the victim's return to his/her initial status and power." (Wachs 1988: 31)

The strongest common themes in these two studies are the prominence of the attribution of crime to leniency and the centrality of the sense of social breakdown as a root cause of crime. The failure of guardians to punish, if perhaps more imagined than real given incarceration trends, speak to a sense of a world without consequences. Social breakdown is also a strong theme in crime legends and the talk about them presented in this study. Additionally, Wachs' attention to the absence of the villain's comeuppance, the observation that the denouements of the narratives end instead with affirmations of the victim's fortitude, enables us to consider some of the contrasts between traditional and contemporary tales of horror, and thus their imputed function. Sasson's distinctions between different forms of support for a given interpretive framework, and the strength provided to that framework by the diversity of those forms (rather than their convergence) in interlocutory settings have provided some guidance in the current study. Distinctive ways of believing in a crime legend appear to add to their resilience.

ORGANIZATION OF THIS STUDY

Each of the three following chapters address a separate crime legend as it has appeared in Internet news group settings and popular culture more generally. What I hope to make clear is the diversity of ways in which these legends can be believed and disbelieved. Moral entrepreneurs and everyday believers take very different tacks, in this respect.

Chapter Two considers the aforementioned "snuff film" legend with its origins in the real-life horrors of the Tate-LaBianca murders in 1969. Here the contrast, and paradoxically, the mutual dependence of fervent or transparent forms of belief ("this particular thing really did happen in the manner described") and more casual or instrumental forms of belief ("this is the sort of thing that could happen, in some fashion") are most vivid.

Chapter Three examines legends surrounding the alleged theft of body parts from the living, especially removal of the kidneys by black-market bio-profiteers. Here, some debunkers themselves play the role of outraged moral entrepreneurs and fervent believers are in retreat. Despite the legend's gory details, a complicating element of humor surrounds it.

Chapter Four takes up a set of legends alleging the routine abduction of women and children from shopping malls and theme parks. This case study demonstrates an unusual linearity of evolution, historically speaking. It is more than 100 years old, originating in its present form alongside the so-called "white slavery" panics aimed at curbing prostitution between 1880 and 1915. At issue thematically is the moral danger posed by the marketplace, particularly for women.

Chapter Five examines the specific role of debunkers of urban legends in the Internet setting. Generally speaking, the role of skeptics and debunkers in shaping popular legend belief has been underexamined. A group of urban legend debunkers at the long-established *alt.folklore.urban* news group have become the standard bearers for the sorting of fact and fiction on the Internet. As such, their influence upon the crime legends considered here is significant.

Chapters Six and Seven consider these legends in two broader social contexts: that of information and belief, and that of crime and personal security, respectively. Both address the somewhat shifting relationships that have emerged between subjectivity, truth, and authority in contemporary Western life.

CHAPTER TWO

The Market in Snuff Films

This chapter concerns the first of three case studies in this project. The legend of the snuff film alleges that films, videotapes, and now Internet webcasts of real murders, usually sex-related murders, circulate in underground social networks. Most versions of this legend include some profit motive attached to these recordings and to the violent actions of the filmmaker murderers. However, in some cases, it is alleged that such recordings are merely passed along for the sexual excitement of clandestine viewers. In most versions, the killers are men and the victims women—women who thought they would be making a conventional pornographic film.

One factor that makes this crime legend distinct from many others, including the other two explored in this project, is that it is often presented as an *explanation* rather than a warning or a narrative. That is, diverse activities in the criminal underworld and their manifestation in above-ground evidence—from seizures of property from organized crime participants to unsolved murders or disappearances to discovered caches of child pornography—are linked to a supposed snuff film industry.

Best (1990: 144) describes the urban legend generally as an "unconstructed social problem," which is quite applicable here. However, compared to other legends, the snuff film legend is somewhat more "constructed" than usual. By constructed I mean that the legend has a degree of institutional presence as a constructed reality, which society is called upon to address as a social problem.[1] This has not always been the case. When the initial snuff film rumors emerged in 1969, they were more the stuff of idle gossip connected with the activities of the Manson family. When the idea of an autonomous market in snuff films took hold, thanks to the contextualization of the problem in a variety of organized claims-making activities, it began to be a social object surrounded by constant speculation and mystery. That is, ironically, the more that moral entrepreneurs took it up as a cause and condensing symbol, the more a shroud of uncertainty began build around it.

The idea of the snuff film is also seemingly more compelling to many who believe in the existence of underground commerce than other crime legends. People who know what an urban legend is still feel strongly, in some cases, that the market in snuff films does not qualify—due to what are often presented as epistemological concerns. They ask: how can one prove that something does not exist? Yet the problem turns out to be less abstract than that if one looks closely at ensuing discussions. What is being put forward is not so much broad epistemological uncertainty, but a specific distrust in social and institutional knowledge. Even debunkers, particularly those who frequent the urban legend discussion groups, are themselves increasingly convinced that "one will eventually turn up" and in many cases only remain debunkers because they have concluded that no one has found one *yet*. The same is true for even the most prominent debunkers from law enforcement agencies.

Among believers we find a wide range of definitional boundaries afloat at the same time with regards to the snuff film. Without exception, all news group discussions that I encountered engaged in intense definitional work in order to sort out disputes about the veracity of the legend and each of its aspects (the victims, the perpetrators and their motives, the recordings, their viewers). Definitions ranged from the "cognate" version—where a person's murder was enacted by the film makers as they filmed, and the subsequent recording traded secretly among some combination of aficionados and prof-iteers—to what I will call a series of "expanded definitions," where a variety of well-documented social artifacts are brought under the rubric of the "snuff film."[2] These include privately held tapes seized as evidence in murder cases, very violent pornography, commercially available recordings of deaths (such as the *Faces of Death* and *Mondo Cane* series which are collections of inci-dental recordings of accidents, assassinations, and so forth), and highly "realistic" depictions of murder (sometimes called "fake" snuff films, like the Japanese *Guinea Pig* series).

However, moral entrepreneurs who have taken up snuff films as a concern generally rely upon the cognate version, recognizing the difference between what they are describing and these latter artifacts. For these "fervent believers" a series of investigations, seeking to document the existence of snuff films, has thus been necessary. It should also be noted, though, that some believers, both fervent and more "casual," question the importance of these distinctions for reasons we shall understand below.

The snuff film is also unique in that it has a significant presence in film and fiction. This fact reiterates its compelling quality as a condensing symbol of all that has gone wrong in the world today. Yet when placed in a narrative context, such as a screenplay, the snuff film, and the good fight against it, enables the characters to be redeemed. Bad girls are dispatched for their deviance, while their avengers, are often alienated but kindly men looking for a redemptive mission amidst a corrupt world. To a lesser extent, the investigation into snuff films in real life has begun to take on this role as well. It is often not just—or in some cases, even specifically— the violence involved, but its status as entertainment that makes the snuff film the compelling social explanation it has been for more than thirty years now.

THE FLOURISHING OF THE LEGEND: 1969—PRESENT

In 1976, the gruesome pornography film *Snuff* was released in New York City. It was a cut-up and re-assembled B-movie. It featured the rape, murder, and evisceration of the lead actress. Not long after, rumors began to spread that the film was in fact a documentation of a real event. That is, that the actress did in fact experience this victimization and died in the making of the film. *San Francisco Chronicle* reporter Rider McDowell (1994) describes *Snuff*'s last scene as a "celebration of hokey latex and stage blood." It is quite clear from all historical accounts that the film's maker, Alan Shackelton, intended to benefit from the pre-existing rumor and from the credulity of his audience. He wrote a disclaimer for the film's marquee ("The picture they said could never be shown ... the film that could only be made in South America, where life is CHEAP!") and even hired his own protest pickets. The publicity stunt enabled *Snuff* to outsell major studio film releases such as *One Flew Over the Cuckoo's Nest* for its first three weeks. (Stine 1999: 32)

Prominent New Yorkers (including critic John Leonard and feminist Gloria Steinem) fell for the hoax and demanded an investigation. It was not until Manhattan District Attorney Henry Morgenthau launched an investigation that Shackelton admitted the scene was a fakery. The film makers made little effort, at first, to dispel the rumors as they brought lucrative notoriety. It was not until the rumor piqued the interest of the District Attorney's office that the actress was trotted out to testify to being very much alive (Strossen, 1995: 190–191) Morgenthau concluded that *Snuff* was a hoax.

But the legend of the snuff film was not quashed; rather it accelerated. Its film and television career began, and the moral outrage against it was taken up by new interested parties. At this time, some feminist groups began to get involved with anti-pornography campaigns, and *Snuff* was a galvanizing force. Since that time, the supposed existence of the snuff film has been integral to anti-pornography activism. Yet it has also earned a tacit acceptance outside those circles as well. To date, no evidence of a market in such recordings has been found. (McDowell, 1994; Caro, 1999; Smith, 2000)

A striking parallel can be found in Edgar Morin's 1970 study of a legend cycle about dress-boutiques in the suburbs of Paris. It was alleged that young women had been drugged and sold into prostitution after having entered the shops. The shops were mainly owned by Jewish proprietors and the rumor cycle took on ominous anti-Semitic tones. Government agencies, major news outlets, and civic agencies rushed to quash it. Morin found that official debunking drove the legend underground. The legend never dissipated fully—rather, those formerly inclined tended to believe that *something* must have happened—or that, "where there's smoke, there's fire." This "repository" of belief, Morin suggests, acts later on to provide the fuel for the revival or another cycle, of the legend. Today, parts of Shackelton's movie emerge in people's accounts of snuff film activity, mixed in or confabulated with other details.

Morin's work suggests one reason why so-called "urban legends" reoccur in cycles and in slightly different, yet consistent forms in different places. Details are made contemporary and local, but the plot generally remains the same. The snuff film in particular does benefit from the advocacy of prominent "moral entrepreneurs" who for different reasons have an investment in proving that a market in snuff films exists. Over time these agents have changed, however.

These moral entrepreneurs give collective shape to the legend that bears more than a passing similarity to the white slavery-abduction legend to which Morin refers, which is more than a century old.[3] The idea of (but usually not the phrase) white slavery is still used today; often with a broader definition that blurs the line between socio-economic coercion of women into the sex trade and actual kidnapping. A similar blurring of forms of coercion has occurred with regards to the hardcore pornography industry, and has set the context for the flourishing of the snuff film legend.

Another factor aiding the salience of the legend was the dramatically increased availability of sexually explicit materials in general by the early 1970s. Porn (and the VCR) came to the suburbs and more of it catering to specific interests became available. Explanations are varied, but certainly the lingering effects of counter-cultural expressiveness, a stronger valorization of free expression across the political spectrum, increased transience and mobility (or, more to the point, the cultural perception of such) and of course, the "sexual revolution" itself in everyday practice, enabled increased social acceptance of pornography. Forces of cultural opposition to these trends seized upon the snuff film because its existence seemed to belie the "harmless fun" attitude towards porn which had become widely adopted in the culture. The legend re-demonizes what had become a mainstream pleasure.

Several specific realities, from the legend's apparent inception to the present day, help maintain a thematic climate for the tale. These realities include the existence of violent pornography which is more difficult to find than regular "adult" films, the prevalence of violence in the United States in general (and the comparatively high rate of violence against women), instances in which it appears that coercion and brutality against women have been tolerated in the adult film industry, and increased knowledge about violent psychopathology in popular culture (for instance, the fascination with serial killers).[4] The snuff film legend suggests an underground industry devoted to the needs of sadists and paraphiliacs, where producers and consumers seem to find one another in a consistent way, and where agents of the law are of no concern.

ORIGINS OF THE LEGEND

In compiling the specific documented history of the snuff film legend, I have relied on three sources: an investigative journalistic inquiry into the topic by

McDowell (1994), a chronology by Johnson and Schaeffer (1993), and the "death-film" history by Kerekes and Slater (1994).

The idea that films recording the actual rape, torture, and murder of people were circulating for the amusement of hard-core pornography aficionados seems to have its major genesis in the aftermath of the Tate-LaBianca murders in 1969, when California media sources speculated on what had happened. Among the rumors that eventually fed into the legend of the snuff film were: 1) that the killers taped their murders at the Tate and LaBianca murder sites and that the Los Angeles Police Department had seized these films; 2) that these tapes were widely screened in elite Hollywood circles; and 3) that the Polanski house, where Sharon Tate and four others were killed, was full of amateur pornography tapes—sex, drug, and sado-masochism orgies—and occultism. (Sanders, 1971: 6–7, 238–239, 262; Bugliosi, 1974)[5] The category label "snuff" appeared then as an artifact of media improvisation: while the term had been in colloquial use as a generic term for murder (to "snuff" someone out) its association with recorded images of real murder began here.

The term would be reinforced by the emergence in 1976 of Shackelton's *Snuff* which was actually a recut b-movie, *Slaughtered* with a tacked on cinema-verité ending, which had been shelved for several years—and *that* original film, made by Roberta and Charles Findley, had been filmed in South America and conceived by its makers as a kind of Manson-family ripoff. In the years between 1969 and 1975 then, the term "snuff" became associated with its "real death on film" meaning and its shaky Manson connection. The idea that snuff films circulated widely for sick thrills and profit on the underground market had not yet become integral.

Actually, the connections between the emergence of the snuff film legend and the Manson murders are both empirical and general—empirical in the sense that the legend grew up around specific Manson-related rumors and general in the sense that the snuff film's current incarnation encompasses several themes in public consciousness about crime having to do with cultural disintegration. The Manson murders marked a turning point in cultural perceptions about society and crime, spawning the idea of a murderous "ritual" underground. More recently, a satanic ritual abuse network as an "underground" has replaced a counter-cultural one in public consciousness about crimes against children for ritualistic thrill. Contemporary discussions of the snuff film do not usually involve the Manson case, and generally regard the snuff film market as a global and profitable, rather than cultish, practice.

MORAL ENTREPRENEURS AND THE SNUFF FILM LEGEND

Over time, the mantle of advocacy for the legend has passed from religious and conservative opponents of pornography, to feminists who seek to link pornography with violence, to famous serial killers and their biographers, and finally to intrepid investigative reporters. I will next discuss the changing role of moral entrepreneurship over the life of the legend to the present, but it should be kept in mind that casual believers and retellers often "mix" interpretive frameworks in a more heterogenous way than do the professionals and moral entrepreneurs who promote the existence of the legend.

In 1974, two years before *Snuff* even appeared, Raymond Gauer, a spokesperson for the conservative anti-pornography group Citizens for Decency through Law, began to circulate a letter alleging that violent pornographers were using real murders. Gauer claimed:

> ... one of my sources is convinced that they [snuff films] exist in quantity, and that they've been screened in the very 'in' circles in Hollywood ... but I'm convinced that they exist because of what I know *does* exist. (Quoted in Johnson and Schaeffer)

The passage presages two themes which will become important via repeated reappearance. One is the theme of populist class *ressentiment*—the idea that the elite and wealthy are consuming depraved materials and are, by implication, inured to the immorality of pornography in general and snuff films in particular. More specifically, in Zurcher and Kirkpatrick's (1976) study of two local antipornography groups in the early 1970s, including Gauer's organization, the participants were found to be "status inconsistent" or relatively high on the income scale while being low in education levels and occupational prestige. Thus the "class" resentment likely reflected an opposition to what is now called the "cultural elite" which is housed in the universities and cultural production centers, rather than the materially well-to-do per se.

The second theme revealed in Gauer's comment is the reliance upon the reasoning that since one or more immoral practices does factually exist (the existence of violent, hard core pornography), other practices whose existences are contested, and which are either on par or worse (such as the snuff film), are likely to also exist. This sentiment is often expressed in the preface "the world is just mean/violent/crazy enough that . . ." In other words, the source of reliable information on the truth of hoaxes, legends, and rumors is whether they are *plausible* given the human capacity for evil. I shall refer to this description of the problem of snuff films as the *inferential* version.

The release of the aforementioned film *Snuff* solidified the rumors. Shackelton re-edited *Slaughtered* and added a section purporting to be the murder and disembowelment of the pornography actress. *Snuff* was distributed nationally, and not long after law-enforcement agencies across the nation began to periodically receive calls from the public with complaints about real murders on film.

The crusade against pornography seems to have then shifted dramatically from a conservative, moralistic one to one given most of its energy by antipornography feminist groups. While the focus shifted from a "vice" framework to a "woman-hating" framework which emphasized the "objec-tification" of women and their sexuality through male-targeted pornography, Andrea Dworkin's (1979) description of the political economy of the snuff film also reiterates elitist and conspiratorial themes mentioned earlier. In Dworkin's version, "organized crime" syndicates distribute films to private collectors. (p. 71) One might assume that such collectors are either wealthy or numerous, and mob involvement would function to "explain" why the commerce in the snuff film persists out of the eyes of law enforcement. Simi-larly, Diana E.H. Russell, in a denouncement of scholarly expert witnesses before the U.S. Attorney General's Commission on Pornography who described the social-scientific research into the harm caused by pornography as ambiguous, speculated that they had been intimidated by the Mafia beforehand (Russell, 163)

So the interpretive context in political opposition to the problem of snuff films shifted in several ways, but preserved certain aspects as well. Orga-nized crime serves as the new "elite" for a somewhat different populist audience. While it is uncertain why conservative groups did not follow through on the snuff film problem, Zurcher and Kirkpatrick's research does imply one reason. Snuff films could not easily serve as a condensing symbol for the concerns of antipornography conservatives. Although this group (surveyed by Zurcher and Kirkpatrick, 251) linked pornography with a host of social ills, violence was not high among them. In one location, only 22 percent of activists associated pornography with the encouragement of violence, while 18 percent did in the second location. Instead respondents couched the problem of pornography in the encouragement of sexual deviance, inappropriate sexual arousal, competition for the family role in sexual education, and personal debasement, rather than crime or violence. So at a time, in the mid-1970s, when sexual mores were changing rapidly and liberalizing, and at the same time crime and violence became a more promi-nent cultural concern, it seemed that feminist opposition spoke to broader populist fears than did conservative opposition.

Yet while the appeal was populist, it also, like Gauer's claims, relied upon insider information about the existence of snuff films. In the case of feminist anti-pornography activism, the historical indifference of law enforcement agencies to various forms of violence against women is used to extend the possibility of snuff films existing, even though no conventional evidence has been brought forward. As Dworkin told the Attorney General's Commis-sion on Pornography in 1986:

> My information comes from a journalist, whose sources I trust, that such films exist, from women who have seen them, whom I believe, whom no law-enforcement official would, that the films exist, that they have seen them. And so far, all that I could tell you is that it doesn't mean we won't be wrong, but so far we have said battery exists and the FBI has said it doesn't, and we have been right. And we've said rape exists and law-enforce-

ment people have said, no; and we have been right. And we said incest is rife
in this country and law-enforcement people first said no, and we were right.
Our big secret is that we listen to the people to whom it happens. And that's
what we are doing here.

At the same hearings in 1986, Linda Lovelace, former porn star, testified:

We have gone from the acceptability of *Deep Throat* in 1972, to child
pornography, to snuff movies, and the mutilation of women in 1983 in
Arizona, to the sexual abuse of young children in our day care centers by
city employees in the city of New York. My question is: what is next?
(Lovelace, 1986: 222)

Likewise, Catherine Mackinnon claims to be protecting sources who have
first-hand knowledge or proof of snuff film commerce, but will not provide
evidence to reporters (McDowell, 1994).

Perhaps because Dworkin and Mackinnon were prominent in the anti-
pornography movement, their claims to have insider knowledge of snuff
films are challenged more frequently. But many popular feminist texts simply
assume that snuff films exist, without much attention to whether proof is
needed. These include Barry (1979: 175), Lederer (1980: 67, 272), Kappeler
(1992: 97), Morgan (1992: 87) and Caputi (1987). Gloria Steinem's *Outrageous Acts and Everyday Rebellions* (1995) relates the story of a senior
partner in a major law firm who included a snuff film with his selections for
his hosting of a monthly porn night for male associates.

One who was present reported that many were 'embarrassed' and 'didn't
know what to say.' But not one man was willing to object, much less to
report this evidence of murder to the police. (p. 250)

Steinem provides no documentation for this incident, rather passing it along
as a telling anecdote about elite acceptance of violence against women. Yet
even if she had supplied evidence, the story raises some interesting questions.
Why would the viewer assume that what he was seeing was a real murder?
Why would a partner trust his associates not to tell? If Steinem knows this
'embarrassed' associate personally, why hasn't *she* contacted the police?
Without suggesting that this event never took place, I am raising these questions to illustrate that interlocutors on the topic of snuff films, even
prominent ones, have difficulty drawing parameters around the implications
of witnessing and evidence. The snuff film seems to work as a condensing
symbol *only* to the extent that it is a reported, rather than verified, practice.

Earlier in the same book Steinem writes:

Though 'snuff' movies, in which real women are eviscerated and finally
killed, have been driven underground (in part because the graves of many

murdered women were discovered around the shack of just one film maker in California), movies that simulate these torture-murders of women are still going strong. (Snuff is the porn term for killing a woman for sexual pleasure. We are not even allowed the seriousness of a word like murder).
(p. 243)

Steinem likely refers to the 1985 Lake and Ng serial murder case, where Leonard Lake and Charles Ng were convicted of killing twelve people in their remote cabin in the Sierra Nevadas. It is unclear who did not take the case seriously. Ng has been sentenced to death for his part in the murders, convicted in part on the videos he made during the perpetration of the crimes.[6] (Deutsch, 1999) These recordings became state's evidence, not commercially available porn videos. It is telling, though, in terms of understanding the interpretive framework which surrounds the snuff film as a semi-constructed problem, that Steinem refers to Lake and Ng as "film makers" rather than murderers who recorded their violence. This choice and the rest of the passage suggest that Steinem's promulgation of the legend rests upon the idea that snuff films are a "normal" enough practice to have once been above ground and then driven below, once the Lake and Ng case broke. It also implicitly suggests that greater moral violation takes place when cameras are present than when they are not; during the time of Steinem's writing, the culture at large became aware of several notorious serial murder cases in which women were the primary targets. In what way does videotape really make this case worse?

The snuff film as an object of feminist distress, though, has begun in recent years to pass, interestingly, back into the hands of men. During the 1980s, when the anti-pornography movement was beginning to wane after serious civil libertarian challenges, the snuff film legend got an unusual boost. Prominent serial killers claimed to have insider knowledge of them. Mackinnon (1993: 18) takes at face value the claim by serial killer Thomas Schiro that he was corrupted by viewing "rape pornography and snuff films." Ted Bundy implicated snuff films and pornographic addiction in his descent into serial murders of young women (Salzman, 1995). David Berkowitz, the "Son of Sam" killer now claims that a convoluted conspiratorial plot involving a cult called The Process and photographer Robert Mapplethorpe led to his spree of murders in the service of a snuff film market, where tapes of the death of Berkowitz victim Stacy Moskowitz fetched as much as $50,000 (Terry, 1987). William Bradfield, eventually convicted of murdering former lover Susan Reinert in Pennsylvania, vainly speculated that she had actually been sacrificed to the snuff film industry. (Wambaugh, 1987: 169) When that failed to convince investigators, Bradford suggested that Reinert had sold her children into "white slavery" and voluntarily disappeared. (Wambaugh, 232)

Notoriety, it seems, brings out conspiratorial explanations in the accused. These claims suggest that each of these convicted men predicted that the public (or some portion of it) might find these explanations compelling.

Naturally, the moral erosion caused by the would-be snuff film industry might help mitigate responsibility for the lethal violence in these cases, and these men could then judge themselves and be judged by others to be only partially responsible and a mere pawn in a much larger and powerful scheme.

Meanwhile, the snuff film legend seems to be passing out of the primary context of feminist indictment and into greater popular culture interest. Here, the moral entrepreneur is a lone wolf investigator fighting a world callous enough to trade in real sex-and-death video, but savvy enough (as Steinem suggests) to drive it underground. The irony, suggests one film reviewer, is that the concern over the depravity of violent sex-and-murder recordings (whether real or staged) does not seem to have been carried forward to the present time when death footage of various sorts has become ubiquitous on stage and screen.

> When was the last time you heard the term [snuff film]? The feminist furor over their existence, which was seminal to antipornography writing in the 1970s and 80s, seems to have evaporated—just as real video footage of horrendous deaths is finding its way onto television. . . . Perhaps because no sex is involved, and because women are rarely involved at all, no one up to now has applied the term "snuff" to the new Death TV. The term now seems a relic of a more innocent age, when we were more concerned with sexual images than with random, insane violence. The idea of the snuff film has disappeared just as the thing itself has passed into mainstream culture. (Smith, 2000)

Yet films and books about snuff films continue to flourish, as the real world campaign against them seems to have faded. It was a visit from Catherine Mackinnon that convinced Yaron Svoray, a journalist, to embark on a global search for snuff films after he reported in a 1994 book that he had viewed one with a child victim during the course of his infiltration into neo-Nazi groups in Germany. "According to her," Svoray (1997: 23) writes, "in eight years of investigating snuff pornography she had not found anyone before me who had ever said in print that he has seen a snuff film."[7] After meeting scores of stock underworld characters claiming grandiose Mafia connections in his search for snuff films, he is brought by an old friend to a group of detectives at the New York Police Department who exhibit polite disinterest in snuff films. He tries to encourage their interest by telling them that most snuff film victims are children and teens.[8] Where Dworkin saw sexist indifference to the snuff film trade, Svoray attributes the lack of law enforcement interest in the topic to sensory and emotional overload in a permeated world of "darkness all around." (Svoray, 127)[9]

In Roman Polanski's movie *Confessions of a Blue Movie Star*, snuff films represent for the film maker "post-humanity." Polanski's authoritative voice in this matter, as the bereaved husband of Sharon Tate, overcomes the unintentionally comic and somewhat amateurish special-effects which are used in the alleged snuff-film segment. Polanski in this instance, becomes the alienated avenger in real life, not just of his wife (a snuff film victim, too, it was once rumored) but of his unborn child as well.

In summary, although the motives for moral entrepreneurship with regards to the snuff film are diverse, they are also ones of quite prominent people and they together form a collective voice of authority on the topic. Throughout the history of this legend, real crimes are linked to the alleged market in snuff films in a number of ways. Moral entrepreneurs promote only the *cognate* version of the snuff film legend, where young women or children are murdered on film, and then the film is shown to aficionados for sexual titillation and for the film maker's profit. The most popular version attributes the snuff film trade to commerce between elite organized crime organizations and wealthy viewers who pay either hundreds or thousands of dollars for a viewing. Another version used by some moral entrepreneurs is the corner-video-store version, where the snuff film is available to people of modest means if they have the right connections and know what to ask for. I found no evidence that prominent moral entrepreneurs currently use the *expansive-definition* or *inferential* versions, which were fairly common among Internet news group participants, and which are discussed below.[10,11]

Moral entrepreneurs have insisted on the existence of a market in snuff films since the 1970s. For feminists, the snuff film typified the totalizing quality of male control of women and the trivialization of their lives and their flesh. It adds a surreptitious element to what is usually plainly visible, as bruises or worse, at the hands of lover or stranger. It speaks volumes about the modern "traffic in women" in a post-modern and most extreme form. It is the perfect backlash crime. However, despite its flourishing as part of a feminist social campaign to socially and legally delegitimize pornography, the appeal of the legend has clearly exceeded those bounds.

HISTORY OF THE SNUFF FILM LEGEND

The idea of the snuff film emerged at the confluence of two major socio-cultural shifts in the United States, in the late 1960s. First was the dramatic rise in reported rapes. By most accounts, the key word is *reported*, although violent crime in general also rose significantly at this time. Owing to the confidence and institutional support fostered by the women's movement, victims of sexual violence began to challenge the stigma adhering to victimization, and challenged police and courtroom treatment. As a result, women in general, not just those consciously influenced by feminism, felt more able to report crimes of violence against them.

Not long after the rise in reported rapes, some feminists began to assert links between pornography and rape. The connection is empirically tenuous and somewhat contentious even within feminism. Social science reviews of studies on the relationship between pornography and sexual violence have been basically inconclusive. (Donnerstein and Malamuth, 1984; Donnerstein et al, 1987; Linz et al, 1987) Out of a fog of causal ambiguity, the snuff film legend seemed to hurdle this problem of inconclusiveness by collapsing *act* and *representation* together. In the snuff film, the vision *is* the violence. As Mackinnon (1993: 23, 26) writes about what snuff films are:

> ... in which actual murder is the ultimate sexual act, the reduction to the thing form of a human being and the silence of women [is] literal and complete.... The most common denial is that pornography is 'fantasy.'... Are the victims of snuff films fantasized to death?

Thus the amorality of all pornography as inherently linked to misogyny and violence is brought forth through the specific and concentrated symbol of the snuff film.

The snuff film legend concentrates fear and rage over relations between men and women in a modern, complex society. Yet would not the really existing genre of violent pornography serve this purpose just as well? The snuff film as a particular allegation (or explanation for crime and black market activities) also speaks to ideas about the split between the legitimate world and the underground, and the distance between those people with things to hide and the agents that are supposed to catch them. In this, like other popular crime legends, police and law enforcement agencies are absent, ineffectual, or behind the curve on innovations in criminality. These are folk-tales from an alternative universe, which appears as a distorted mirror to the ordinary one. In this alternative universe there are perpetrators, victims, witnesses, the warned, the unlucky—but no guardians and no recourse.

Indeed if a bona fide market in snuff films and secret screenings of them exists, and law enforcement agencies, including Scotland Yard, the FBI, and local police departments cannot find one, this state of affairs would imply one of two things. First, that an elaborate and air-tight conspiracy among law enforcement agents at all levels exists to destroy any evidence that might come to light. Or, instead, that we live in a society in which it is possible to kill young women, film their deaths, sell tapes and screenings of these films— which, according to the diversity of accounts, occur all around the globe—and yet no evidence is left, no tapes or films confiscated, no arrests made, no one even specifically accused of making, possessing or viewing such a film. One model suggests a world tightly controlled by unseen forces, while the other suggests a world without justice or safe havens. As I found few interlocutors who alleged the former, the latter interpretive framework seems more appropriate in describing their ideas. However, these ideas about the invisibility of the snuff underground were often tacit ones.

This interpretive framework assumes that there is no reliable guardianship and an insufficient amount of moral outrage within civil society to prevent it from happening. Indeed if anything goes, as Polanski suggested, we may be, living in "post-humanity." However what is also interesting is that *skep-*

tics and *debunkers* of the legend also allude to such a state of affairs possibly existing in the near future.

DEBUNKERS OF THE SNUFF FILM LEGEND

As with urban legends in general, the snuff film has spawned a relatively well-organized group of debunkers, aided enormously by the growth of Internet talk groups. Structurally, then, it is fair to say that the snuff film legend benefits from its high-profile vectors, with a countervailing force in law enforcement that is reactive rather than proactive. Only in the 1990s has the popular media addressed the issue, mainly from a debunking viewpoint. (McDowell, 1994; Caro, 1999) The only more organized set of debunkers exist on-line, mainly in the Internet news group *alt.folklore.urban*, and even they do not devote as much energy to debunking snuff films as believers do in promoting it.

Debunkers of the snuff film legend summarize their skepticism in a simple "habeas corpus." Get us one. Let's see it. Where are the recordings? This generally describes a debunker's response in the on-line news group *alt.folklore.urban* and others. Debunkers demand positive evidence of a conventional sort: tapes, law enforcement records, newspaper accounts. Although their stance necessarily tends to be deconstructive and negative as compared with believers, their presence in the public conversation about the legend means that the promulgation of the legend tends to be responsive to it. Organized believers, such as moral entrepreneurs, exhort people to believe in the face of apathy and skepticism, while casual believers accommodate skeptics by changing the definition of the legend or challenging the notion of "knowability" about the social world.

NEWS GROUP INTERLOCUTORS AND THE MEANING OF THE SNUFF FILM

Discussions in News groups

During the years for which such data was available, I found 945 individual posts to Usenet news groups that mentioned snuff films in 1996; 2,165 such references in 1997; and 2,835 in 1998. Of these postings, only 93, 170, and 155 of these, respectively appeared in groups dealing with folklore.[12] Thus most references were found outside the "ground zero" for urban-legend debunking on the Internet. As with most searches for specific topics on Usenet, the "signal-to-noise" ratio favors the noise: duplicate posts, conversations ("threads") which have drifted from the topic but still contain text picked up by the search engine, and brief non-substantive replies dominate. In addition, the search for the phrase "snuff film" specifically brings up a number of metaphorical or in-passing references which were not addressed specifically to snuff films per se. The same is true of news media references, which will be discussed below. Not surprisingly, then, most of the substantive discussion of snuff films (particularly their existence, and what their would-be existence means) was found in folklore groups, followed by feminism and "erotica" discussion groups.

In this section the general character of the debate surrounding snuff films that takes place among news group interlocutors is sketched through examples, particularly examples of debates. The purpose here is to understand the shifting contexts in which the snuff film legend is and has been understood. These contexts constitute a departure from those discussed above surrounding the legend's moral entrepreneurs. There are several interwoven themes. The first concerns debate over the existence of the "cognate" version of a snuff film—where women or children are assaulted and killed in front of the camera, and the resulting recordings traded in an underground market or network. The second considers whether the definition of snuff films should be expanded to include practices and recordings about which much more is known and which "exist" in the conventional sense: violent pornography, underground videos of animals being killed, inadvertently filmed violence (such as the Zapruder film), and videotape made by serial killers of their victims (but which are not apparently available to the public). The third concerns the question of whether it matters that snuff films really exist; some ask, is the demand for such a genre enough by itself to legitimate concern over the "problem" of snuff films?

The Cognate Version Expands

Snuff films, as a semi-constructed social problem since the 1970s, represent a sense of the ultimate depravity within a larger context of misogyny. Prominent feminist concerns about them are often accompanied by accusations that society as a whole and male law enforcement officials in particular accept snuff film making practices and refuse to prevent them. News group discussions include this general understanding, as well as a number of others which are less often found among moral entrepreneurs.

For example, in *alt.feminism*, snuff films appear in a broader discussion of the objectification of women's bodies in artistic representation. In the following exchange (12/17/97), the specter of the snuff film serves as a fulcrum for the more general problem of social harm produced by pornography in general.[13]

> *David:* I've purchased pornography, and it is becoming increasingly clear to me that I've given the matter of objectification a lot more thought than you have.
>
> *Carol:* Actually, the making of a snuff film could also contain "artistic content" however, it doesn't alter it's claim to fame as a snuff film.
>
> *David:* Ah yes, the knee-jerk invocation of the great nonexistent phantom, the "snuff film" And um ... just where did you learn of the existence of such material, Carol?

David approaches the problem of debunking by demanding evidence; Carol, though, pulls the snuff film into the discussion rhetorically as a symbol representing extremity in "art." It almost serves as a "what-if?" challenge to those who fail to respond to existing sex or violence images without enough moral outrage.

It is often the case, though, that debunkers serve the role of defending and reinforcing the cognate version of the legend. Believers (or one might more accurately say, in this case, proponents) in the market in snuff films in on-line discussions engage in constant challenge to this definition.

On the previous few days, David argued with another *alt.feminism* participant about the status of video recordings made by Lake and Ng of their assaults upon their victims. Meri challenges David's claim that no law enforcement agency had found any evidence of a snuff film market. (12/16/97)

> *Meri:* So David L—was, of course, incorrect when he implied that, merely because he was unaware of these developments, snuff film pornographers had never been arrested and convicted, their products used as evidence.
>
> *David:* All of this exciting recitation is entirely beside the point, which is that nowhere has anyone apparently shown that the films were made specifically for the purpose of sale to other users, and nowhere was any evidence provided that it WAS sold to or seen by anyone else but its manufacturers. What is the significance here? Simple. That gruesome home movies made by psychotic killers really have nothing to do with the pornography industry, and no legislation is going to prevent such horrific behavior from occurring again in the future.

For Meri, the snuff film exists anytime that real violence is recorded, even where no market is involved. This is the most common definitional dispute found on-line about snuff films. However, as we shall see below, some debunkers also subscribe to this broader definition, thus sharing the sense that the outrage stems from the recording, rather than the would-be distribution, of these real images of violence. In few cases was the redundancy of morally indicting a serial killer for filming his or her violence ever raised.

It is of some interest, too, that David wishes to fully detach the problem of lethal violence against women from the pornography industry, and make such deviance the province of the mentally ill. While this choice has much to do with his cause of challenging the snuff film mythology and defending ordinary pornography, it also has to do with a more general sense that the snuff film has been used rhetorically as a symbol of the logical conclusion of an unimpeded flow of sexual and violent images in modern, otherwise non-psychotic societies. However, like many debunkers he relies on a highly evidentiary argument against their existence: no one has found one yet. What is left unaddressed, or at least unaddressed directly, is the plausibility of a market in snuff films.

Believers present lurid descriptions of sex-and-violence in the real world as evidence of what evil is clearly possible to do with the film running and for money. So why shouldn't the snuff film exist? Just because no law enforcement agencies have found any? Believers think debunkers naive about how secretive and devious this underground practice is. Brett wrote defensively in *rec.arts.comics.misc*:

> Snuff films unfortunately DO exist. They are (rightfully so) SO illegal that you would have a very difficult time finding a copy. Probably one of the sickest forms of so-called entertainment to ever be conceived! (10/22/97)

Not surprisingly, respondents describe their own forms of evidence and argumentation and those they agree with as more rational and logical than those who opposed their point of view. But there was a great deal of diversity among respondents in terms of how they felt about being asked by others to defend their positions. I asked news group participants how they would "summarize the dispute about this issue [snuff films] in the news groups that you've participated in." Louise, 42 years of age and a lawyer, says:

> Frustrating. The dispute is not satisfying as there is a demand for proof of something it is illegal to own. If genuine snuff films exist, how would it be possible to prove their existence if it is not legal to admit having one? As to fake snuff films where it is pretended to kill someone, those films can be purchased in NY for $10.

And BT, 27, a health consultant, is equally frustrated.

> People won't believe they exist until they see it with their own eyes. This is the basic premise of the Urban Legend news group—people argue about what they have heard of but never seen or experienced. 99 percent of the stuff in there is B.S.

What were some of the definitions offered?[14] Louise offers what I would describe as typical definition proffered by a believer in the expansive definition, "a person is murdered, in reality, to make a film designed to sexually stimulate." Likewise, BT says, "A snuff film is where a person (usually female) is violently and sexually abused and eventually killed for the sexual gratification of the viewer of the film." Contrast Louise and BT's responses with that of David, who's a skeptic:

> A film or video during the manufacture of which a person's life was taken, and which has been made specifically for the purpose of entertainment and the making of a profit by sales or rentals.

Yet David, as a skeptic, also confirms BT's insight that the criteria for evidence is too narrowly limited to what can be experienced directly. When asked in an interview whether he thought snuff films existed, David said:

> For practical purposes, no. One cannot locate them anywhere on the open market. But I have read Yaron Svoray's book *Gods of Death*, which suggests that they do exist ... in extremely rare, carefully controlled instances. [. . .] People who claim snuff films exist base their argument entirely on hearsay from the publications of anti-pornography activists. . .

David's skepticism about the legend is tempered by Svoray's book, which is a first-hand account of the author's search for a real snuff film. One scene describes an exclusive screening of such a film that Svoray was invited to attend and this constitutes the main proof offered in the book.[15] In any case, what leads David to make an exception to his skepticism is the testimony of someone who claims to have seen one first hand. Similarly, in a heated news group discussion in *alt.cult-movies*, a debate emerged over the existence of snuff films.

JmcClennan wrote:

> I have not seen a snuff movie. No one I know has seen a snuff movie. No one whose views I take remotely seriously has seen a snuff movie. No police department in the world has ever found a snuff movie. There is no actual evidence that snuff movies exist. Any of the above would be a start, I guess [*to convince the writer that snuff films exist*]. Until then, I think I'm free to pour scorn upon those tabloid TV suckers who believe in the existence of snuff movies. I'm sure they also believe in massive Satanic cults, alien abductions, and the tooth fairy.

JmcClennan's post is actually an interesting mixture of the standardized snuff-film debunking (no law enforcement agencies have found any, after decades of searching) and subjective skepticism (nobody I know. . .) which, like David's remarks, reflect a willingness to take first hand testimony more seriously than some skeptics might. To which a fervent believer (Zodiac) remarks:

> I can't believe you are so wrapped up in your warm western world view to actually make such a ridiculous statement? Paul Bernardo was caught RED-HANDED with videotapes of him, and his wife, Karla Homolka, raping, torturing, and mutilating teenage girls. There are also reports (I admit unconfirmed) that more of these videos starring Paul and Karla have been found in Japan. If someone made a movie like this, is it not conceivable that someone else probably has, and included the final seconds of his 'star's' life, especially considering the demand for such a thing (admit it, people are sick, why do you think they slow down at accident scenes?). . . (9/17/96)

Zodiac refers to a 1992 case in Canada where a husband and wife were arrested and videotapes made by the couple of their victims were confiscated by the police. The ability of Canada's courts to secret away much of the trial and evidentiary proceedings meant that rumors about the case were rampant. What was it about JMcClennan's post that caused Zodiac to regard it as "warm, western?" As far as Zodiac is concerned, what Bernardo and Homolka did should have put the issue to rest. These were real tapes, with real victims, spilling real blood, and screaming in real pain. It is clear that Zodiac attributes JMcClennan's dismissal as naive about what's really "out there"—and it's cold as hell ("Admit it!").

Despite its rambling form, I included Zodiac's protesting post because it has several typical "believers" elements in it. First, it asserts the primacy of several indisputable facts as though the others in the group were in deep denial about the cruelty possible between human beings. Second, it reasons that one only need prove that "people are sick enough" in order to prove the existence of the nefarious act at hand, namely the snuff film. Zodiac's post also underscores the degree to which believer's ideas about the cold-heartedness of the world they live in are developed and articulated compared to the world-view of debunkers.[16] Believers are certain that it could happen, and that is often good enough.

Adam K. joins in, pointing out that the Bernardo tapes don't fit the definition of a snuff film:

> Correct me if I'm wrong, but isn't part of the definition behind "snuff film" that the people who make these videos WITH THE INTENT OF SELLING AND MARKETING them? To my knowledge, all the cases you [*Zodiac*] cited were just people videotaping their crimes for their own use, not for a wide distribution. (9/18/96)

Brian R. concurs:

> But those are NOT snuff films, they are simply fucked-up videos made for their own sick pleasures, not to be marketed or sold to foreign video companies. Someone may have gotten a hold on the Bernardo/Homolka tapes in Japan, but its very unlikely that Paul and Karla planned on mass-marketing them underground. . .(9/18/96)

Zodiac has actually run afoul of *alt.folklore.urban*'s definition of a snuff film, as it appears in their on-line archives. It's not uncommon for other news groups to turn to the popular *alt.folklore.urban* as the final arbiters about what's true and what's an urban legend. Of course, the elements that go into *alt.folklore.urban*'s definition are based on the recollections of people who helped build the archive. They and other debunkers, like David, are the ones that place a heavy emphasis upon the underground marketing aspect of the legend, to separate it from the numerous times in which police have discovered films, photographs, and videotapes of violent activity. However, the folklore group's definition also conforms to the cognate version offline, and that of moral entrepreneurs who promote the legend. But it appears that for others not loyal to *alt.folklore.urban*, the preferred definition of the snuff film is expansive—any recording of violence made with prurient intent regardless of its commercial worth.

In fact the debate has not even been settled in folklore circles. In a discussion within *alt.folklore.urban* (12/2/97) about how and whether the definition of the snuff film should evolve, Angus, a regular participant, offered a summary of the previous working definition:

> The standard afu [*alt.folklore.urban*] definition of snuff involves an onscreen murder staged as a business enterprise. A few months ago, I argued that the way the story has evolved in the camcorder age necessitated a slightly broader definition—snuff being a movie that—a) depicts a murder, b) was filmed by one of the perpetrators, and c) has been sold by someone involved in its production for d) entertainment viewing by a non-partici-pant. This definition places the emphasis on the production and sale, rather than on the motivation of the film maker.

Another commonly referred-to definition is one offered by Barbara Mikkelson (1999) at the *Urban Legends Reference Pages*, which removes the "market" angle altogether.

> Some will further claim that a profit motive must exist, that the final product has to be offered for sale (as opposed to being passed around without charge within a select circle, or remaining solely in the possession of its maker). That detail is extraneous. It's the recording of the death itself which consti-tutes the "snuff" in snuff films, not who makes a buck out of it. Likewise, claims that the film maker must have had no other motivation than the production of the film should be dismissed. A psychopath who tortures and murders solely to satisfy his personal demons but who videotapes the event to create a relieveable record of the experience has produced a snuff film.[17]

Mikkelson's article goes on to describe several notorious incidents in North America where serial killers did film their victims being assaulted, but did not include their murders in the filming. Therefore by this definition, a snuff film would only have been created had the victim died in front of the camera rather than later. Since no such evidence has as yet surfaced, the article regards the snuff film as a "myth."

Mikkelson notes, probably referring mainly to regulars at *alt.folklore.urban* that, "purists will tend to dismiss this footage [possible future discovered footage of murders] because it does not conform to an overly-strict definition involving the necessity for a profit motive." Thus even among the most seasoned of debunkers, the snuff film presents definitional problems with real consequences for the perception of how likely we are to know about such films. Mikkelson's definition allows the possibility that a snuff film maker exists but is not yet discovered; the *alt.folklore.urban* version mostly does not, as it is the distribution angle of the legend which would allow the perpetrator to be caught. Interestingly, then, fervent believers and moral entrepreneurs such as Dworkin, Mackinnon, and Svoray have a much stricter definition than many skeptics do.

Some of the braver regulars to *alt.folklore.urban* have suggested recently that since the group is devoted to the study of contemporary folklore, that it should not dismiss new "versions" of the tale out of hand, as something merely to be debunked in its cognate version. If folklore is a living, developing thing, they argue, maybe multiple definitions should and can exist in the group's tightly-held archives.

This issue is hotly contested, and has to do with two thematic conflicts that reflect *alt.folklore.urban*'s subculture. The first thematic conflict is between *study* and *debunking*, the second is between different sorts of "worthy opponents." Some skeptics in *alt.folklore.urban* see themselves as aligned against prominent vectors such as journalists who claim to be "tracking down snuff films" or Catherine Mackinnon. Others seek out *alt.folklore.urban* as a refuge from a world of gullibility and are more concerned with gathering the tools to debunk urban legends in their immediate social surroundings. The first group especially regards those who propound an expansive definition as "grasping at straws" at best and disingenuous at worst. A small group, inclined to value the *study* of such legends, may not be very impressed by the believers, but question the point in having a non-evolving archive. Shell, for instance, asks fellow debunkers:

> In debunking one specific myth, the AFU [*alt.folklore.urban*] definition of snuff is reasonable and defensible. But I think that the myth has mutated; we no longer believe and fear that women are being coldly murdered for gain. We fear that the murder of women could be used for gain, and that people we know would pay the price to see it. I think this discussion would have taken off anyway; but mea culpa for my part. I won't argue for a change in the definition for AFU purposes at this time; but count me among the heretics. (9/30/97)

From the point of view of the strength of the legend, the fact that some skeptics like Shell are willing to bat around the idea of an evolving archive definition also gives a structural advantage to proponents of the snuff film legend.

Indeed there are many approaches for the believer when engaging a skeptic. The first is to rely on one's own provincialism to make the case; to employ humbleness: the world is big, diverse, dangerous—who's to say it does not happen? The second is to emphasize one's worldliness: "I've seen things just as depraved, and I know three different people who told me about various snuff films." These informants, to the believer, are qualified or credentialed as sources in some way: film maker, pornography aficionado, investigative reporter, residents living near the old Times Square. The legend, as do many urban legends about crime, undergirds a belief that law enforcement agencies don't really know "what's going on."

Part of what allows the snuff film to hide in plain sight, is the involvement of underworld figures. Theories of elite conspiracy to distribute the films appear in many, but not all, versions. Mafia or underworld figures are said to make, distribute, and screen snuff films for aficionados with money to burn. This element introduces class *ressentiment,* taking the form of both blame and envy of the rich, exclusive, and depraved into a story which is on the surface about gender power, social chaos, and lawlessness. The role of Hollywood elites, referenced earlier by Gauer, is particularly central in this formulation. This *elite-conspiracy* version of the tale contrasts with both the *expansive-definition* version (which includes the freelance work of serial killers) and the *can-be-found-easily-and-locally* version. The elite conspiracy version seems to be associated with the cognate version, whereas the democratic version, emphasizing the ubiquity of such films, is favored by most believers on-line.

Believers of a less fervent or noncommittal sort will say they've heard it, believed it, but never really thought about how true, false, or exaggerated it was. Like the fervent believers they will say that the world is sick enough to produce snuff films. The difference between the fervent and the casual believer is that the latter are unable to account for the absence of evidence with an elaborate theory of conspiratorial activity. At this level of belief, however, it is fairly common for the believer who is sparring with a debunker to attempt to expand the term "snuff film" in some even-broader-yet definitions. Filmed violence of any sort now "counts." *Depictions* of sex-murders on film, when outside the narrative context of a full length film or television episode, counts. The part about being sold on a black market drops out.

Authors, journalists, and political activists that believe in and use the snuff film legend generally adhere to the cognate version and feel, like the on-line skeptics, that the expansive definition is perhaps irrelevant. They may not in fact, know that such an expansive definition of the snuff film has gained a foothold in popular culture and is becoming the predominant one.

However, an even more basic question has been asked by some proponents of the legend: does it matter whether snuff films are real, and can we know? Some have come to define the salience of the legend by *inference* from the fact that the desire to watch them exists. If people want snuff films, won't they eventually, if they have not already, get them? One of the interesting things about this formulation is that this desire makes the "snuff film" real to them.

The second problem is one of imputed uncertainty: where "I don't know whether they exist" equals "one can't know whether they exist." While the function of this formulation is to make room for the possibility that snuff films exist, and as such can be treated as a real social problem, it also contravenes the method of moral entrepreneurs. The latter seek out investigations and proof that they exist, sometimes charging others with complicity and silence—and they would be loathe to suggest that it simply does not matter or that we cannot know. In fact, in some cases, the "casual" believer prefers not to know with any certainty the depth, truth, of scope of the problem. During a contentious debate about the morality of violent fantasy in the group *rec.arts.movies.erotica*, Bob M. chimes in:

> In my just post-college days when I worked in New York I was at a party in the early 70s when, along with other pornography, a said-to-be-real "snuff" film was played as background enhancement to the drugs and booze we were all using. There were some interesting rumors at the time that a lot of these movies were being made in Mexico and Central America, where life was cheap and drugs prevailed. Whether I saw a real snuff film or not, I'll never know ... I was haunted for weeks. (5/10/97)

Bob continues to criticize those who like violence in their pornography. For him, not knowing for sure whether it was real is central to the atmosphere and climate of decadence that he was trying to convey about his past. The world from which this evil came must remain shadowy so as to be understood as separate from the world in which he lives. This imputed uncertainty is not limited to on-line discussions. Sociologist Diana Russell's allusions to the snuff film underground are equally shadowy.

> There are of course many notorious cases of such home videos being filmed by femicidal murderers, such as Leonard Lake and Charles Ng. Who knows how many of the everyday amateurs are also trying and succeeding in marketing this new cottage industry? (Russell 1993: 15)

Such a vague statement from a prominent researcher in the field of violence against women supports the idea that the snuff film explanation functions only insofar as it is depicted as of unknown prevalence. Likewise, with the women who perform in pornographic films, Russell claims (p. 18) that

> No one knows what percentage of them are also being beaten up, tortured, raped, or even killed, before, during, and after the photographic or filming sections.

The assertion that no one knows is rather strong. Certainly if one does no serious research on the subject, then it would indeed be difficult to hazard a guess. But not knowing and asserting that no one else can know keeps the matter fertile for speculation.

It is the inferential and expansive-definition versions of the snuff film legends that most often provoke angry responses from the skeptics on-line. In fact, *alt.folklore.urban* periodically publishes a routinely ignored "frequently asked questions" for newcomers, and the section on snuff films implores:

> Note to the new reader: please don't send or post e-mail saying 'snuff movies could exist, because people are naughty enough'—this is not in dispute; the point is that no examples have yet come to light. (10/24/96, posted by E.H. Kelly in *alt.folklore.urban*)

Expansive-definition believers are more worried about the depravity involved in recording violence, whether real or staged, than they are about the general veracity of the snuff film legend. Skeptics tend to regard any recording of violence that might go on in a case like the Bernardo-Homolka case as incidental to the violence itself. Believers tend to regard recording devices as extra-depraved, and they are much more concerned about the *demand* for snuff films, whether they exist or not. Louise said in an interview:

> My argument is that the fact that there is a MARKET for fake snuff films is, in itself, disturbing, whether or not real snuff films exist. In other words, whether or not they exist is not as important to me as that there is a market.

According to the expansive-definition believers, and even to some skeptics, the technological democratization of recording and broadcasting devices can and will likely eventually produce something like a snuff film, perhaps involving the Internet. When asked in an interview whether he thought snuff films existed, BT said:

> Yes. And we will be seeing more of them move through underground circles (or stills/video clips showing up on the net) in years to come as technology makes it easy to copy and distribute them.

Likewise, Vicki Lou, age 43, an health administrator from Australia, who participates in *The Urban Legends Listserv* fairly regularly, and who finds the debunking evidence compelling while also wondering whether some snuff films' existence is "possible, maybe even probable" concurs with the analysis of increasing social depravity specifically aided by media technology shifts.

> That means now exist to satisfy appetites through the use of mass media, which previously would have been pursued by individual fantasies or acts. Acts, fantasies, appetites, and interests which become "realised" in mass media (even if in strictly limited circulation), are shared and therefore validated. At the same time, moral responsibility is dispersed and consequently dissipated.

This scenario is echoed even by the nation's most official snuff-film debunker, FBI agent Kenneth Lanning. It was Lanning who informed the public about the agency's collaboration with Scotland Yard in an investigation of alleged snuff films, and about their failure to uncover any. (McDowell, 1994) "It's just a matter of time before one is made and it surfaces. Camcorders make this scenario possible." Likewise, Sergeant Don Smith of the LAPD, who debunked the original Tate-LaBianca related rumors, told McDowell:

> My feeling is that if snuff existed on film or video, it would be so far under-ground the average person would never see it. For years there's been talk of a Las Vegas dealer selling snuff films for $100,000 a pop.[18] For that you get the original film. I've never believed this, but with all the unsolved murders in this country (more than 8,000 in 1992 alone), it makes you wonder. Certainly the possibility is there.

Finally, the most thorough snuff film debunkers of all, Kerekes and Slater (1994: 246), suggest:

> Snuff is a means by which the media can prick public morality. Despite no such film ever being found, in any place, anywhere the media continues to indiscriminately nurture and promote the myth as fact. Perhaps in so doing—reiterating its potential monetary value and projecting potential markets—it will one day succeed in making snuff a true commercial reality.

Chuck J., commenting on the *Urban Legends Listserv's* quest for a work-able snuff film definition, asks:

> All the attempts to define what is and isn't a snuff film, and all the exam-ples and counter-examples, are kind of missing the point, since the question isn't a purely academic one. The relevant point isn't whether or not the films exist, but rather what would it say about people and the nature of evil if they did? And what does it say about people just that we can conceive of such a thing? (February 25, 1999)

Chuck's quote reveals how much questions of *inference* and *meaning* around the snuff film have come to concern even those who are serious skeptics. Indeed debunkers do tend to have the facts on their side about the existence of classic snuff films, but are increasingly being called upon by even very sympathetic voices to consider what it means that the culture at large seems so taken with the idea. The concern about the emergence of snuff films worries event the most vocal skeptics. In this case study and in the other two, this theme of *debunking* versus *interpreting* reappears time and again.

MEDIA TREATMENTS OF SNUFF FILM LEGEND

Newspapers

Newspaper references to the snuff film in the years 1989 to 1999 were sought by using *Lexis-Nexis Academic Universe*, which indexes articles from the 50 U.S. newspapers with the highest circulation as well as major dailies from Canada, Australia and New Zealand, and Great Britain and Ireland.[19] A total of 130 were found. Of these, most made reference to snuff films in the course of relating other subjects. Four were specifically directed at investigating the snuff film legend as a general rumor. (Souster, 1990; McDowell 1994; Roeper 1999; n.b., *Toronto Star*, 1999). Sixteen reported on plans to investigate, or drop investigations of, alleged snuff films associated with actual reported crimes. No follow-up articles on these cases appeared in the index. Twenty-eight refer specifically to the film *8mm*, while another 22 refer to other fiction (movies and books) that contain snuff film plots. In these 40 movie-related cases the market in snuff films is neither described as real nor as an urban legend—but the strict, cognate definition of the snuff film is used. Ten used the phrase "snuff film" to describe any footage of death or depictions of death in fictional films. Two referred to the airing of a fake snuff film on a public access cable channel in San Francisco. Two referred to the general question of whether pornography is socially harmful, mentioning the snuff film in passing. Four used the snuff film as an argument for greater Internet content regulation and for limits to the First Amendment. Eight referred to the 1989 case of Daniel DePew and Dean Lambey, who were charged with plotting to make a snuff film in Virginia by soliciting young boys on computer bulletin boards. The remainder (17) tended to refer to snuff films in passing, or for rhetorical reasons, for example, something might be "as unpleasant to watch as a snuff film."

In these cases, it could be argued, the existence of a market in snuff films tends to be implied by lack of comment or metaphorical use. There were numerous occasions in which the specter of the existence of snuff films was raised (for instance, as the plot of the film *8mm* in film reviews) without any remarks about whether snuff films really existed. In only a few instances did media sources use the occasion to look into the snuff film legend and get differing opinions on their existence. As for metaphorical use, the term abounds in any reference to recorded death. I found instances where the Zapruder film was referenced as such, as well as the *60 Minutes* episode showing Dr. Jack Kevorkian assisting a man's suicide. In these ways, the idea that there is a market in snuff films is a tacit assumption in many media stories that use the term. This practice *in effect* broadens the definition, as well, while paradoxically reinforcing the cognate version at the same time.

Magazines

Of magazine articles indexed in the *Reader's Guide to Periodical Literature* between 1989 and 1999, only five referred directly to "snuff films."[20] Millea's 1999 article in *Premiere Magazine* used the release of the film *8mm* to discuss the legend of snuff films. Stine (1999) wrote a history of the rumors for *Skeptical Inquirer* magazine. Articles by Cohn (1998) in *New Republic* and another without a byline in *Newsweek* referred to the airing of one of Dr. Jack Kevorkian's assisted suicides on television and a videotape sold in the United Kingdom with footage of state executions, respectively. Both articles address the public desire to see death recordings. Spitznagel (1994) describes in *Harper's* a performance art piece in which the author placed casting calls for a snuff film in order to see how desperate out-of-work actors were.

Thus, the small overall number of references as the tendency towards metaphorical use of the phrase "snuff film" are underscored in the case of popular magazines.

Broadcast References

Lexis-Nexis Academic Universe found 87 broadcast (North American English language television and radio news) references to snuff films. By far the largest portion of these (42) were instances where the term was used as a metaphor for any death on film. Four suggested ongoing investigations into allegations that snuff films were associate with reported violent crimes, while six debunked the legend.[21] Twenty concerned fictional movies about snuff films, including *8mm* and *Mute Witness* without any debunking. The rest were passing references, including seven about animals being killed on film. Again, the assumption that the audience knows what snuff films are, and that they are a real world phenomenon, is often passively implied. This mode of dissemination is considerably more important in the case of broadcast messages than in active promulgation.

Fiction: Movies and Television Crime Drama

Snuff films act as condensing symbols in both films and television crime drama. The cognate version of the legend is almost always used, and the status of the snuff film as urban legend is almost always mentioned—usually in some way to be overturned by the progression of the narrative. Almost all of these treatments place the current state of morals within society on trial and find them wanting. However, this is often accompanied by the heroic intervention of exceptional individuals who are, interestingly, often themselves flawed characters. Film versions generally attach a bleaker message to the problem of snuff films than do television crime dramas, although there are some exceptions.

NBC's 1995 *Law and Order* episode "Performance" finds the detectives (Mike, who has poor control of his temper; and Lenny, a cynical recovering alcoholic) in possession of what appears to be a snuff film. They set out to find the apparent young victim, only to find that she is alive, but the victim of a group of male high-school classmates who are competing in a points-for-sex club.

At a bachelor party, some young men play a videotape that they thought would be amateur pornography. Instead, it is a video of a girl being raped and shot to death. A shaken partier brings the tape to the police, remarking, "I heard about those things, but I always thought they were an urban legend." While Mike notes that there were several snuff film fakes floating around in the 1980s, he and Lenny both agree that "she's not acting." As with Svoray's experience with similar videos and with film protagonists discussed below, the sincerity of the actress' fear and pain are what convince the investigator that the snuff film is real. Echoing frustration with a society too decadent to prevent a market in snuff, the detectives upbraid the video store owner responsible for the rental. "Many have rented it," the owner insists, "and no one has complained." Yes, they mutter to one another, and no one called the police, either. "This is America" Lenny sighs. Ultimately, the snuff film myth is both underscored and debunked. It has been rentable without previous complaint, reinforcing the independent effect of demand upon the supply of would-be snuff films. Is it a snuff film if the viewer thinks it is? Further, as it turns out, the detectives' sense that the girl's pain and fear were real was correct: the death scene was faked, but the sexual assault, at the hands of classmates, was not.

What few earlier treatments of the snuff film legend on television that could be unearthed used it in a straightforward plot device manner. In the first season of *Charlie's Angels* (1977), for instance, an episode called "Dirty Business" calls on the Angels to rescue a woman from a pornography ring intent on making a snuff film out in the desert.[22] The camera is specially equipped with a bullet chamber which will kill the actress. The Angels arrive just in time, as always.

Snuff films are shown materializing in the newest of mass media, the Internet, as the premise of a 1998 episode of the Fox-TV show *Millennium*.[23] In the episode entitled "The Mikado" two teenagers browsing the web for pornography are tipped off to a 'special site' called the Mystery Room. What they see is a woman tied to a chair on an empty stage, blindfolded, and then slashed across the neck.[24] A curtain on the stage then closes. The boys are distraught—"call someone!" screams one. Another responds, "We need proof!" But the web site disappears, can't be printed out, can't be reloaded. For the rest of the episode, the Millennium group, who are a secretive group of private investigators, try to locate the source of the net broadcast. Somehow it's not technically possible for the people running the computer servers to know who's doing it. Meanwhile, the Mystery Room creator goes on killing, and thousands of people around the nation are somehow tipped off to the newest murder site. When enough people call up the page, the murder show begins again. The show's protagonist, Frank, who works with the Millennium group, suggests that the web surfers around the country, by tuning in, are "practically accessories" to the murder of the girls. Eventually they rescue the last girl but the killer escapes.

One might be tempted to shrug off the story as a kind of gimmicky update of an old tale. But in the update we learn a lot about fear of the future. If we accept that the role of the Internet here is to represent unknown technological possibility, then it is also interesting to note that when the snuff film emerges there, it represents almost complete untraceableness, which is the quality of the completely ephemeral that it has lacked in previous versions. The democratic nature of the medium means that anyone can broadcast anything, and can as quickly make it disappear without a trace.

What made the boys think that what they were seeing was real rather than staged? How did word get out to people, in successive waves, to tune in to a certain web page at a certain time? Why was possible for the server personnel to not know it was being used to host a murder? On one level these are pedantic questions, but in another they go right to the heart of the snuff film's conjectured future. It is a future where the boys just knew it was real. Where law enforcement is the last to know what will happen and where to go to look for trouble. Through informal ties, people learn about the web site, and Frank implies that the viewers are complicit in that they go to the site knowing what they'll see. And they won't tell, either. Thousands, maybe millions of them share a vicious secret with one another, and can successfully keep this secret from those with a conscience.

This tendency couldn't be truer for the recent film *8mm* starring Nicolas Cage (Joel Schumacher, 1999). *8mm* simultaneously affirms and debunks the snuff film legend. Inasmuch as the cognate version of the snuff film requires a functioning market, the film actually debunks it. A widow, Mrs. Christian, discovers among her dead husband's personal possessions an eight-millimeter film which appears to document the violent stabbing death of a young woman. Desperate to be reassured that the film is fake, she hires a private detective, Tom Welles, to find the girl, she hopes, alive. Welles tells her and her family lawyer that he knows snuff films only to be "urban myths" but nonetheless agrees to view the film. He is shocked by its intensity of violence and is himself haunted by the victim's fate.

Treating the case as a missing persons case, he follows her trail to Los Angeles' seedy pornography underworld. Welles finds an accomplice in a young pornography store clerk who leads him through the underbelly, and they attempt to buy snuff films with little luck and end up paying $1,200 for what turn out to be fakes. Another underground vendor assures them there's no such thing.

Canvassing low-end pornographers, he finds one who reacts nervously to the girl's picture and tracks his associates to New York. Posing as a wealthy man interested in a privately commissioned film, he approaches them with an offer, but they discover his true purpose and try to kill him. In the mayhem that follows, he finds out that it was Mr. Christian's lawyer who had originally arranged for the commissioned snuff film to be made. Christian paid one million dollars. He was willing to pay that amount because, having searched for an already existing snuff film, he couldn't find one. Thus while following out an elaborate plot based on the snuff film idea, the film simultaneously implies that no snuff film market really exists, such that one wealthy man had to make one happen to get it.

But Welles becomes interested in more than finding the girl in the film—he is interested in the "why" of the snuff film, even its fakes, its pseudo-markets, the latent demand for it. To everyone whom he encounters along the way he asks same question, "why?" His accomplice, the pornography-shop clerk, tells him there are three rules in life: one, there's always a victim, two, don't be it, and three, well, he forgets what three is. The ultimate engineer of the girl's death on film, the lawyer Longhorn, finally explains to Welles why. Mr. Christian wanted to have a real snuff film, "because he could." Thus in both of Welles' worldly informants we see the recurring themes of the snuff film and other crime legends: in the first case, that the world is a manichean place of victims and perpetrators, without witnesses, bystanders, guardians, or recourse; and in the second case, that the emergence of a real snuff film is borne from the synergy between the power of money and the power of depravity.

8mm, darkly shot throughout, even in sunny-day scenes, aims to show the viewer Welles' descent into an underworld that he did not know existed, and ultimately into his revenge-torture and killing of the girl's killer. In a final scene his above and below ground worlds merge when his wife, harping upon his absence from the home all along, validates his journey. By writing a letter on his behalf to the girl's mother, a lonely and heartbroken alcoholic, and assuring her of the demise of the killers without the involvement of the police, Welles' wife writes a virtuous moral narrative of revenge around his actions; he is so haunted by what he saw and what he did that he could not put a coherent spin on it himself.

Welles' series of decisions not to involve law enforcement at any stage of his pursuit also speaks to a world without reliable guardianship. Indeed in *Hard Core* (1979) the wayward Midwestern daughter Kristin goes missing from a "Youth Calvinist Convention" trip to Knotts Berry Farm amusement park in Southern California. Compared to the noticeably derivative *8mm*, *Hard Core* almost seems like a reflection of, as the cliché goes, a more innocent time. Jake Van Dorn, a pillar of the Dutch Reformed church in Grand Rapids, Michigan, sets out to find Kristen since it seems no one else really cares. Before setting out on his journey, Jake tries contacting the police, who in a jaded manner imply the department's boredom with missing kids, claiming that most aren't runaways, and that he should hope Kristen is. So sets in motion the idea that she's been abducted from an amusement park, and Van Dorn's next move is to hire a private detective.

The detective is another bearer of ominous news. He's found Kristen—sort of. He screens for Jake a hard-core pornography film, a genre which he ambiguously describes as now legal and ubiquitous, and yet impossible to track down, "like it doesn't even exist, one showing to the next." Kristen stars in it. Why, Jake wants to know, didn't he contact the police? The detective tells him that he now knows more than the police do and, by way of explanation, "a lot of strange things are happening in this world; doors that shouldn't be opened." Still on the case, the detective, who is abrasive, brash, and expensive, goes back to Los Angeles and is soon followed by Jake. Jake tracks him to a motel where he bursts in on him having sex with a young woman, perhaps a teenager, and after a fight the detective retorts, "go find your own daughter." The retort is like a motto for the new post-social, post-guardianship world. Everyone has to find their own daughter. The detective cannot understand Jake's motive as anything but as corrupt as his own. Likewise, during Welles' journey in *8mm* no one understands why he cares about the girl, either, without having his own base motive.

In *Hard Core*, the Calvinist father, with the "perseverance of saints" eventually triumphs, finding Kristen just in time before she is slaughtered in a snuff film, although not without first being drawn through the degradation and corruption of underground Los Angeles, almost scene for scene inspiring Welles' walk twenty years later. Kristen, it seems, walked away from the amusement park herself, eager to break free of her repressive home life. Jake and she agree to meet each other half-way. Confirming, almost, the existence of snuff films while undermining the specter of theme-park abductions, *Hard Core* is laced with overt social commentary about a failing, chaotic society in which heroic men can save their own daughters so long as they are willing to know the sins of the world in all their monstrousness.

The roles shift somewhat in *8mm*, perhaps reflecting twenty years of even more suspicious terrain and sense of dislocation. Welles cannot save the girl, although he does get revenge. Nowadays, it seems, the corruption is even more deep. The murder of the girl in *8mm* is set in motion by the violent lust of a respected businessman, who happened to be named Mr. Christian, facilitated by a trusted lawyer, carried out by two miscreants, one of whom nonetheless lives with his mother in Queens and sees her off to her church group outing. Like *Hard Core's* Jake Van Dorn, Welles is an innocent, that is to say naive, who is forever scarred by his journey into the heart of darkness. In fact, Welles initial belief that snuff films were merely "urban myth" gave him hope that he might indeed find the girl alive—as Mrs. Christian had hoped but fearfully doubted. It turns out, in a way, that she knew better than he did—in this sense his skepticism made him naive. When Welles reveals to Mrs. Christian that the girl was indeed dead, she commits suicide, leaving some money for both her mother and himself, and a note that said simply, "forgive us." We have seen the enemy.

Skepticism puts nearly everyone in danger in *Mute Witness* (1996), a film set in Moscow that follows the perilous journey of Billie, a young mute woman employed as a technician at a film company. Inadvertently locked in late one night, she sees a pornography film turn into a snuff film when the actor kills the actress with a knife. Billie knew the whole thing was real, like Welles in *8mm* did, because of the authentic expression of pain on the face of the victim. (She was never really close enough to know otherwise, and the body disappears.) Secreting a diskette with the digital version of the snuff film on it, she goes to the police. When they investigate, the film company managers convince them that Billie is crazy and that the snuff film was a fake. Billie seeks help from her sister and her skeptical brother-in-law. Every disbeliever puts Billie in more danger. Someone enters Billie's home, trying to kill her, but an undercover cop arrives and kills the murderer instead. Even he doesn't have enough pull to arrest anyone or stop the production of the film. He decides to fake Billie's death in an explosion to keep her safe, and the diskette intact. The snuff film makers assume the diskette has been destroyed with her. The only "happiness" in the end is that Billie is still alive and that someone believes her, yet nothing can be done. Thus she would in a sense be a "mute witness" even if she could speak. Who can be told? Does anyone care?

In the futuristic *Strange Days* (1995), themes of the anomic, post-social, and post-guardian society are so prominent that they are quite nearly background assumptions. In this future America, no one seems particularly concerned with morality, and the fight against crime and violence against persons has simply been given up. Money buys the only security that is available as the outside world has devolved into victims and perpetrators. Indeed the little heroism displayed by the protagonist flowers out of his status as that rare breed: someone who is merely a bystander or witness.

In *Strange Days* the streets are in chaos and the country has devolved into a spectacular entertainment-based culture. Illegal traffic in virtual reality, point-of-view disks flourishes. These disks record the activities of the wearer: what the wearer sees, does, and hears. The disks are then sold to underground consumers who then experience the recorded activity as if it was nearly their own. Buyers, we are told, seek out more and more extreme disk material: sex, crime, and physical stunts like parachuting. Lenny, our protagonist, is a dealer of these disks, strictly a profiteer with little emotional interest in the material himself, until he comes across a disk that disturbs him. The disk is a life-recording from the point of view of a rapist-murderer who has tortured, raped and killed a prostitute named Iris. Iris (as in the iris of the eye, perhaps) is also forced by the attacker to watch her own brutalization and death with a projected disk. (Indeed at times the movie even questions how selfless Lenny even is; he is also motivated to find and destroy Iris' murderer because he is infatuated with her friend Faith, a rock singer, and this would be a way for him to gain her attention and love.)

Like many other movies that take up themes raised by crime legends, *Strange Days* grapples with the snuff film in an ambiguous way. Yes, society is so eroded that the disk could be made and passed around with impunity;

after all, Iris is a low status victim. But at the same time, Lenny, the jaded bystander is deeply jarred by its appearance, implying that not much like this has passed his way before. And when the police begin looking for the disk, it is only because the same recording also captured murders secretly carried out by the police themselves, and they wished to destroy it for that reason. Police are really just another self-interested gang of thugs roaming the street, trolling for victims. The movie also confirms the theme that within a morally corrupt society, demand creates its own supply of brutality-as-entertainment, and as such all barriers of circumstance (onlookers, agents of civil society, juridical authority) will be circumvented. There is no civic infrastructure to detect, let alone prosecute, a virtual-reality snuff film.

Conclusion: Post-Humanity as Tacit Knowledge

Do we live in a society where such underground activity is possible without interference from law enforcement or the conscience of civil society? Where this underworld is so totally separate from mainstream, ordinary society that it can carry on such a trade? Maybe not now, say some fair-weather skeptics, but perhaps in the future. As news group participant BT and the *Millennium* episode suggested, perhaps the snuff film will finally become realized in the newest of mass media, the Internet.

Yet even among skeptics, the plausibility of the legend is rarely addressed. The debunkers' categorization of the snuff film as a myth or legend seems to be based upon that fact that none have yet surfaced. Yet it is rarely questioned how this practice could elude authorities more than other proscribed practices. Child pornographers, drug dealers, and other traders of forbidden materials—as well as perpetrators of violence—are routinely caught. For the snuff film to go undetected now, it must have some special quality that is never really specified. This unspecified quality is implied by the aggregate set of news media reference to the snuff film, which endorse the legend in a number of passive yet effective ways, if likely inadvertently.

Perhaps the fear of snuff film production is more tied into a basic social distrust. Have we, or will we, grow into a world of amoral viewers of Internet flotsam and jetsam, alone in our houses and at liberty to do what we will with camcorders without fear of being caught by authorities, and yet able to sustain real life underworld connections, networks of aficionados, that tip us off to glorified violence events such as these? If so, then, perhaps, finally the snuff film can be born.

This point is undergirded by films about snuff films—where they represent so much more than misogyny taken to its logical extreme. For fallen patriarchs, they enable singular redemption in a world otherwise too decadent to prevent snuff films.

The idea that snuff films will someday exist as an illicit commercial genre testifies to ideas about the social structure of modern Western countries, either now or in the near future. Just as with those who believe that it is possible, currently that such a market exists without attracting the attention of law enforcement, the belief in a potential market of this sort suggests that the surveilled and unsurveilled worlds will be increasingly split apart, or are already. And the future version adds a fine point—the desire-drives-reality view. People want more extreme video consumables, so they shall have them. BT worries:

> As people become increasingly desensitized by the violent pornography available to them, they will increasingly demand more intensely violent content. The very extreme of this is the snuff film.

The fact that debunkers tend to eschew further discussion of the snuff film based upon its non-appearance as evidence to date has bothered a number of interlocutors concerned with the subject. In a heated exchange about the existence of snuff films, Mitcho ventured into heavy debunker territory (*alt.folklore.urban*) and taunted the group: "One of these days some sickoes really will make and distribute one or more bona fide snuff films, and that day will be an interesting one in AFUland." (3/26/98) Bo, a group regular, replied, "I think I am not the only one who has pointed out that if that ever comes to pass, it will not go back and retroactively make twenty-five years of snuff mythology true." It is fair to say, though, most debunkers are fairly uninterested in *why* the legend resonates with believers like Mitcho, who generally have a kind of thematic monopoly on future speculations. They are certainly more explicit in their low expectations of civic integrity.

I should reiterate that the themes discussed in this chapter, such as loss of guardianship, a radical split in society between everyday life and the underground, increasing levels of depravity coupled with indifference to this depravity within bureaucratic law-enforcement and civil society, and the high favorability of information derived from claims of "insider" and "underworld" knowledge are most often implicit, and not overt. That is, they represent tacit knowledge about the social structure of modern Western societies and not explicit, highly structured world-views.

Both believers and debunkers of the snuff film use accusations of naivete and gullibility to defend their positions against critics. In the process, they articulate what is *plausible* in the world we live in and what is not. Plausibility is a key feature in the vitality of an urban legend, according to contemporary folklorist Jan Harold Brunvand (1986). This ingredient of plausibility allows what is not true to be passed along as true. A search for evidence and counter-evidence is then set in motion, and very quickly the original tale picks up a pre-emptive assertion of truth to silence skeptics.

With the snuff film in particular, re-assertions of the core and cognate truth of the existence of snuff films—where films and videos are made of real-life murders of women and children, then sold or screened for profit along the lines of an underground market—are tied into some clearly defined political agendas. There appears to be a rather complicated symbiosis between the snuff film legend as told by moral entrepreneurs and the snuff film legend as told by less well-aligned believers. The latter are likely to use the *inferential* and *expansive-definition* version of the tale, thus giving the tale cultural support where it might otherwise fall at the lack of evidence.

Skeptics spend much more time explicitly discussing epistemology, and therefore have a sort of rhetorical advantage over believers, but only when it comes to dealing with the cognate version of the legend. When the snuff film develops a kind of symbolic truth through inference and expanded definitions, the playing field gets a bit more even because few debunkers assign social, moral, or psychological meaning to the snuff film legend. The only thing sociological that debunkers and skeptics are willing to say about this or any urban legend is that it is evidence of widespread gullibility and that such tales are designed to make us more afraid. Believers, by contrast, have a whole context of meaning that can be drawn on to explain the tale's social salience. As such, the performative, narrative, and meaning-producing repertoires available to them are much more numerous, flexible, and varied.

CHAPTER THREE

Stolen Body Parts

This chapter concerns the forced extraction of vital organs from living people by people aiming to profit from the resale of the organs for transplant. One of the versions currently circulating has a man lose one or both of his kidneys to a seductress who drugs him in a hotel room. When the man awakes on a bed of ice in a bathtub, he sees a note that informs him, "Call 911 or you will die!" When he does this, the 911 dispatcher asks him to look at his back to see if he has stitches. He does, and it is determined that his kidney has been stolen. The victim does live to tell.

This version contrasts somewhat with organ theft rumors that circulate globally, particularly in the Third World. In these versions, organ thieves are said to leave their victims, often street children, to die after stealing their hearts, kidneys, livers, or eyes.[1] In a manner similar to that of the snuff film rumor in the First World, the Third World organ theft is a semi-constructed social problem. Reports of organ theft routinely surface in Latin America and Asia, promote investigations, but are followed by less-publicized findings of evidence that such practices did not occur. International media sources have given these allegations credibility on occasion, ignoring follow-up reports (Radford, 1999: 36–38; Genge 2000: 64). Like the snuff film legend, the Third World organ theft rumors appear as *explanations* (for missing children or foreign adoptions, for example) rather than narratives.[2] By this I mean that the form of recounting need not adhere to a discrete narrative form as described in the above paragraph, with a set scene, event, and denouement. In the case of Third World organ theft rumors, the allegation is offered as an explanation for children gone missing, or for the presence of white foreigners, or for general ill-health in children.

In this study the version described at the beginning will be the focus. This "First World" version appears to circulate somewhat independently of the Third World version, and does not appear to have any on-record partisans at all. It is told as a discrete narrative, and that narrative has become highly standardized on-line even where the local details have been altered.

The following features characterize the currently popular text: first, the legend merges an older femme fatale legend with the new menace of stolen body parts; second, debunkers of this legend take a proactive stance and accuse promulgators of causing social harm; and third, the legend includes the tacit assumption (here, perhaps less tacit even than in the snuff film legend) that a large network of underground facilities and corrupt personnel exist to process and deliver stolen organs. Additionally, talk about the legend revealed that a strong undercurrent of humor accompanies the story. This is also absent in the Third World version and is only marginally apparent in the First World folk text itself.

All varieties of the legend speak symbolically to the expendability of bodies at the hands of modern, technologically advanced profiteers. If the snuff film speaks in part to the expendability of women and children to a global trade of images to be consumed by a depraved public, the most recent rumors surrounding the illegal procurement of organs from those still using them brings the systematic victimization of men into the fold as well. But while an invisible profiteering network seems present in producing both crimes, the alleged market in stolen body parts takes its victims only out of ruthless necessity rather than jaded amusement. As such there is zero-sum political theme that runs through all organ theft legends. This zero-sum theme is highly apparent in the Third World versions, where the health and life of poor people, usually those who are brown and black, is sacrificed for the prolonged life of wealthy, and often white, would-be organ recipients. However, there is some element of the zero-sum theme in the First World version as well.

The global profiteer angle is complicated by the contemporary tale's "femme fatale" aspects. Earlier femme fatale legends were about revenge, while this merged version has women seducing men out of their kidneys purely for profit. In one of the earlier folk texts circulating in the 1980s, "AIDS Mary," a woman seduces a series of men, bringing them each to a hotel room. When they awake, she is gone, having left behind a note that says, "Welcome to the World of AIDS." The legend further explains that the HIV-positive woman seeks revenge against all men for the one who has infected her with the deadly virus. (Brunvand, 1999: 133–134; Fine 1987) The "AIDS Mary" legend is itself a version of one that may date back to syphilis victims in the 1500s.[3] The transformation of the vengeful victim to one who is purely instrumental, and who takes the time to make sure her victim is sewn up, raises some interesting questions about the changing social roles of women.

The emergence of proactive debunkers also shapes the talk about this folk text in interesting ways. These debunkers have claimed the moral high ground and could be considered themselves moral entrepreneurs, promoting both faith in medical practitioners and voluntary organ donation. A some-what different, but in this case overlapping, group of debunkers, including those found in the on-line folklore groups, see this stolen kidney legend as an exemplar of all those conditions within our societies that produce credulity towards urban legends in general. Generally, this latter group also finds the legend very amusing.

CURRENT STOLEN KIDNEYS LEGEND TEXT

The University of Texas "Daily Texan" newspaper has tried to stop it, as have the New Orleans police, the National Kidney Foundation, the United Network on Organ Sharing, and a small software firm in Florida. Medical personnel cannot get rid of it, and this latter group seems frustrated that it keeps reawakening in different spots. Much commotion has been made over a mass distributed e-mail message:

This story came from the "Daily Texan"—the University of Texas newspaper. Apparently it occurred during Fall Premier—a UT tradition that is a celebration of the end of midterms.

"Reason to not party anymore"

This guy went out last Saturday night to a party. He was having a good time, had a couple of beers and some girl seemed to like him and invited him to go to another party. He quickly agreed and decided to go along with her. She took him to a party in some apartment and they continued to drink, and even got involved with some other drugs (unknown which). The next thing he knew, he woke up completely naked in a bathtub filled with ice. He was still feeling the effects of the drugs, but looked around to see he was alone. He looked down at his chest, which had "CALL 911 OR YOU WILL DIE" written on it in lipstick.

He saw a phone was on a stand next to the tub, so he picked it up and dialed. He explained to the EMS operator what the situation was and that he didn't know where he was, what he took, or why he was really calling. She advised him to get out of the tub. He did, and she asked him to look himself over in the mirror. He did, and appeared normal, so she told him to check his back. He did, only to find two 9 inch slits on his lower back. She told him to get back in the tub immediately, and they sent a rescue team over.

Apparently, after being examined, he found out more of what had happened. His kidneys were stolen.

They are worth 10,000 dollars each on the black market.

Several guesses are in order: The second party was a sham, the people involved had to be at least medical students, and it was not just recreational drugs he was given. Regardless, he is currently in the hospital on life support, awaiting a spare kidney. The University of Texas in conjunction with Baylor University Medical Center is conducting tissue research to match the sophomore student with a donor.

This similar crime ring has been targeting business travelers. This ring is well organized, well funded, has very skilled personnel, and is currently in most major cities and recently very active in New Orleans.

The crime begins when a business traveler goes to a lounge for a drink at the end of the workday. A person in the bar walks up as they sit alone and offers to buy them a drink. The last thing the traveler remembers until they wake up in a hotel room bathtub, their body submerged to their neck in ice, is sipping that drink.

There is a note taped to the wall instructing them not to move and to call 911. A phone is on a small table next to the bathtub for them to call. The business traveler calls 911, who have become quite familiar with this crime. The business traveler is instructed by the 911 operator to very slowly and carefully reach behind them and feel if there is a tube protruding from their lower back. The business traveler finds the tube and answers, "Yes." The 911 operator tells them to remain still, having already sent paramedics to help.

The operator knows that both of the business traveler's kidneys have been harvested. This is not a scam or out of a science fiction novel, it is real. It is documented and conformable. [sic] If you travel or someone close to you travels, please be careful.

Sadly, this is very true. My husband is a Houston Firefighter/EMT and they have received alerts regarding this crime ring. It is to be taken very seriously. The daughter of a friend of a fellow firefighter had this happen to her.

Skilled doctors are performing these crimes! (Which, by the way have been highly noted in the Las Vegas area). Additionally, the military has received alerts regarding this. This story blew me away. I really want as many people to see this as possible so please bounce this to whoever you can. (Circulating via private e-mail lists, Spring 1998) [4]

The text is at first glance just another variation on an age-old cautionary tale about leaving one's drink unattended and following a seductive stranger to their lair. Such cautionary tales have functioned to encourage chastity and monogamy, for both men and women. This time, however, the victim is just one nodal point on a vast underground syndicate, merely an expendable and exploitable pawn, rather than the hapless prey of a disturbed predator. One's college classmates may be either the victims or the perpetrators. The 911 dispatcher is so familiar with the practice that he or she is able to direct the victim towards the stitches in his back. The inclination towards skepticism is specifically challenged in the text, and doctors are explicitly accused. The elements of humor and pathos ("Reason not to Party Anymore") seem designed to produce a text that is somewhat non-judgmental towards the victim—at one time this would have been okay, but one just should not stray this way anymore. It is a crueler world, and at the same time one in which the traditional function of the cautionary tale must be expanded.

After all, to run such a ring one needs more than depravity, desperation, and the willingness to trick a man out of his kidneys. One needs: surgeons skilled enough to remove the organ and sew up the victim tidily, a system of transport and preservation for the kidney, a way to tissue-type it, then a network of corrupt clinic practitioners who will then purchase the organ, perhaps make up a story about where it came from, deliver it *only* to someone who can pay a premium and needs one conforming to the stolen organ's rough size and exact tissue-type, and—who can keep a very big secret and only use underground medical services for the surgery and recovery.

OTHER VERSIONS OF BODY-PART THEFT LEGENDS

Unlike the snuff film legend, the stolen body parts legend has been approached in social science before (at least the Third World version). Veronique Campion-Vincent (1990; 1997) addressed body-parts theft legends in Latin America, and Nancy Scheper-Hughes (1998) also has examined organ trafficking myths worldwide. Both argue that while the stories of organ theft have so far always been debunked and appear to have no basis in real events, they express a symbolic truth about the expendability of third world bodies in a global capitalist marketplace.

In Latin America the legend most often concerns infants and children. In Guatemala white tourists are suspected of adopting local children in order to harvest their body parts. These rumors have led to the beatings of at least two American women tourists. (Kadetsky 1994) Although apparently contemporary Guatemalan tellers do not make the connection, it was the case in the 1500s that the Mayans thought the Spanish *conquistadores* intended to drain their babies' blood to cure their anemia. (Fox et al, 1996: 8)

While there is some evidence that the current Latin American story had its origins in a Soviet disinformation campaign (Leventhal, 1994; Bailey 1990), Campion-Vincent emphasizes the resonance of the tale with perceptions of real-world conditions.

> The baby-parts story was initially accepted in many intellectual circles, not because of the propaganda machines, but because of its own exemplary value. It was a horror that was plausible to convinced anti-imperialists or to committed enemies of capitalism because this plundering and dismembering of innocent humans seemed to parallel the plundering of raw material by developed countries.
>
> Born from faraway causes and enhanced by triggering events, the exemplary story operates through the transformation and resurgence of a legendary tale that presents a systematic interpretation of a dysfunctional situation and denounces a conspiracy. An implicit moral thus seems to be naturally expressed.(Campion-Vincent 1990: 23)

Campion-Vincent's categorization of the baby-parts story as an *exemplary tale* with an implicit moral parallels my own formulation of the term *inferential belief* in categorizing some tellers and hearers' verbalized interpretations of crime legends. Primacy is placed with the symbolic truth of the tale regardless of its roots in real events. However, beliefs that are constructed through inference need not be connected to a specific tale per se, but may instead serve as a belief orientation that can "explain" why a given

tale is salient. That which elites would be capable of, considering their indifference to the conditions of most of the world's population, is drawn into the
formulation of this tale's plausibility.

> As in South Africa, rumors about organ stealing can be heard among poor
> people in Brazil. The rumors are based on similar perceptions—equally
> grounded in social and biomedical reality—that their lives and those of their
> children are dispensable. Because of these rumors, shantytown residents in
> Brazil try to avoid public hospitals, where they fear they will die prema-
> turely so that their organs may be harvested. The Brazilian rumors are also
> fueled by unscrupulous operators involved in international adoptions. In
> many people's minds, the active market in babies, with its occasional scan-
> dals involving corrupt officials, police, doctors, and mafialike
> intermediaries, is indistinguishable from the market in spare organs for
> transplant surgery. (Scheper-Hughes 1998: 52)

Both Campion-Vincent's and Scheper-Hughes analyses emphasize the role
of the real structural inequalities and associated corruption, which generate
and sustain the circulation of false rumors about organ theft. There is here
a similarity to the compelling argument of Turner (1993) that rumors and
conspiracy theories sustained in African-American communities are improvised from historical, but in some cases contemporary, instances and
circumstances of racial oppression. For instance, the prominence of bodily
incapacitation (such as soft drinks that are alleged to cause impotence or
infertility among black men) as a motif in these African-American tales
connects with the injuries of slavery and later events such as the Tuskegee
syphilis experiments and the era of lynching. In all cases discussed above,
then, folklorists attribute the rumors and legends to real underlying conditions, concerns, fears, and conspiracy. However, the legend itself as a specific
narrative at the same time substitutes for a much more abstract analysis of
suffering and stratification. The role that forcible body disintegration plays
on a symbolic level tends to make more concrete the more subtle erosions of
marginality and inequality upon the physical body.

Using a quite different analysis, Goska (1997) examined another first
world incarnation of the organ stealing legend. She discusses several standard
versions (the Texas student, the traveling businessman) circulating in 1996
and one variation where a white tourist is the victim of local organ thieves
on a Jamaican beach.[5] She analyses the stories as "projective inversions" of
power relationships in modern society—where a woman randomly victimizes
a man and perhaps symbolically castrates him, leaving him helpless and in
some versions, dialysis-bound. Goska further describes the emergence of the
legend as part and parcel of the "angry white male" syndrome, where the
story serves to indict the femme fatale figure as part of a larger profit-oriented
conspiracy. The tourist version serves as a projective inversion of core-

periphery capital and race relations—it is the tourist's body victimized and appropriated for a world commerce in organs. In other words, Goska's analysis depends upon identifying a *disconnection, or inversion* between the premises of the tale and the surrounding global-economic reality in which it circulates.

Both arguments are compelling, but as such, a problem is raised analytically. Symbolic truth or projective inversion—when can we apply each analysis, and to which contemporary legends? They are somewhat logically opposed arguments about stories which have some basic narrative similarity; at the end of the day in both versions someone loses a kidney due to depravity and greed. Is it really quite fair to say that the North American version of the story has no impetus in symbolic truth, or that there is no projective inversion at work in Third World tales, or vice versa? In the current study, both explanations are only partially useful. The unique quality of contemporary folklore is its tendency to constantly challenge and exceed these otherwise logical explanations. The "First World" version especially presents a problem—it appears that both victim and perpetrator hail from the same milieu.

It might be useful to think of the stolen body parts tale as what Turner calls a "Topsy-Eva" tale. Turner explains that tales of malfeasance, such as suspicions of cannibalism, were told by both blacks held in slavery about their white captors, and by whites about their captives (Turner, 31) [6] Turner explains that the existence of two opposed versions of the same tale reinforces, concentrates, and narrows suspicion about the nature of the Others' threat (Turner, 149).[7]

First and Third world versions of the tale exist, but the kidney thieves in the University of Texas version seem to be victimizing "their own kind." Hence even the suspicion of the Other becomes overly generalized. Yet this does not imply that the fear or threat is perceived as less serious. The symbolic castration element of the stolen body parts tale appears here as a kind of peer affair. It is probably useful to examine some common elements to the First and Third World versions of the tales. First to consider is the alleged underground world market in organs. There are elements of truth here, albeit without much functional use for theft as a part of the equation.

ORGAN TRAFFIC WORLDWIDE

Mainstream clinical complicity in expropriating bodies has at least one real-life historical root. In the 1700s corpses were robbed from graves in England and Scotland and sold to medical schools. By the early 1800s, medical students in Edinburgh and later in London, made cadaver-purchasing deals with men who, in turn, murdered vagrants to produce fresh corpses for medical experimentation. Historians speculate that as many as seventy poor and homeless people were murdered this way. (Richardson 1996: 71–73)

Cadavers now are plentiful and easily preserved, but it is still the case that surgeons have taken organs from cadavers without permission, usually for research. (Gorman and Folmar, 1999)

Organs for transplant remain scarce. People die waiting for them. Waiting lists themselves are hard to get access to. Tissue types of donor and recipient must match in a number of ways—sometimes even blood relatives will not match. (Paradoxically, the above version of the legend alludes to this when the victim's recovery at Baylor University Hospital is discussed.) This is the reality context in which the tales of theft thrive. It is, of course, the involuntary or premature removal of organs that promotes fear of theft.

In the industrialized world commerce in body parts is generally prohibited. In the case of China, there is always a fresh supply of recently executed prisoners to harvest them from. In fact, people from all over the world who are wealthy enough to fly to Beijing can usually get a needed transplant faster there than they could expect to on a waiting list in their home country. Likewise Belgium has a "default consent" rule, which assumes that upon death a citizen of Belgium is willing to donate organs unless she or he carries papers that specifically say otherwise. Thus Belgium is a magnet for people needing transplants, especially those from countries where widespread religious or cultural taboos contribute to a low rate of organ donation: Italy, Israel, and Japan. Due to international imbalances of this sort, con-artist brokers claiming to have access to transplant centers and donated organs have approached people on recipient queues. (Wendling 1998)

If, as has been recently reported, there is a market for the excess organs of executed Chinese prisoners (Drew, 1998), then the only thing that makes kidney theft improbable there is the overstock of prisoners. Elsewhere, too, there are literally millions of poor people willing to part with a kidney or eye such that theft is really redundant. There is little role for theft of organs in places like India, where they can easily be bought for a few thousand dollars. (Rothman 1998; Youngner 1996: 40–42) Those who sell them right out of their own bodies are so desperately poor, and in debt, that the money they receive for selling a kidney or eyeball lasts only a couple of years, maybe less—subjectively, these existential circumstances of a poor organ-seller must seem very much like theft. (Barraclough 1996)

In September 1999, the University of California at Berkeley opened the Organs Watch center to study abuses of the worldwide extraction of organs, under the co-direction of Nancy Scheper-Hughes. Although the center plans to focus upon inequality in recipient queues and unfavorable and exploitative live donation by poor people, unconfirmed rumors from around the world about organ thefts were also a partial impetus to the center's founding. (Associated Press, 1999b)

Of course there are also significant technological barriers to making theft a viable and profitable option for would-be organ thieves, and this is the primary medical objection to the plausibility of a black market in organs. Hospitals attached to Chinese prisons are perhaps the only worldwide example of a facility appropriate for separating an unwilling donor from his or her organs and preserving those organs for a paying recipient. The rifle is a key part of the process. Most other methods of execution ruin the organs, and since the Chinese government profits from selling the organs of executed prisoners to wealthy people in need who check into Beijing hospitals, most are executed by gun. In the United States the "best" dead people to remove organs from, medically speaking, are gunshot victims. However, gunshot victims here—mostly young men, poor, marginal, and disproportionately Black and Latino—rarely sign organ donor cards.[8]

Given that vast inequalities exist in health care systems around the world and in recipient queues, it would seem logical that the organ theft legends, both First and Third World versions would, in interlocutory settings, use the expansive definition process so prominent in the case of the snuff film. The fact that scarcity is dramatic, that people can be ruthless especially when they are desperate, would seem to suggest a linkage between real-world practices and the "idea" of organ theft. Yet this does not seem to have taken place.

If fear of having one's organs stolen for the black market are global, and it appears they are, then what explains the specific elements of the American version? The seduction, the drugging, then the suddenly courteous sewing up and warning note for the victim? We notice that in the dominant version of this kidney-theft legend the culprit is female and the victim male. This provides a contrast with the usual pattern (in reality—and in the majority of fictional crime drama) of cases of bodily mutilation—where a *lone* male serial attacker, such as Jack the Ripper, mutilates, deforms, or dismembers his female victims. Here, as well, our victim lives to tell, stitched up in the back so as not to bleed to death: this element seems symbolic of guilt-ridden traces of either a woman's domestic touch, a surgeon's skilled hand guided by the Hippocratic Oath, or both. The victim has been caught up in an elite criminal network that nonetheless does no more harm than necessary and aims at invisibility.

INTERLOCUTORS IN NEWS GROUPS AND THE STOLEN KIDNEY LEGEND

Absence of Fervent Believers and Promulgators

I found 398 posts to news groups related to kidney or organ theft in 1996; 973 in 1997; and 1,698 in 1998.[9] Of these 80, 183, and 369 respectively were found in the *alt.folklore.* * hierarchy. Generally, then, about one-fifth of all references to the story were found in folklore discussions. This is a large portion compared to that of the snuff film. Those in the folklore groups would often use the kidney theft legend in off-topic jokes and as a kind of exemplar of contemporary urban legends in more general discussions.

The legend seemed to have few true partisans. Since the narrative, which has often appeared in a very standardized form like the Texas student version described above, has circulated widely, it was odd that so few news group participants seemed to "own up" to being believers in the kidney-theft legend. It is possible that its standardized narrative form has made Internet promulgators more elusive; they could simply pass on the story anonymously or via third-parties without having to back them up. Those who held some suspicion that it was likely to be true nonetheless had no elaborated interpretive context for it, such as conspiratorialism.

Promulgators may also be more elusive because they are embarrassed, having been accused of causing social harm by passing the tale along. By contrast, snuff film legend believers display more self-righteousness than snuff film debunkers. Here the poles are reversed. Medical students, doctors, surgical nurses, and health care nonprofit foundations are very concerned that such rumors will discourage the signing of organ donor cards, or perhaps on some level, because the legend implicates medics.

The *Daily Texan* debunked the story in December 1996, but nonetheless that same version circulates still in its core form unscathed.[10] It is possible that more "believe this!" type details were added later, such as the Houston firefighter and "Michele Shafer" endorsement that appears in some versions of the electronic mail tale.

The "warning to businessmen" version is fairly standardized as well. So the paradox here is that while the debunkers of the stolen-kidney legend are very pro-active and have set up debunking websites and campaigns, the net legend continues to spread while appearing to be debunked much more than it is positively promulgated.

How is this formally possible? Well, first because of the difference in the way that debunkers and believers regard and use the legends. Debunkers, being the more pro-active pole in this case, are very concerned about any appearance whatsoever of the legend. These are not just medical students who use the Internet groups but also have overlapped with those who are part of the subculture that debunks urban legends regularly. The kidney-theft legend is thus a case-instance of proactive debunking in action.

Debunkers on the Moral Highground

Mike H., a medical student, is very clear about why people tell such tales. While the *alt.folklore.urban* regulars are more likely to cite gullibility and irrationality of belief as a reason for the sustenance of urban legends, Mike H. clearly feels that the believers are malicious and careless. In direct contrast to the split over the veracity of the snuff film tale, here it is the *skeptics* that argue from (as they see it) a moral high ground and about the impact that the tale could have on public health. Casual, "inferential believers" dominated where they appeared at all. However, believers often simply pass the story along on private e-mail lists and publicly accessible news groups without very much sense of *commitment* to the truth or falsehood of the tale. Gayle, age 36, living in New Zealand, who was frightened by the kidney-theft tale ever since she first heard it in 1996, surmised:

It's just too whacky to be something sucked out of a thumb and it's been circulating for too long now in one form or another.... People will do anything for money. Some people will also do anything to live longer. I should know—being in the nutrition business and seeing people suffering all sorts on a daily basis. Some are desperate enough!

Skrybe, a 26 year old Australian man, reported:

I read about it in a magazine or newspaper ... I tend to believe they [the kidney thefts] did take place because the information I read was from a fairly reputable source. I made (I think) only one post along the lines that I believed it was true. I don't remember particularly feeling anything about this topic. It was more or less something I posted in an idle moment.

Stuart, age 27 and living in England, who once believed the story, a version with a female victim, but now is skeptical, is still nonetheless haunted by it:

When I heard the story in a bar from a new friend, it depressed me because I felt that the poor girl (victim)'s life had been destroyed for the sake of money, merely that she was in the wrong place at the wrong time. I felt she would have been better off dead than having to spend her life on a kidney dialasis [sic] machine. It actually ruined my whole night, and it is only intellectual belief that the story is not true. In my heart I still think that the poor girl (even if she is fictional) is suffering through no fault of her own.

This tale seems to provoke a sense of helplessness in the face of sophisticated victimizing forces even when it is intellectually disbelieved. It is this vague discomfort, which Stuart acknowledged consciously but is much more often likely to be unconscious, that scares "moral" debunkers. The latter worry that organ donation and necessary hospital stays will be affected.

As for fervent belief that a ring of kidney thieves was operating, little of it was to be found and it, too, was also based upon inferential belief. Only a few people that I identified were willing to argue with debunkers. Kontac, in *alt.drugs*, blended a kind of inferential argument with a technical one in pushing the probability of unauthorized organ extractions.

Money Talks and when people are dying they get desperate. Kidneys will last quite well for a wee while on ice but yes it must be quick. But it is a reality and will become more frequent in the coming years. a Doc experienced with a theatre in the right country could retire after a year of such work. When you look around you life is cheap in fact almost worthless to those with piles of money. Do you think they care your [sic] dreaming. (10/20/98)

Like similar inferences with the snuff film, only greed and financial resources are really necessary to make stolen organs a reality. One of my respondents, Milky Way, insisted strongly that my failure to specify *which* organ-theft legend I meant in the questionnaire I sent meant that my study was "off to a bad start." His contribution was the only instance of someone dismissing the First-World story out of hand while insisting that the Third-World version was true.

> An urban legend, as far as I'm concerned. (Re: the particular story I believe you are referencing, about a "Businessmen's Alert.") BUT, it's important to understand that organ theft is a big problem and does occur. For good documentation on this, read Brian Freemantle's book, "The Octopus.".... Sorry to sound rude, but your study is off to a bad start. You are not adequately distinguishing between a particular urban legend story ... and the actual occurrence of organ theft.[11]

This was unique. Belief or skepticism about organ stealing in the news groups was generalized among those I observed and interviewed. Either, it happens, or could happen or it doesn't, and it is therefore, according to the tale's detractors, an urban legend or a hoax.

In sum, social support for the kidney legend among news group participants is broad, persistent, but not terribly deep. I found no one who would vehemently argue for the existence of organ thefts, in contrast to the case study of snuff films. Nor did I find the practice of "expansive definition" belief to be present—where the boundaries of the discussion about the truth of the tale are bent to include tenuously related phenomena—as was true of discussions about the snuff film legend. For example, an expansive definition of "organ theft" might logically include underpayment or social coercion within the legitimate organ donation realm. Yet nothing of this sort was raised here.

Reactions of skeptics further showed that many take a whimsical stance toward the tale that only reaffirms that lack of seriousness that surrounds this particular tale. A number of them, although not all, described their emotional affect towards the tale, and discussion of it, as one of amusement, rather than Stuart's lingering sense of horror. Perhaps the ribald humor, however, is itself a displacement of discomfort. Charles, age 30, thought the story was "totally hilarious" and attributes its popularity to sensationalism. Gayle, who thinks it could be true, told her husband about it and he "laughed it off." Mothra, age 51 and mother of two, thought the Internet discussions were fun and didn't "think anyone took it seriously." Joseph, age 23, found his Internet encounters on the topic "a bit frustrating, but not terribly. I sort of feel like I'm spoiling a fun story, but it ain't true.... I used to get annoyed by stuff on Usenet, but life's too short."

Actually, references to the kidney-theft legend figure prominently in the plentiful joking, ribbing, spoofing, and wordplay that goes on at *alt.folk-*

lore.urban and the debunking websites. Two of my respondents even mentioned the easy adaptability of the kidney-theft legend to jokes within the group. It was exemplary to what made the story compelling—to debunkers. Greatbrit, age 45, born in England but now living in the US, said:

> [While it's] frustrating that people can be so gullible and that they don't think these stories through before making a decision to believe them, ... [it's] fun to use it for follow up humorous posts.

He also said that off-net, he had only ever referenced the tale "as a joke in conversations." Jupiter, age 38, thought it served as fodder for a good practical joke. "I jokingly brought it up to my niece, a college student, as if I believed it. She said, you silly, that's an urban legend." It seems that there is something humorous in the tale to its debunkers. However, there is no evidence that angry debunkers confront the amused debunkers about their handling of the topic with humor; angry debunkers likely rely upon those who frequent the debunking sites to get the word out about its untruth. Nonetheless, the current Internet incarnation of the story itself is titled "Reason Not to Party Anymore," suggesting that humor isn't wholly absent even for those to whom the story is more real and more threatening.

The opposite was true of the snuff film legend. Not only were the *believers* the ones to claim moral high ground (the practice as described by that legend meant a conspiracy to murder women for profit), but in that case it was they who were more organized, with prominent feminist writers using the snuff film as an example of the kinds of dangers the modern world holds for women. Commitment to that legend's salience, thus, was comparatively high, and the snuff film's debunkers often had to apologize rhetorically for their skepticism so as not to be branded callous to the world's real misogyny. And nobody thought it was funny.

The snuff film debunkers may seem to imply that the world may not be quite as dangerous as one might have thought, at least the wild side of it. Similarly, the debunker of the body parts legend suggests that "partying" may not cost you your kidney after all. Thus the common tendency exhibited by debunking practices in these cases seems to be, intentionally or not, about deviance being less dangerous after all. But the debunker of the body parts legend has a virtue advantage: he or she can present the possibility that *the legend itself* is dangerous; that the promulgation of the legend may cause people not to donate organs or to avoid needed medical treatment.

P.J. Geraghty, age 27, a paramedic who works with transplant teams and has visited a number of Internet news groups with an offer of a month's salary to anyone that can produce proof of an organ theft in the United States, told *bit.listserv.transplant*—an email list which itself is devoted to medical, ethical, and logistic issues on organ transplantation—as well as the regulars at *alt.folklore.urban* that:

Many urban legends are funny, this one is dangerous because it could possibly undermine organ donation and cost thousands of lives. In short, it never happened, and never will. Anyone who says differently is either substantially misinformed or a liar. (4/17/98)

Mike H. does not feel the need to back up his fear and anger about the legend's dangers (it would probably be difficult to do so) in part because exhortation often suffices in this context. In a heated debate about the believability of this tale of underground commerce in kidneys in *alt.folklore.urban* (8/16/94), Mike H. provides an excellent example of the moral self-righteousness of the debunker in the stolen kidney tale. He also uses a variety of forms of argumentation about why the tale couldn't be true and also speculates about the motivations of tellers.

The British law making the sale of organs illegal was not prompted by forcible removal of organs but by the desire to keep India's practice of payment for live kidney donation from spreading. Its similar to laws in most western countries now.

The belief that you can take an organ from anyone off the street and put it anywhere is extremely ignorant and extremely harmful. Urban legends of "organ theft" make transplantation appear gruesome and is a major cause of lost donations. Potential transplant patients are dieing [*sic*] because some asshole thought an "organ theft" story was entertaining. Anyone interested in more information is invited to read the *bit.listserv.transplant FAQ*.[12]

Mike's post distinguishes the "moral" debunker in this case. First he cites the illegality of trade in organs in Western countries, perhaps assuming (although it is not completely clear here) that illegality would prevent such commerce. Favoring a kind of facts-and-science bent, the second paragraph is likely more appealing to traditional debunkers: he provides a reference. The organized debunkers such as those on *alt.folklore.urban* tend to attribute the genesis and maintenance of such legends to generalized fear and ignorance about technology issues, which create a fertile seedbed for a variety of science-related legends, instead of specific ill-intended actors desiring to "entertain" others.

The United States' National Organ Transplant Act of 1984 (98th Congress, Public Law 98–507) specifically stipulates that donors and recipients may not be treated by the same medical personnel, perhaps precisely to address this fear. In attempting to debunk the stolen-organ legends, "moral" debunkers often invoke the existence of the law to suggest that such schemes are impossible. The use of this argument tends to feed accusations from believers that debunkers are naive; that they only disbelieve the legend because they don't know how cruel and greedy people can be, and that they have too much munificent faith in institutions such as big medicine and the government. Other debunkers might bring up illegality only to imply that if something like this were really happening, law enforcement would certainly have an interest in pursuing it and in publicizing this pursuit, and that the tabloid media would exploit it.

P. J., the paramedic, described what he observed to be the tenuous nature of organ-theft belief in his encounters both on and off the Internet:

> Depressing, that so many people would believe such an obviously contrived story ... the discussions [off the Internet] tended to be about the same. People have heard the story and while they may not believe it absolutely, they attached some belief to it. Again, very depressing. People will believe anything, especially if it sounds like a conspiracy-type story.

Yet one of the interesting things is that the story implies a vast conspiracy without apparently being connected with a well-elaborated conspiratorial mindset. Most believers stop short of accusing medical personnel involved in these debates of complicity.

Australians on-line have been treated to their own version of the kidney theft legend, nearly identical to the UT-Austin "reason not to party anymore" story but set in Australia. "Michele Shafer, " featured in the some American versions as an attributed source from Alachua, Florida also makes an appearance as an attributed source—but now her outfit is located in Camperdown, Sydney.

> Sadly, this is very true. My friend's husband is a Sydney EMT and they have received alerts regarding this crime ring. It is to be taken very seriously. The daughter of a friend of a fire-fighter had this happen to her. Skilled doctors are performing these crimes! (which, by the way have been highly noted in the Brisbane area). Additionally, the military has received alerts regarding this. This story blew me away. (Sent to *alt.folklore.urban* by Brian C. from Canada who received it via e-mail, 7/14 /99)

Darrow, an *alt.folklore.urban* regular noted the similarity to the American story in a post to the group:

> So, the text is virtually identical, except for the Australiocentric additions (000, Brisbane, and contact info). I have a hard time believing that these changes were accidental, since it would take a conscious effort to edit the story in the text form. Word-of-mouth can suffer a lot of changes, but email? Strikes me strange, like someone deliberately attempting to hoax out Aussies. Opinions? Interestingly, the address given for the woman who allegedly sent this out is rather close to that of Royal Prince Alfred Hopsital [sic], one of the nation's foremost teaching hospitals. 99 Missenden Rd, Camperdown, is the address either of the hospital's attached private medical centre, or of one of Sydney University's residential colleges. If this person were in fact attached in any way to RPAH or its medical centre, I think

she'd be advertising that fact. My conclusion is that someone has used this address so that people like me (who recognise it) would be more likely to be fooled. I am unceasingly amazed at some people's attempts to gain self-importance through spreading stuff like this! My 2c worth!

Certainly it is the case that someone had to consciously adapt the story for local consumption and send it out. The company that "Michele Shafer" worked for sent out an email post to a number of diet, fitness, and travel interest news groups that had received the kidney-hoax tale.

> The article which was posted to this news group relating to kidney thefts is a hoax. Please be advised that Medical Manager Research & Development is a software development company which has no knowledge or information concerning this matter. An e-mail was sent by an unknown party who apparently used Medical Manager Research & Development's address to perpetrate this hoax. If you have any questions, you may contact the FBI, your local law enforcement office, or visit the National Kidney Foundation web site at: http://www.nkfg.org/kidlegnd.htm"
> Please do your part to help dispel this hoax.
> Thank you,
> Corporate Legal Department
> Medical Manager Research & Development, Inc.

A standard legal department disclaimer at first, and then oddly stern instructions to contact the FBI or local law enforcement for more information. The ease with which MMR&D made these suggestions seems to me, once again, to reflect the feeling of empowerment and righteousness on the part of debunkers, who often take the supposed dangers emanating from the spread of this rumor as seriously as a believer might take an actual kidney theft. Again, as well, the sense of the legend as a "hoax" rather than a legend reflects a desire for a specific actor to blame. As for the desire for self-aggrandizement attributed by Darrow to the person who revamped the legend in Australian clothes, it is confounded by anonymity, not just in this instance but in nearly all others; both origins and the source of transmutations are untraceable.

Media and the Stolen Organ Legend

News media coverage of the First World kidney-theft legend has been fairly uniformly one of debunking. The same cannot be said for the Third World version. This distinction likely has some implications that will be discussed below. Print media news reported very little upon the topic and what reports did occur tended toward skepticism. By contrast, broadcast reports were more numerous and their overall stance more ambiguous.

Newspapers

Using Lexis-Nexis a search was made of major newspapers between 1989 and 1999 for articles on stolen kidneys or other organs.[13] Fifty-four articles were found. Ten of these specifically debunked the current First World version, often referring to the matter as a "hoax," connecting its circulation to a general uncritical mindset promoted by the Internet, and passing along pleas from agencies involved in transplant for readers not to forward the message any longer. Two others debunked the First World kidney-theft story in more general articles on urban legends. Ten reported upon allegations of theft abroad (four in India, where surgeons are accused of removing organs during other operations; one in Albania, where rumors that children are being taken to Italy and their organs harvested, one in Nigeria where sorcery was blamed for the alleged theft of sexual organs, and four were duplicate reports of the above). Eight considered ethical issues related to the existing organs market worldwide, including presumed consent law, poor terms of compensation for the impoverished donors, and differential cost burdens upon recipients. Two reported upon the violence associated with baby-parts rumors in Guatemala. Three reported upon the theft of organs from cadavers and one described a science-fiction novel with organ theft as a subplot.

Magazines

Only seven magazine references were found.[14] All but one concerned only the Third World version and each debunked it. These included Scheper-Hughes (1998), Barry (1995), Chelminski (1996), Scanlan (1994), Schreiberg (1990), Lopez (1994), and Radford (1999). None reported on the First World version, with the exception of Radford, who considered both versions and debunked them.

Broadcast News

Using the same search approach as described above with print news, the Lexis-Nexis database of broadcast news (television and radio) reports between 1989 and 1999 was searched. Initially 745 reports fit the search criteria.[15] A subset was constructed by choosing every tenth entry (n=74). Of these 74, a full 65 were unrelated to the topic. Of the nine remaining, four were "teasers" (preview announcements) for upcoming stories which would feature "stolen kidneys." Three concerned rumors and allegations of organ theft worldwide without evaluation. One debunked the First World version. One concerned the theft of organs from pet animals who were then left to die (Schroeder, 1996). One report concerned a murder in which a fetus was taken from a woman's womb and the woman died (Eyewitness News, 1996). To the extent that the subset is typical of the total of broadcast reports, then credulity seemed to be higher in this medium and inadvertent confirmation (such as might be suggested by the teasers) may or may not have enhanced this effect.

However, even if broadcast reports had been more uniformly critical, it is unlikely that they would have impeded the rumor greatly. Debunking may draw more attention to the legend. Scheper-Hughes (1992: 233–235) found in researching organ theft legends in Brazil that public service radio reports about the falsehood of the rumors would often fuel another round of rumor circulation, this time with the imprimatur of one having "heard it on the radio." This may not be as much of a problem in developed countries.

As for the idea of organ theft, the idea is expansively applied to a number of practices when it is discussed in broadcast settings, whereas there is no evidence that anything but the cognate version is used elsewhere. For instance, descriptions of the Zauhar-McNutt case employed a "stolen organ" angle. In this civil court case in 1997, McNutt needed a kidney. His fiancee, Zauhar, offered hers but was not a match. Zauhar's brother offered his on the condition that McNutt pay his expenses and make his sister happy. McNutt received the kidney and broke the engagement and Zauhar alleges theft by swindle. (Goldstein, 1997)

Fiction and Organ Theft

Where a high-tech organ theft scenario has emerged, it appears entirely limited to fictional representations. Here the technical impracticalities of forced organ removal are overcome through present-day medical corruption or future technological development in science fiction settings. The high-tech version contrasts with the current First World legend, which involves seduction and off-site organ removal (typically in the bathroom of a hotel), and also with the Latin American version.

In an episode of *Star Trek: Voyager*, "Fury" (2000), the specter of organ theft is first introduced as an updated version of the current Texas student tale. The captain tells an anecdote about a cadet's first time on leave at a vacation planet, who awakes after a night of partying to find his kidneys missing. She tells the story as an urban legend, but it serves as a segue to a plot involving a threat from an alien group species who are desperately ill and must harvest human organs to survive.

Yet even without the transfer of setting to the 24th century, American popular culture has generally dealt with the specter of organ theft in a high-tech manner. The threat that doctors may hasten the death of someone to get to their organs is a staple of medical and crime drama on television, as well as in Robin Cook's 1977 medical thriller novel, *Coma*. But in the mass media, as with the current manifestation of the kidney-theft legend, the victim-perpetrator dyad is not portrayed in racial or ethnic terms, although sometimes class issues are raised. *Coma*'s victims were mostly healthy middle-class young people, just like our Texas student.

In *Coma* a medical student becomes a sleuth when she observes an aberrant pattern of young people coming in for routine operations and ending up in comas due to adverse reactions to anesthesia, after which they are sent to a special hospice. It turns out that they are to be "warehoused" for the harvesting of their organs. Cook's author's note at the end of the novel warns, "This novel was conceived as entertainment, but it is not science fiction. Its implications are scary because they are possible, perhaps even probable." (Cook, 304) L.L. Stookey, in a critical companion to the works of Robin Cook, observes:

> Cook here is referring, of course, to the scenario of the black market trade in human organs that he has envisioned in his novel ... His novels expose technological possibilities that are mainly held in check by assumption of good will. The law, he believes, h(as) not adequately addressed a growing need for transplant organs, and the long lists of those who currently await transplants suggest that he is right. (p. 47–48)

In this analysis, the feasibility of such a scheme is portrayed in such fictional drama as prevented only by good will on the part of transplant clinicians, and by really no other social or structural factor. No wonder then that organizations like the National Kidney Foundation and groups of medical students have become "moral entrepreneurs" acting forcefully to debunk this legend.[16]

Another novel based upon the current First World version, Will Baer's *Kiss Me, Judas* (1998) has the victim, a private eye, fall in love with his surgically skilled victimizer, a woman named Jude. Both have deep connections to the criminal underworld.

NBC's *Law and Order* has dealt with the topic in two different episodes, and referenced it in still another. In the episode entitled "Sonata for Stolen Organ" (1991) a man is relieved of a kidney and left in the park, bleeding, whereupon a plot to deliver the stolen organ into the dying daughter of a wealthy developer is uncovered.

Beat cops find the man huddled on a bench and take him to a hospital. He is examined by a surgeon who concludes that the surgery done on the man was semi-professional and that his bleeding came from an apparent "rookie mistake." The detectives ask if his kidney could have been stolen, as per the cognate version of the urban legend. The surgeon scoffs and explains how complicated and technology-dependent transplant surgery is. So the police at first assume the man has amnesia about his own legitimate surgery. The man insists otherwise and so they continue to investigate, and corroborate his story when they can find no record of his surgery in area hospitals.

They retrace the transfer of organs for transplant in the region, using the records of recipient hospitals, and then compare them with ones registered by the "organ transplant network." They find a discrepancy, where a hospital receives an organ that was a match for a young woman patient who has registered under a pseudonym. The patient received that kidney. Her staff doctor has also recently ordered heavy-duty monitoring and anesthesia equipment and had it delivered to a nurse's apartment. It seems the doctor and nurse have been paid by the patient's wealthy father to perform the illegal transplant. She was not otherwise eligible, as her body had rejected two previous kidneys. A tissue match was found with the involuntary donor by bribing blood lab employees. When indictments are handed down against the doctor and father, there is massive publicity. The family tries to pay off the man whose kidney was taken.[17] The defense tries to present the patient's family in a desperate and sympathetic light while the prosecution reminds the jury that a man was stalked, violated, and left for dead. When convictions are secured, one prosecutor remarks that she feels sorry for the patient and understands the father's motivations. The other counters by asking what would have happened had his daughter needed a heart rather than a kidney.

This episode underscores a common theme in all legends involving an "underground": wealthy people can have whatever they need or want. All barriers—even if stubbornly logistical —fall away. However this *Law and Order* episode, like the novel *Coma*, is also noticeable for its contrasts with the folk version raised by the detectives at the beginning. The crime is transferred from a seductress' bathtub to a true surgical setting. Corruption, especially bribing, is necessary to make the profitable crime work—lest too many other witnesses emerge. And most of all, in the cognate version no one is ever caught and tried for kidney theft.

In another *Law and Order* episode, "Harm" (1998) a gunshot victim slides toward brain death and a surgeon prematurely takes out her organs for another patient in need at a neighboring hospital, where he is also on staff. The district attorney's office is only able to build a case when they discover that the doctor administered morphine to the donor, indicating that he knew she might be sentient enough to feel pain. In each case, doctors, nurses, high-tech equipment and surgical theaters within major hospitals are utilized.

Finally, *Law and Order* in 1994 ("Precious") used the specter of body parts theft as a red herring. When a baby disappears from a park, one of the Guatemalan nannies in the park offers the detectives her theory about kidnapped children: stolen for their organs. The theory is simply used in the narrative to set up a *Rashomon*-like opening scene: the detectives ultimately pay little heed to the idea, although it is never specifically debunked either. Ultimately the child's family is accused of making up the abduction tale when in fact they have already killed her themselves.

As is also the case with the snuff film, the specter of body parts theft seems intriguing to news and fictional media alike. Broadcast news media seem to be most likely to report allegations of organ theft without evaluation. Paradoxically, fictional representations seem clearer about the logistical barriers to organ theft and create narrative pathways around them. Still, they also seem to endorse the idea that it is "good will" which is largely responsible for the theft organs by doctors being rare.

PROACTIVE DEBUNKERS AND THE QUESTION OF INTENTION IN CRIME LEGEND PROMULGATION

Traditionally, the role of the active hoaxer has been downplayed in folklore research. Perhaps because there is usually no way to trace the origins of the initial flurry of email, word-of-mouth stories, and badly photocopied flyers, folklorists regard the hoaxers' intentions as secondary to the importance of believers and retellers in the spread of the tale. There are two issues here: the difficulty in tracing the origins of a legend, and the philosophical commitment to believers and recounters as the more important part of the social life of the tale. The latter sometimes seems to stem from the former. Contrary to what people who get angry at the spread of a particular hoax or rumor might hope, the origins of these legend episodes appear to be multiple and partial: they appear to snowball from piecemeal origins (a variety of combined motifs and narratives) rather than an initial, identifiable event that became exaggerated and detached from its original context. As discussed in the introductory chapter, it is difficult to affix blame and it is rare for hoaxes and rumors to be deliberately started and successfully perpetuated. Although they may be analytically separable, promulgators and casual believers are not so distinct in real life. Very little is thus actually known about the motivations of originators and embellishers, such as those people who add authoritative-sounding details to warning flyers. Brunvand's guess is consistent with that of Shibutani's case study analysis—it attributes embellishment to a somewhat natural process. Folklorists, like Brunvand, have simply noted that since we cannot find these people, we cannot assume their motivations are malicious and intended to be *fully* deceptive, as we might say of some hoax perpetrators. While the embellisher must know that they are adding information, they may still believe that the story itself is true.

About.com (formerly The Mining Company), an information and encyclopedia-like website with a large file on urban legends, provides an example of an attribution of origins based on maliciousness and a desire to deceive and frighten any and all unknown others:

> *Someone* initiated that cavalcade of faxes, email and phone calls earlier this year, causing panic among prospective travelers to New Orleans. It's hard to imagine what the hoaxer's motivation was, if it wasn't to spread a climate of fear. In succeeding, he or she induced others to do the same. An epidemic was born. (Emery, 1997)

About.com's website description of the kidney-theft hoax then goes on to couch the interpretation of the event in a metaphorical framework of "memetic" or "virus-like" behavior, referring to the urban-legend forms' ability to mutate, adapt, and spread across cultures.

Likewise, the United Network on Organ Sharing, or UNOS, worries:

Many people who hear the myth probably dismiss it, but it is possible that some believe it and decide against organ donation out of needless fear. If you receive questions about this story, you may wish to mention the Washington Post story. The WP first ran a story about the kidney heist myth on April 2, 1991 in which the writer traced back the origin of the myth to a rejected movie script.[18]

The Public Affairs Department of the New Orleans Police Department has also threatened to pursue anyone passing along this tale. (Pursue them with what, exactly, it is unclear.) Nonetheless, the Department posted a notice on its website that with regards to alleged kidney theft:

The warnings that are being disseminated through the Internet are FICTI-TIOUS and may be in violation of criminal statutes concerning the issuance of erroneous and misleading information.[19]

It is here that the disjunction between a hoax and an urban legend is vital. The dissemination of urban legends is one that relies upon sincerity of belief for its development, rather than intentional deception. It is certainly possible that interested parties began the circulation of the story with the worst of intentions, be they biomedical interference or a kind of vicious, albeit secret, joy in getting people scared over nothing. Yet the mutation of the story to different locations suggest an "urban legend" rather than a "hoax" model applies.

CONCLUSION/SUMMARY

More likely, though, the legend is a mutation of older legends. Underlying fears combine with *inferential belief* in the kidney-heist legend, as well as the snuff film legend. This combination is vital to understanding the social life of the legend: the meanings attached to it, its ability to fade and then return another day unscathed by previous debunkings, and the disputes over everyday epistemology that surround it.

Thematically, the tale feeds on the fresh oxygen of Brave New World technophobia and feared social disintegration. Yet Rothman (1998) suggests that the reluctance of Americans to donate organs (generally about half refuse or claim they would refuse) stems less from Frankenstein associations than from a general discomfort with collective care. "Americans are unaccustomed to sharing resources of any kind when it comes to medicine." (p. 6) In this sense, the fear of theft just takes the stinginess one step forward, transforming the personal conflict over the potential removal of one's organs after death to an outright victimization during life by the pleading forces.

Promulgators and believers do not expect the police or mass media to warn you about such hazards—although your office mate who likes to forward such email just has. Perhaps here the guilt associated with the fantasized pursuit of sex and drug pleasures characterized by the tale legitimates the absence of warnings. When you stray this way, expect "anything" to happen—lose your kidneys, star in a snuff film.

It is also tempting to couch the impetus for the stolen body parts legend—in its more generic form—in the extreme inequalities and inadequacies of the private free market health care system, where one may find oneself suspicious that one's organs might be more valuable stuck in someone else with more social status. One could argue that in the same way that the snuff film legend "concentrates" fear about violence against women, the stolen body parts legend concentrates fear of having one's life literally reduced in worth to the sum of one's parts. Such fears aren't totally absent from the legend's promulgation, except that the health care arrangements in countries around the world that sustain the legend are vastly different—from Latin America where arrangements for the care of the poor is rudimentary at best to Europe where universal health care is the norm to the United States, the pinnacle of high-tech medicine but a bifurcated market for haves and have-nots. When medics object to the spread of the legend and take offence at its implications, they reveal a heightened sensitivity to the underlying resentment directed towards them—in all of these places and for a variety of reasons. There is a commonality to the First and Third world versions of the tale—and that is its evocation of a clandestine network of doctors gone bad, because of the lure of profits. The legend could be seen, in a sense as what Knapp (1944) characterized as a "wedge driver" casting suspicion upon the medical establishment. Yet overall the class politics are not overt. The formal properties of the tale itself seem to also exhibit more "snowballing" (Peterson and Gist, 1951) than condensing characteristics. In this case, the primal fear of bodily disintegration picks up elements of class suspicion, puritanism, social distrust, and pessimism about ever knowing for sure about the nature of the threat.

The stolen body parts legend endorses the idea—not even very subtly or in a tacit manner, but overtly—of an international organ-theft conspiracy that operates with impunity. Grafted here onto a pre-existing femme fatale legend, it appears nonetheless to be losing its Us versus Other particularities. This international elite is purely profit driven, their network of operators is wide and likely diverse, and the victims are Anyone.

In retrospect the same could be said of the evolution of the snuff film legend. Once only possible, it was thought by believers, to be made "in South America, where life is cheap" the snuff film market now spans the globe, exists comfortably in the United States, and even could, as the television show *Millennium* suggests, go unstoppable on the Internet. Again, here, we find the notable absence of swarthy perpetrators, implicating instead a multi-faceted criminal elite. Thus the zero-sum scheme feared in the Third World version seems to be pulling the "ordinary American" into the realm of the undefended.

Still, the absence of specific threatening Others in this particular iteration of the stolen body parts legend does not mean that the threat is any less frightening. In fact the Anywhere and Anybody quality of this and a number of other crime legends seems to generalize the anxiety. There is no indication beforehand that our drugging seductress was anything but an ordinary temptress, our college student or businessman being rather ordinary too. Consider the level of detail offered about how the crime took place and why it happened, compared with the level of detail about who the perpetrator and the victim are. This is especially borne out in the text, but isn't at all contradicted by the talk about the text.

As with the snuff film legend, the discussions that surround the body parts legend are somewhat different in emphasis than the tale itself would suggest on its own as a semi-mutable text. There is a deep sense of organized wantonness and unimpeded profit-driven predation that provides the cognitive context for the fair-weather belief in First World organ theft. The only voice of authority is the already-in-the-know 911 dispatcher—after the fact. Hence the need to pass along the warning "just in case" it is true. The importance, then, of inferential belief based on the idea that the story "could" happen and thus should be kept in motion and heeded only reveals itself in full flower in the talk *around* the text rather than the text itself, which appears to have few, if any, fervent partisans.

Finally, the persistence of the legend in the face of two types of active debunking (moralistic medical danger and ridiculing, respectively) supports Morin's notion that legends can be "driven underground" to smoulder until the next wind of circulation. The existence of a moral prohibition against spreading the tale does not impede it, nor does the absence of fervent believers in it. The legend has encountered, in both its incarnations, a fair amount of mass media debunking only to rise again and again. In these ways, the social life surrounding this tale confirms Morin's pessimism. Official debunking has also taken place in the current case without clear results. As such, the elusive policy implications of the sociology of rumor studies is supported here.

CHAPTER FOUR

Shopping Mall and Theme Park Abduction Legends

The purpose of this chapter is to examine an amalgam of abduction legends that have, for more than a century, traveled together more often than they have done so apart. The legends center around the forced abduction of women, usually by means of trick or drugging, for the purposes of forced prostitution. Enhanced by periods of moral panic over so-called "white slavery" which peaked in the 1880s in Britain and the 1910s in the United States, the legend core has been challenged and debunked nearly from the beginning (Billington-Grieg, 1913; Massachusetts, 1914), and as a result was "driven underground" from time to time but never really dissipated. In fact, it has shown itself to be a resilient legend with a great deal of flexibility, seemingly strengthened by its remission periods.

By the post-World War II period, the legend, having been quiescent for several decades in the United States, attached itself to new-found anxieties about the modern marketplace. The idea that modern women were being kidnapped from shopping malls, cinemas, boutiques, and theme parks by means of drugging and/or disguise, and then spirited away into sex slavery and prostitution rings appeared again in the 1960s. Morin (1970) studied the outbreak of a rumor panic around abduction and white slavery charges in the summer of 1969 in Orleans, France that held that young women were being drugged in dress boutiques, and sold as chattel abroad. During the summer of 1969, rumors to this effect reached such a fevered pitch that violence nearly broke out. Some versions of the rumor implicated Orleans' Jewish shop owners specifically, giving the whole affair an anti-Semitic effect, as had some versions of the earlier white slavery legends in the United States and England.

In North America in the 1970s, the legend attached itself to shopping mall restrooms and the alleged victims were also teenage girls. Transported to new modern locations, the narrative nonetheless varied little from the one at the turn of the century, which fretted over the fate of women lured out of other public accommodations, in particular the "candy store." Then as now, there is a clear symbolic association between a drastic and unanticipated danger at the heart of a location that has seduced the modern woman into leisure, consumption, and self-fulfillment.

From the 1980s onward the legend shifted again: from a story naming young women as victims to one that most often names children as the intended prey. While to some extent this shift reflects a similar shift in focus of the public's general concern with the dangers of sexual exploitation and abuse, from woman as primary victim to child as such, it also reflects an expanding legend with varied versions that resonate with different audiences. This shift is not uniform, however, since some versions still describe women as the primary prey.

Of the three case studies presented here, this drugging-disguise-abduction legend probably has the most linear of histories. The legend's basic narrative conforms closely to those similar legends attached to white slavery panics. Disguise of the victim as a motif plays a particularly strong role in the narrative. At the same time, however, an apparently new series of shopping mall-related abduction legends has emerged, focusing upon elaborate deceptions as the cause of abductions of children and adult women.

THE MODERN LEGEND

Let a child venture into a restroom by him or herself, and they might fall prey to a predator, perhaps more than one, cleverly able to spirit the child past a guardian who is none the wiser. How? By disguising the child—drugging her, changing her clothes, dyeing her hair, and carrying her out of the restroom and out of the shopping mall undetected. To where? Unclear, but it can't be any good place. Most current versions often involve the foiling of the plot by an observant mother who recognizes her child's shoes. Fathers tend to be altogether absent; neither rescuer nor distracted parent.

The same notable absence of chivalrous men characterized the slightly older version of the mall legend involving teenage girls, as well. Girls were captured from shopping malls, it was alleged, for procurement into local prostitution rackets. (Brunvand, 1984: 80–81) While the term 'white slavery' was never used in this scenario, the story amounts to an Americanized version of the legend panic that Morin investigated in France. That the current version usually carries no information about the ethnic background of perpetrators is of considerable curiosity considering the legend's weighty history of more than a century. Some current versions, however, do implicate procurers of Middle Eastern descent.

Brunvand terms this legend "The Attempted Abduction" and notes that while it was routinely debunked in local newspapers during the 1970s, it has maintained its basic narrative structure. (Brunvand, 1984: 79–82; 1999: 316–317). In some versions it is also maintained that other bystanders did nothing to intervene in the kidnapping because they believed the captors when they explained that the hysterical or unconscious victim was their relative who had fallen ill in the restroom. The bystander is thus exonerated from complicity by the shrewdness and complexity of the capture scheme, and simultaneously admonished for a lack of *hyper*vigilance in the face of these new criminal techniques. Alternatively, some versions suggest that security personnel in the stores are so used to this sort of kidnapping occurring that they instruct the mother to scan the exiting crowd for her child's shoes. In either case the implication is that little safety is provided by numbers.

Katherine Samon's 1993 article on urban legends in the popular women's magazine, *McCall's* featured the one of the more common versions.

> A good friend of mine told me this, and it still gives me chills. A young mother and her four-year-old daughter were shopping, and while the mother was busy trying on clothes, the little girl disappeared. The frantic woman called security guards, who combed the mall for the missing child. They were about to give up when one of the guards found the girl standing on a toilet in the men's restroom so you couldn't see her feet. Her long, dark hair had been chopped off and dyed blond, and she was dressed in boy's clothes! Apparently she had been abducted by a notorious child-snatching ring who abandoned her once they realized the search was on.
>
> Gotcha!
>
> There's no truth to this story. It's just one example of what is known as an urban legend ... (Samon, 1993, p. 120)

Another current version involves similar abductions from Disney theme parks. Despite the fact that in reality it is fairly easy to lose a child in a theme park, no such incidents have been reported to Orlando or Anaheim police (Miller 1994). This means either that no such abductions have taken place there or that a massive conspiracy cover-up campaign exists involving parents, media, the Walt Disney Corporation, and the local police departments. Here is a query from a park fan on the news group *alt.disney.disneyland*:

> Has anyone heard about the kidnapping [sic] that almost took place at DL [Disneyland]? Apparently a woman and her child (either age 4,5,or 6) were sitting on the curb on main street, the mother turned her head just for a second and looked back for her child and he was gone. She then frantically allerted [sic] security. They took her to an office where there were quite a few t.v. monitors to look for her son. She was so out of breath and distraut [sic] security told her that they didn't have much time, that to look closely at faces not at the clothes her child was wearing or his hair. From the time she entered the office, they found her child in a matter of 3 minutes. He was headed out the entrance by a couple of Iranians. When they grabbed him they took him to a restroom and changed his clothes and shaved his head, all in a matter of minutes. That way he wouldn't be noticed. There [sic] reason for taking him was so that they could sell him.
>
> This just sends chills up my spine. I have 3 children 7,4,2. The moral of this sad story is that when ever you are in the park keep your child at your side at all times, to prevent this ever happenning to you.
>
> A Truly Crazy Disney Fan!—Kim (9/22/96)

The *Urban Legends Reference Pages* summarizes versions of the Disneyland kidnap story by noting that they are often accompanied by dour forecasts of the victims being sold into sex slavery.[1]

Yet the fact that these modern versions, involving children, often fail to specify an ultimate nefarious purpose for the elaborate abduction, opens up a great deal of leeway to the creative hearer and reteller. Here as with the snuff film legend, weaker (in the sense of less organized) forms of belief may actually be the strongest suit in maintaining the salience of the legend today. One may believe the abduction story without believing that a kidnapping and prostitution ring was operating; perhaps, to fill in the blanks, one might imagine black market adoption or sexual abuse at the hands of the perpetrator himself. That is, one may substitute a more plausible ending for the tale than the traditional one as a way to support the overall plausibility of the bathroom abduction. At the same time, though, the scenario of drugging and disguise remain remarkably stable despite its lack of necessity. Indeed, as will be discussed below, this is a legend in which promulgators may themselves doubt the truth status of a tale while choosing to pass it on for its exemplary value.

This tendency is also in keeping with the tale's roots in the white slavery panics of the turn of the last century. A brief history of those episodes and the associated abduction rumors are provided below.

WHITE SLAVERY LEGENDS, 1880–1915, UNITED STATES AND ENGLAND

Frederick Grittner's examination of the so-called "white slavery" myth in American and British history suggests that apocryphal tales of forcible abduction of young women accompanied more general social reform campaigns against prostitution. As such, there is a consistent tendency among moral reformers and interested journalists to conflate social coercion into the sex trade with the specter of actual abductions for such a purpose. Stories abounded, then as now but then to a much greater degree, about "the forced prostitution of white women and girls by trick, narcotics, and coercion." (Grittner, 1990: 3) Procurers were often portrayed as non "white" meaning usually non-Anglo-Saxon and non-Protestant. (Grittner, 5, 20–21, 62–63) Civic reformers and rescuers were, by contrast, precisely of this background and male. One cannot but notice the degree to which the modern tale has preserved the core of the forced procurement narrative, while having jettisoned the patriarchal rescuer.

> In another story a girl at a soda fountain observed a man dropping a powder in her glass. After drinking the soda she became dizzy and semiconscious, and the man took her by the arm, saying to the attendant, "This is my sister. She often has these fainting attacks. I will take her home in a carriage." The girl was sufficiently conscious to object, was rescued by a bystander and escaped.

> Another account alleges the administration of a narcotic drug by the use
> of a hypodermic needle by a procurer, who plies the needle on his victim as
> he passes her on the street ...
>
> Every story of this kind has been thoroughly investigated, and either
> found to be a vague rumor, where one person has told another that some
> friend of the former (who invariably in turn referred the story farther back)
> heard that the thing happened ... (Massachusetts, 1914)

But the underlying moral panic was really a reaction to the explosion of
prostitution in general, owing to the development of a desperate urban industrial working class and a simultaneous period of renewed calls for chastity,
monogamy, and purity for middle and upper-middle class white women.
"The elaboration of the myth of sexual slavery," Grittner writes, "attempted
to balance the moral didacticism characteristic of Victorian culture and the
allure of forbidden sexual encounters." (P. 32) The reality was that many of
the poor women who were the subject of the purity campaigns in the United
States from 1909 to 1914, were immigrant women who saw prostitution as
the best of a series of bad choices for survival wages. (P. 63) Generally
stymied by an inability of academics and pundits to see class, male domina-
tion, and poverty as a primary motivation for women thought to be held in
"white slavery" its popular image split along two paths of explanation: the
idea of otherwise pure girls being tricked or drugged, on the one hand, or
loose morals on the other.

Both the broader moral panic and the forced abduction scenario are
presented in the 1913 film "Traffick in Soul" which was used for a time as
an instructional film for female immigrants at Ellis Island. Widely regarded
as one of the first social problem exploitation films, it now is included in the
National Film Registry for its historical interest.[2]

The film opens in a candy store owned by a wealthy man, Mr. Trubus,
who is chosen to address a citizens' commission on the dangers of white
slavery. The scene switches to a brothel where young women are locked in
their rooms. A man from the brothel spies on a young woman working in a
candy store, while across town police are briefed on forced procurement. At
the harbor, two Swedish girls are lured to a phony "employment agency."
The man from the brothel courts the candy store clerk and plies her with
gifts, dancing, and finally a drink. Falling unconscious, she is dragged to the
brothel. We find out that the "Office of International Purity and Reform
League" of which Mr. Trubus is a part is in fact a front for the brothel. After
the police raid the brothel and rescue the girls, the newspaper headlines note
that "50,000 girls disappear yearly into the clutches of the white slavery
trade," and ask, "is it possible that our candy stores are used for this infamous market?" The twist here is that the town patriarchs, deeply involved
in the public campaign to stop white slavery, are themselves not to be trusted.
It is the ordinary police who rescue the girls.

"Traffick in Soul" shares the generalized anxiety which accompanies this legend, both then and now. One should not only fear the "Other" as procurer and despoiler, but rightly also the pillars of the community and moral entrepreneurs like Mr. Trubus. This more generic predator appears often in crime legends, and such an example so early in the century suggests that this depiction may be characteristic of middle-class promulgation contexts rather than post-social or postmodern ones as suggested by similar examples in the previous case studies. Grittner's analysis of middle-class reformers in the anti-white-slavery movement underscores this point. Movement activists were anxious to distance their purity campaigns from incipient nativist movements, fearing a loss of credibility. (Grittner, 6, 55) Nonetheless the fear of nativist influence in the movement reflects the tendency of the topic, by its nature, to conjure images of swarthy exploiters and pure, white girls driven to prostitution against their will.

White, or Sex Slavery Legends Today—Confusion and Overlap with Trafficking in Persons

The conflation of socio-structural and direct coercion continues to surround accounts of abduction for sex slavery today in the West. Many women are indeed trafficked from Eastern Europe to more prosperous nations and once arrived, pressured to succumb to the sex trade, although it is largely a myth that these women had grand illusions as to what would await them, and perceive themselves to have few economic alternatives in many cases. There is no evidence that such labor has become so scarce and so prized that an abduction ring has emerged.

The white slavery myth described by Morin and carried through the boutique-abduction rumor panic of 1969 in Orleans, France did not die with the dissipation of the panic. Stories of French girls trafficked to Arab harems found their way into popular exploitation books like that of Barlay (1977). Sources for these claims were, as usual, elusive. The claim also appears in a widely read feminist text by Barry (1979):

> Several thousand teenage girls disappear from Paris every year. The police know but cannot prove that many are destined for Arab harems. An eyewitness report that auctions have been held in Zanzibar, where European women were sold to Arab customers (p. 33)

Barry further claims that debunkers of the white slavery myth were engaging in "hair-splitting" by treating socio-structural and direct (i.e., abduction, drugging) coercion of women into the sex trade as logically distinct. (p. 28) Most commentators who wished to follow this line of inquiry, however, by the 1970s dropped the term *white slavery* in favor of the terms *sex slavery* or *trafficking in women,* the latter being a somewhat confusing phrase that also includes pandering, debt bondage, smuggling of illegal immigrants, and coercive conditions for industrial labor. Indeed, today the term *white slavery* seems to appear only in white supremacist circles, such as in the infamous novel by Andrew Macdonald, *The Turner Diaries* (1978). A search for the term in use in Internet news groups drew mostly instances in racist news groups. The term has not completely disappeared, though. Syndicated sex advice columnist Dan Savage printed an inquiry he received in his column, "Savage Love" (December 17, 1998) in which the author claims that her sister was told by locals while in Europe ten years earlier that rich Arab men have white women kidnapped off the street in Western Europe, or when traveling in Egypt, and force them into harem-servitude. The term "white slavers" was used. Was this true, she wondered, and should she alter her travel plans? (Savage debunked the story.)

With or without the term "white slavery" attached, in each version of the story, the common denominator is: young women taken to sexual exploiters against their will—in fact, procurers who go to extraordinary lengths to capture and secret them away. Up through 1980, according to Brunvand (1984, 78–82), the shopping mall abduction tale was still mainly attached to young women and included an explanation of procurement. Simultaneously, the tale spoke of a wider world, mysterious, dangerous and exciting—almost a world apart.

To conclude from more than one hundred years of cyclical moral panic and debunking investigation in Europe and the United States that such allegations of abduction for the purposes of sex slavery are basically mythological is not to say that women and children are not trafficked for such a purpose in various parts of the world. But even in the case of highly coercive prostitution schemes in areas of the world that are truly without reliable guardianship and in which virtual sex enslavement does exist (via debt bondage and law enforcement collusion in the illegal confinement of sex workers), there is little evidence that stranger abduction plays a role in it. Here, as with the Third World market in donated organs, there is little chance that such risk-taking on the part of procurers would be necessary given the dire economic and social circumstances in which millions of young women find themselves. In a report on one of the largest procurement markets in the world, the trafficking of Nepali girls to Indian brothels, the organization Human Rights Watch describes a system in which destitute women are lured into forced prostitution schemes by offers of marriage or legitimate work. In other cases, young women are sold by their equally destitute families to procurers and agents. (Human Rights Watch—Asia, 1995, 14–15) There are rumors of stranger abduction for such purposes, but as with the Western rumor there is no substantiation by any of the reform groups working on the problem or Human Rights Watch. (p. 30)

INTERLOCUTORS AND THE ABDUCTION LEGENDS

Both the updated "traditional" disguise-abduction tale and new variations appeared in news groups between 1995 and 1999. There were 220 references to shopping mall abductions found in Internet news groups during 1996; 361 in 1997; and 580 in 1998. Additionally, references to abductions at Disney theme parks were counted: 287 in 1996; 591 in 1997; and 690 in 1998.[3] At the very least, then, the Disney version of the legend has become as popular on-line, if not more so, than the shopping mall version. Additionally, very few of the these posts were found within the folklore groups: in reference to the Disney park posts, 38 were in the folklore groups in 1996; 7 in 1997; and 41 in 1998. In the shopping mall posts, 15 were in the folklore groups in 1996; 13 in 1997; and 37 in 1998. Thus stories related to the feared abduction of children from malls and Disney theme parks mainly took place outside of the skeptical orbit of the folklore groups. However, as we shall see below, this does not mean that skeptics or debunkers were absent from the related discussions in other groups.

Cognate Versions

Concern about the abduction of a child by strangers haunts many on-line parents' groups. Parents routinely argue about whether and to what extent one should worry about it. In the on-line news group *misc.kids*, a discussion developed about leaving children unattended. One participant, Jennifer, expressed anger at parents who were oblivious to their children's whereabouts in public places and cited the threat of stranger abduction. Cindy responded by suggesting that parents overly worried about stranger abduction would do better to be concerned about more common risks to children like car accidents.

> JENNIFER: What if you left your children unsupervised in your own yard and they were abducted or assaulted by a stranger? I know of cases where this has happened.
>
> CINDY: I know of lots of _stories_ about this happening to a "friend of my neighbor" but they have always fallen apart when investigated further. There are lots of urban legends about this happening (like the story of the child who was abducted from Disney World or one of those giant discount stores, got new clothes and a hair dye job, but the parents allegedly recognized the child by his/her shoes...). But the truth is that, in the countries where most of us are sitting—and yes, that includes Canada, and the US too—the vast majority of abductions are carried out by someone known to the child, often the parent who didn't get custody or a close relative following a messy divorce case. The same is true of abuse—the perpetrators very seldom snatch a strange child from their own backyard; more likely they are related to or know the child already, or will take the time to make friends with the child first. This is not to say that there are no dangers associated with leaving a child unattended—but losing sleep over the very unlikely possibility of an

abduction while forgetting about dangers like climbing the fence and wandering out into traffic is a serious misjudgement.

JENNIFER: Cindy, I'm not talking about urban legends. Here in Ottawa, Canada, where I've lived for nearly 30 years, the very reliable local media have documented 2 stories:

> 1. bout 10 years ago, two preschool brothers were playing unsupervised in their own fenced yard. A mentally disturbed young man, a total stranger, abducted them from their yard, sexually assaulted them, and threw them into the Ottawa River. The younger boy drowned, and his brother was rescued by a passing woman jogger. The surviving boy grew up to be severely disturbed, and recently murdered a local newspaper vendor for money.
>
> 2. A preschool girl was abducted from her own yard by teenage boys who sexually assaulted her. She suffered physical and psychological trauma. These boys lived in the neighborhood and were known to the girl's family..... [*three more stranger abductions are recounted by Jennifer*] The only way I know of that any of these incidents could have been prevented is to supervise your small child closely. This could also prevent him/her from climbing the fence and wandering out in traffic, a danger I would never forget about. (*misc.kids*, 8/6/96)

While engaged in a kind of contest about who has the right idea about what to lose sleep over, Jennifer and Cindy's exchange reveals the wide nets cast by both interlocutors on the issue of stranger abduction. Cindy, armed with a repertoire of risk-rationality arguments approaching that of a social scientist and Jennifer, clearly prepared for such a moment by a scrupulous list of brazen abduction incidents, talk right past each other. Cindy is also a regular at the debunking group, *alt.folklore.urban*. Taking pro-active debunking to full tilt, she introduces an urban legend not yet raised at all, let alone raised as true, to debunk a more generalized panic about missing and abducted kids.

Cindy employs what might be called "expansive debunking": a process by which the legend is actually introduced into the conversation by the debunker or skeptic, perhaps to provide evidence that irrationality exists around a given topic, specifically around a given social problem. This exchange provides quite a clear account of the different ways in which debunkers and non-debunkers identify the "problem" out there. Jennifer amasses evidence about real threats to children while Cindy is mainly concerned that some level of irrational panic or gullibility might be lurking in the discussion. Both are mothers of small children.

It should be cautioned that in the present study, the identification of gullibility and irrationality as "the problem" is characteristic only of "strong" debunkers, ones who might be described as part of a debunking subculture, rather than situation-bound or casual skeptics. The latter tend to either be alarmed and angry at the specific content of the legend (like Mike H. in the kidney-theft discussions) or be so apologetic when suggesting a certain story is not true (such as those in the snuff film discussions) that the issue of a greater gullibility out there threatening to engulf society is really not as prominent.

Yet *misc.kids* had engaged this same disguised-child tale before. In a discussion about appropriate levels of protectiveness, Kellie offered the story in a familiar form:

> Better to be overprotective than to not care at all. At a mall in our home town, a woman had turned away from her shopping cart 'for just a second'(!?) and her child was stolen from the cart. When she noticed, she was lucky in the fact that there was a mall security guard close by who closed down the exits and had security people go to the washrooms. When mall security found the person and the child in the washroom, the woman had already changed all the child's clothes, was in finishing up a 'dye job' on the child's hair and had drugged the child, so that they would appear like a mother with a sleeping child.
>
> All this happened in less than 5 minutes—It can happen that fast! :-{ If I lose sight of any of my children, I'm not ashamed of yelling out their names—just in case! (11/28/95)

Naomi responded by joining in a somewhat skeptical reaction that had emerged:

> I often hear things like this described as "just a second", and suspect that it's more like a minute. It MUST take more than a second to undo the buckle, lift the child from the seat, and disappear out of sight! .... Again, if she'd turned her back for "a second", and immediately contacted security...how could the person have, within "a second" made it to the wash room, changed the child's clothes, dyed his hair, and drugged him! I'm guessing it was more like a minute or two. (Misc.kids, 11.29.95)

Rosalie, who identified herself as a grandmother, was skeptical about the idea that many stores really had store detectives and restrooms; to her this made the story "a most unlikely scenario."[4] Thus the argument shifted to whether such an abduction could possibly happen, with what sort of child, with what sort of drug, with what sorts of disguises, time elapses, and digressions on the new portability of hair dye. Here, a weak debunking inflates the authority of the believers, and their ability to sketch in details, collectively, to move the story from possibility to plausibility. Not at all a "debunker's debunking" this example shows that 1) skepticism is not limited to the places where debunkers gather, but appears in a variety of forms *in situ* 2) that debunkers enter conversations where such sparring has already taken place, enervating or aggravating believers, and 3) discussions about a variety of dangers are often bifurcated: the two options presented by Kellie are over-protectiveness (what debunkers might think of as paranoia) or "to not care at all" (what debunkers are often charged with by believers).

Here Kellie reiterates a theme that seems important to defenders of the truth of all crime legends—the alternative risk of "not caring at all" about the threat described in the narrative of the crime story. That is, the believer is not so much a strict "believer" as she is one who finds a valuable lesson in the story regardless of its relationship to event or fact, and surmises a greater danger in skepticism, that of "not caring at all." The value of the lesson infuses the promulgation process with a vigor of righteousness regardless of the truth status of the story. Thus the legend's truth status will not so much be defended as declared irrelevant.

As will be discussed below, it is likely that the resonance of this legend has been enhanced by the missing children panic of the 1980s. Shopping trips with children are often cause for concern in parents' groups. Wal-Mart stores have initiated a program called "Code Adam" which is an emergency practice put into play when a child is lost in a store. As the company describes it, "A brief description of the child [is given] to all associates, who immediately stop their normal work to look for the child. Store associates also monitor all exits to ensure that the child does not leave the store."[5] It is clear that the Code Adam system has overlapped to some degree with the bathroom-abduction legend, even though it is simply an exit blocking and search system for lost children. Anne, whose daughter wandered away at a Wal-Mart store, told the other news group participants at *alt.support.step-parents* that the bathroom abduction scenario dominated her fearful thoughts as a realistic threat.

> Yesterday in Walmart I needed to change Charlie's diaper, and I took Brooke with me to the restroom, which is located inside the layaway room. I opened the door, took Charlie in, laid him on the changing table, looked around for Brooke, and didn't see her. I quickly opened the door back up to make sure she wasn't stuck out in the layaway room, she wasn't. So I went back into the bathroom to look for her. I looked in every stall, calling her name, she wasn't there. I realized that she must not have made it into the bathroom with me, and raced back out to the layaway room for a more thorough search. When I didn't find her, I checked the three aisles to the right and left . . . she was gone. There were three sales associates there, I called to them, "My daughter's gone! She was wearing a striped sweater and blue pants! She's two and a half!" And ran back out to look for her, calling (screaming?) her name. I heard the announcement go over the PA system, "All WalMart Associates, we have a Code Adam. Code Adam for a two and a half year old girl named Brooke, wearing a striped sweater and blue pants. All WalMart associates, drop what you're doing and look for this child." My heart, at this point, I think might have stopped. I remember thinking dully, "What's the point of saying what she's wearing? She's not wearing it

anymore if somebody took her." I just thought, she NEVER could have gotten far away from me in those few seconds alone. Somebody must have seen the opportunity and snatched her up. It was about ten minutes of searching, before the announcement came over the PA system, "WalMart associates, please inform the parent, we have the child. Code Adam is canceled, we have the child." But right before that an associate had come up to me and said, "They have her." And I didn't really understand, I guess, I thought she meant kidnappers because I said, "WHO has her?" and started to cry. They started to bring me over to where she was, and this guy was carrying her and she was crying. He told me that two of the WalMart people had to chase her down, she was all the way on the other side of the store! I don't know how long it would have taken me to find her, by the time I did she really COULD have been gone. She kept saying, "I couldn't find you?" and I just was shaking and crying when I realized she was actually safe. I've never been so scared in my life. This lady put her arms around me and I think I just fell to pieces for a minute and people were patting Brooke and saying they were glad she was safe ...> >When it was all over, this woman told me a few things, which is the point of this. She said that when your child is missing, always tell the store people what shoes they were wearing right away. Because kidnappers always change the clothes, but they don't usually change the shoes. And then she said, to say to the store people, "My child is missing, she was wearing XYZ, have somebody check the bathrooms!" because apparently I guess the WalMart Code Adam announcement didn't direct the associates to the bathrooms. Anyway, I thanked the manager profusely and he told me that the lady had come to him and made the same suggestions and he thought they were good ones too, he's going to do some training. But I just wanted to let everybody know this. I had never heard it, and most of the people on these lists have young kids, or know people with young kids they can pass it on to. Did you know that they don't let anyone with children in the right age group leave the store during a Code Adam?! (11/14/99)

Vicki R. in the same group cautions gently about the disguise legend aspects of Anne's worries, while relating sympathetically to her panic.

The shoes idea figures prominently in a number of child-abduction urban legends. In reality (the way I understand it; I'd be interested in seeing some research on this), most abductors wouldn't bother to change shoes or clothing; their aim is to get the child out of the store as soon as possible, and they're much more likely to just either scoop them up and head for the exit, or ask for the child's help to look for a lost kitty and just gently walk out the door with them....(11/14/99)

Vicki's intervention is unusually diplomatic. For the debunker this particular tale is so deeply linked with the general social overemphasis of the risk of stranger abduction that their responses are often much more bombastic. Though to some extent, as with the debunking of the snuff film legends, skeptics often need some way to establish their moral right to critique, which may influence Vicki's strategy, too. Both Vicki and Cindy, as the skeptical parents, run the risk otherwise of, in Kellie's words "not caring at all" even when merely objecting to one facet of a discussion.

Variations on the Contemporary Versions

This legend, a coherent narrative with a considerable history, has now also spawned a series of new versions. More precisely, it seems to have broken down into dispersed, autonomous parts. There are tales of abduction, tales of drugging and disguise, tales of procurement for forced sex work, and trickery, but these components are now less often seen together.[6] Morin (1970: 146) calls this a breakup, under pressure of debunking, of a tale into its "constituent elements." Here perhaps the splintering is even more extreme, with parts completely drifting off in some cases.

> I just got this sent to me and figured I better pass it on. It's pretty scary.
>
> Have you ever noticed those guys in the mall, pushing an empty baby carriage loaded with bags, coats, or whatever? Did you ever notice that half the time they're alone, with no wives or kids around? Well, keep your eyes on them, because you don't know what they might be doing. According to a story in the American Press wire, a woman with her four kids was shopping for summer clothes in the Woodbury Commons (a mall in New York), when one of the kids was tired and asked if he could sit on a nearby bench.
>
> She looked out and saw a man with the above description sitting there. She figures that he's a parent too, so it should be ok for the four year old to go sit on the bench. It was in her line of sight, so she did what most of the rest of us would do, she said ok. Next time she looked around, both the child, and the man were gone! According to eyewitnesses who saw what happened, the man picked up the child, put him in the carriage, and ran pretty quickly for the door. Everyone figured it was his own kid who was protesting having to go into his carriage (and how many times has that happened to the rest of us? makes sense to me), and went out the door quickly to get the kid out of the store for punishment. No one thought anything was amiss until the frantic mother called for security and everyone was questioned. When the local police arrived, they told the mother that this was not the first time, and it's a new trend going around. The kids are put into the carriage, covered partially with a coat or bags, and rushed out of the store. No one thinks twice because most people have seen fathers do that with their kids before.
>
> Pass this story along to everyone you know who has kids! I talked to a friend of mine who works for the police department here in Springfield, and he told me that it's happened out here, too.

This new trick seems to be passed along amongst pedophiles everywhere
because of its success. Very few of the children have ever been recovered,
making the tale even more tragic. Make sure you let everyone know about
this, so we can stop these sickos from having any more success at this! Mall
security forces everywhere have been alerted to this, but if you see a man
hanging around with a carriage with no kids, or see a man trying to get a
screaming kid into his carriage and/or leave the store, call security to stop
them! It's better to call on an innocent man than let the guilty get away!!!—
Jeanne Luther, Springfield, IL

(Of unknown origin, received by Joe Y. and posted to the Urban Legends
listserv, 5/12/99)

Here the ruse is slightly different, but the motive dramatically so. The
child is snatched not to be sold, but to be exploited by a pedophile. Still the
idea of a "ring" or conspiracy remains; the trick is passed from offender to
offender by some mechanism. By the time Joe received the story, it had traveled very far from any real or fictitious Jeanne Luther, let alone from
Woodbury Commons in New York.[7] Other list members responded by
noting that a similar tale about a California mall was broadcast on the religious program "700 Club" (no corroboration has been found yet), with
homosexuals and satanic cults at fault.[8] As is typical for crime legend texts
that widely circulate on news groups, lists, and email pathways, a tamer
version simply blaming "pedophiles" emerges and circulates, with debunkers
being the ones sensitized to more hateful versions. The debunkers' list
members were probably primarily motivated to discuss the "700 Club"
version simply because it was a broadcast story of an urban legend that they
knew about. Additionally, however, list members are likely to find a more
inflammatory or outlandish version of particular interest, confirming the
pernicious quality they see in many crime legends, as well as the limitless
gullibility of believers.

A similar dissonance was reported by Morin at Orleans. Several versions
of the boutique abduction circulated, some of which were explicitly implicating Jewish shop-owners, and other which generically identified
"shopowners" or "dress merchants." The acts of formalized debunking by
media, government, and civic organizations were what solidified the idea
that the tale was an anti-Semitic swipe. That is, the *debunkers* restored and
stabilized the scapegoating elements of the text when they denounced it,
placing a uniformity upon it which it did not have *in situ*.[9]

The fact that debunkers are also *generally* skeptical about stranger-abduc-
tion worries means that, for them, a variety of diverse stories may be
regarded as just new versions of "The Attempted Abduction." As a result of
the dispersed quality of the abduction legends now current in the news
groups, the responses of skeptics and debunkers, in turn, tend to be overly
general. Debunkers, as if trying to slap away flies from different directions,
and faced with a new abduction legend, often promulgate a kind of vernac-

ular version of the social constructionist view of social problems, often leaving believers and promulgators of the tales bewildered about their overly general response. It may be that the legend has unraveled to the degree that believers and debunkers have a totally different experience of what is being talked about—in sharp contrast to the kidney theft legend and to a lesser extent, the snuff film. As with Jennifer and Cindy's exchange, the point of contention itself is often decentered.

A recent mutation of the women-as-victim at the shopping mall was no doubt inadvertently encouraged by a piece done by television tabloid news magazine "Inside Edition" in August 1998. The following warning has been circulating since then via email and was posted immediately after the airing to a number of Internet news groups.

> Women be Aware
>
> Last night on Inside Edition there was an article that is of interest to all women. There is a new scam to abduct women. A man comes up to a women in a Mall or Shopping Center and asks if she likes Pizza, when she says she does he offers her a $100.00 to shoot a commercial for Pizza, but they need to go outside where the lighting is better, when the woman goes out of the mall she is abducted and assaulted.
>
> Another ploy is a very nicely dressed man asks a woman if she would be in a Public Service Announcement to discourage drug use. The man explains that they don't want professional actors or celebrities they want the average mother to do this. Once she leaves the mall she is a victim.
>
> The third ploy, a very frantic man comes running in and asks a woman to please help him, his baby is not breathing. She runs out of the mall following him and is also a victim.
>
> This has been happening in well lit parking areas in daylight as well as nighttime and the abductor usually uses a Van to abduct the woman. Inside Edition set up a test in a Mall and 10 out of 15 women went out of the Mall on the Pizza scam and the Drug scam.
>
> Please pass this along to your friends and family as now that it has been shown on nationwide TV there are bound to be copy cats of this.

In fact the *Inside Edition* piece (8/8/98) only showed a videotaped experiment they conducted to see if women could be lured out in such a way. The segment's narrator then claimed that 200 to 300 people per year are abducted and in about half the cases, the abductors were strangers. Of course, no clarification was made that these people were not abducted by the pizza scam.[10] Val, who posted the story with a warning to the group *misc.survivalism,* ended up arguing with regulars on *alt.folklore.urban* who saw her post. [11] As with discussions on the existence of snuff films, and *unlike* those surrounding the body parts theft story, here the believers assert the moral primacy of even a false warning which is thought to help prevent a future abduction. This is favored over skepticism, which merely concerns itself with the "fact" or "event" and not the expansive threats of "possibility." Lon from the folklore group challenged the mall scam story, making Val incensed.

> As for what I posted, I thought that some might find this information valuable. Why would you have a problem with reminding women that there are predators out there, and that some of them can be very creative, is something that makes no sense to me. (5/12/99)

Here is an excellent example of symbolic or curative legend belief, where passing along the tale is thought to provide a valuable social act, regardless of its basis in fact. In fact, it is unclear that Val even believes these "Pizza Scam Abductions" have taken place. Instead, having been questioned on the story, Val seems to accuse Lon and other skeptics of interfering with the protection of women. Viv, another debunker, picks up on the implicit charge.

> Ah, you see, you are assuming you know what our objection is when in fact you couldn't be wronger. Our "objections" have not been to your motivations but to the truth of the scarelore ... (5/12/99)

Viv goes on to proffer an explanation of her own motives in debunking the tale, and speaks collectively ("we" and "our") for those who have objected to Val's post. Viv argues that such posts create more danger for women by focusing their attention upon threats that are relatively rare and rely on convoluted ruses, as compared with the considerably more common threats in which violence towards women lacks such cleverness. Thus Viv is making some claim to be protecting women, too, and not simply casting aspersions. Val has, after all, basically accused Viv of being insensitive to the potential for violence. (Elsewhere, she has also implied that Viv and the other debunkers are encouraging foolhardy, carefree behavior in women, in defiance of reality.) In subsequent exchanges that continued through the next 48 hours, Val and Viv continued to spar. Viv even questions Val's understanding of what the *Inside Edition* episode even showed. After all, Val had passed along the warning as a perceived good deed, not sent along a verbatim report as a first-hand viewer of the broadcast. Of course, Viv had not seen it either.

> Did the "Inside Edition" show actually show women getting into a van with a stranger? I haven't heard that. I heard it showed them going outside the mall. Just outside the entry doors. Different thing. Actually getting women into a van without raising a hue and cry would be much more practical and unlikely. Why would an abductor attempt something with potentially hundreds of witnesses rather than just following someone to their home, waiting his chance, and abducting her from there? Truly creative predators are less obvious than this scarelore attempt. (5/11/99)

In fact, the show did in fact show about ten women willing to get into a van under such circumstances. Viv is accurate in her assertion that no such epidemic of abductions exists; the segment simply showed that it could happen, and in fact the real-life singular case cited in the segment was four years old. Here, though, is another form of "expansive debunking" where Viv feels compelled to question every aspect of promulgator Val's assertion. Unlike the other two case studies, the snuff film and the kidney thefts, the abduction legends tend to provoke general, thematic debunkings: skeptic Viv, like Cindy in the *misc.kids* exchange, engages in a general polemic about excessive worry about stranger crime and relative inattention to threats that are much more common. In the process these debunkers often end up disputing that which "sounds like" an urban legend. (About this tendency more will be said in the next chapter.) For Viv, the show's segment resonated with her as a version of the old mall abduction tale. This was not the context in which Val understood and offered it. The dispersed, disaggregated nature of the basic abduction tale seems to encourage these "blanket" debunkings. In one specific case, as we shall see in a following chapter, the on-line debunking community found themselves attacking what turned out to be a real-life horror, which in turn provoked a bit of soul searching in that community. This tendency is another way in which debunkers shape the social meaning of crime legends in tension with believers.

Encounters with debunkers often provoke more elaborate versions of abduction tales to emerge. For instance, debunkers will often ask why a supposed kidnaping incident did not make the papers. Generally, crime legends are passed on without benefit of such an explanation. It is really the challenges that come from debunkers that create, for instance, a conspiratorial explanation—where Disney has paid off everyone to keep the story quiet. Joe, 30, is a business development director from Florida who had visited urban legend sites on the Internet sporadically, at first to clear up some suspicions about stories that he had heard, and later for the entertainment value. When asked about some of his off-line, face-to-face experiences with the abduction stories, he alluded to the dynamic elements of story building inherent in the debates about the truth status of the legend:

> Yes, the discussions in a public/non-internet setting were often more detailed because the other participant had not heard the story at all and many details were required. In addition, the public discussions necessarily evolved into other discussions, whether about the true power of corporations to control the press or to other "urban legends."[12]

Here Joe acts as both emissary and debunker at the same time, much the way Cindy did on-line, but in a less heated environment. As Joe's passage suggests, the process of debunking itself is a productive enterprise in the shape and meaning of the legend.

MEDIA AND ABDUCTION LEGENDS

I could find only two news media references to the disguised child abduction scenario, both debunking the stories. (Samon, 1993; Miller 1994) Once again this may be an artifact of the difficulty in the specification of appropriate search terms for use with the *Lexis-Nexis* and *Readers' Guide to Periodical Literature*. However, another possibility is that the *conscious* public concern with the stranger abduction of children remains so prominent that these particular legends have a difficult time competing. This is to some extent underscored by a striking surge in the number of broadcast references to "abduction" in relation to locations of shopping during the year 1996. In 1995, 98 references were found; while in 1996, 1,238 references were found; followed by a drop in the year 1997 to 182 references.[13] Since the year 1996 figures prominently in this study, this surge may represent some influence upon the shape of conversations about abductions. Print references in newspapers to abductions in or near shopping malls numbered 725 between 1989 and 1999. Narrowing the search further to include only those mentioning also "hair" or "shoes" 129 articles were found; none related to the present legend text.[14] Similar searches in journals and periodicals resulted in 32 articles; none are related to the "Attempted Abduction" legend. I could also find no fictional references to the tale.

ABDUCTION LEGENDS AND MORE ORGANIZED CLAIMS-MAKING

In the following section, the abduction legend will be considered as an occupant of a hypothetical ecological "niche" of fear. Rather than being threatened by debunkers, the legend appeared to be on the wane in the late 1990s due to "competition" from conscious, highly organized, and well-publicized abduction fears, where alternative explanations are offered for disappearances. Hilgartner and Bosk (1988: 58–59) have suggested that to some extent public arenas for social issues are limited, and thus organized claims-makers must engage in competition to define social problems within their favored categories of analysis. Best (1990: 17) further suggests that those actors who are most able to draw on existing cultural resources in providing the content of their claims are likely to be successful. The abduction crime legends, lacking an organized partisan force, had to, in recent years, compete with more highly organized claims about abduction. These include alleged alien abductions and the overall public campaign to save "missing and exploited children" which began in full force in the 1980s.

Alien Abductions

It would be difficult to say with certainty that the relative remission and "break-up" of abduction legends on the Internet reflects a parallel process in the "real" world. Nonetheless, it appears to be in relative remission compared to other crime legends. Perhaps the legend has also begun to face competition from a different set of stories about abductions: alien abductions. Alien abductions certainly have a dramatically higher media profile than do mall abductions. In addition to being a staple of tabloid television programming, the topic has been considered with some seriousness on occasion in more "responsible" fora like the Discovery channel and public television. The fact that such treatment is often ultimately skeptical does not detract from the topic's overall high profile. When one of the 1990s most popular television dramas, the "X-Files" continually returned to a story line in which a classic believer and a classic skeptic investigate a vast and confusing conspiracy to cover-up evidence of alien abductions, it can be said with some confidence that alien abduction, even associated as it is with marginal culture and suspected collective delusion in the minds of many, has had a grip on the popular imagination. The "X-Files" also placed the question of truth at the heart of its drama: the identity of its protagonists, the problem of evidence, the boundaries of scientific fact and faith, and epistemology are not sideline plots; they were fundamental to the storyline.

Alien abductions as a popular interest may have supplanted the old mall/boutique abduction tale in some ways, particularly as anti-government sentiment has gained ground in the last ten years. Alien abduction offers a much more vast and powerful conspiracy than does the earthly abduction scenario. It also creates an aura of mystery around the kinds of powers that these captors would have; human abductors, by contrast, must hew to the same scientific limits as everyone else. As interest in the topic of aliens broadened on a conscious level in the 1990s, it may have competed for attention with legends involving human exploiters. Alien abduction also generally addresses adults' fear for their own safety. Were aliens to abduct children, parents and bystanders would be helpless to intervene; whereas the current human abductor legends do offer that hope through hypervigilance.

Missing Children and Abduction

Alternatively, as the country emerged from a moral panic about "missing children" in the 1980s the public became much more sensitized to the role of psychopathology as an attribution in stranger abductions of children. Vastly overestimated as it was, the focus upon crazy men stealing children off the street nonetheless provided greater exposure for mental illness and sociopathy—as opposed to the profit-motivation of sex slavery rackets—as a cause for the abduction of children by strangers. That is, individual psychopathology, rather than coordinating rings of child and women stealers, became a popular explanation for alleged abductions.

One possibility is that the twin child-worries of the 1980s, missing children and child sex abuse, combined to enhance the profile of the lone psychopath as the primary image of the abductor. This *conscious* fear, fed as it was by the media and opinion leaders, may actually compete with the mall legend in some ways. While the over-emphasis on stranger abduction is a distorted view of the reality of violent threats to children, it may be supplanting the idea of a profit-motivated "ring."

Just as destitute Nepali girls have their parents to fear most in a world in which they may be forced into prostitution, Western children are most likely to face exploitation at the hands of their own trusted adult guardians rather than strangers. Yet for many years, residents of the United States and United Kingdom were told by opinion leaders that tens of thousands of children were "abducted" each year, implying that kidnappers operated with impunity right before our own eyes. U.S. Senator Paul Simon, using statistics provided by the National Center for Missing and Exploited Children, claimed that 50,000 children per year disappeared and described his statement as a conservative figure. (U.S. House of Representatives, 1981). Other organizations promulgated similar statistics, attributing the disappearances to a variety of fates depending upon their agenda: prostitution, pornography, satanic ritual abuse.[15] (Best 1988: 23) Milk cartons everywhere sprouted pictures of cute kids. Numbers like these held currency until the mid-1980s when the *Denver Post* launched an investigation into the claims. The FBI and local law enforcement reports seemed to suggest that the numbers of children missing had to be drastically revised downward. Today, the figure of about 100—300 cases of true long-term or fatal stranger abductions per year is widely considered accurate. (Best, 1988; Ove, 1999) The likelihood of one's child being abducted by a stranger is less that the chance that she or he will choke to death on food. (Griego and Kilzer, 1985) When children are abducted by strangers, there is little evidence that procurement for any sort of ring (pedophile, satanic, prostitution) is involved. (Lanning, 1992)

Parents routinely overestimate this risk extravagantly as compared with others, particularly with regards to the threat posed by automobiles to children. And along with this fear, the psychopathic sexual predator has become central in the imagined story of stolen children. As such, claims that such fears among parents are "natural" are only true to a limited extent, given the number of considerably more common threats to the health and safety of children that do not generate moral panics. Thus, the specificity of the fear embedded in the threat of stranger abduction, and of abduction legends in particular, has much to do with cultural themes: trusting no one, fearing all, and the emphasis on self-reliance without benefit of bystanders or guardians to help. In discussing another crime legend and related moral panic involving children, that of deadly tainted treats at Halloween, Best (1990: 147) suggests that, "Nor was it clear how collective action might stop Halloween sadism; parents who worried about the threat found the best protection in individually curtailing their children's trick-or-treating or inspecting their treats." Like the Halloween sadism legend, the "Attempted Abduction" provides a set of actions that can be taken to control the threat. However, since the 1980s the organized campaign against stranger abduction has offered many more such actions including fingerprinting of children, leashes, and milk-carton scrutiny. The latter had been made a public problem rather than a private issue. As such it may have temporarily supplanted the former.

Public and Conscious Discussion of Abduction Causes

Alien abductions and mall/theme park abductions do share some character-istics. First, both occurrences rely upon the notion of a pattern of capture. For those that hold credible first-hand accounts of abduction by aliens, the similarities between the stories add to their believability. To skeptics looking on such resemblances are attributed to cultural diffusion and suggestibility. Mall and theme park abductions, although never first hand, also rely upon the idea of a pattern. Criminals interested in grabbing kids or women develop new patterns, and while the supposed victims may be random, the "method" of capture attributed to the perpetrator is highly patterned, and in some instances those who pass on the legends explicitly suggest that criminals share such information somehow or "copycat" each other without the benefit of press coverage.

Both aliens and sexual predators have gained ground in the popular imag-ination as abductors, relative to profiteers. Secondly, both alien and mall/theme park abductions rely upon ideas of conspiracy and coverup—although the former does so explicitly and by way of primary accusation (the conspirators are the problem) and the latter implicitly (the kidnappers are the problem) where it is a tacit assumption. Here, in both cases, the loss of guardianship theme is prominent. What good is a government that cannot or will not protect its citizens from abductors from outer space? Or a mass media that fails to report upon the patterned practices of abductors at our very shopping malls and theme parks? The alien abducted are often taken from their beds, the mall and theme park victims from enclosed and protected spaces of leisure and free-flowing consumption: the happiest place on earth. Victims of alien abduction and their supporters, though, often accuse their government of something worse—active collusion. (Dean 1997, p. 166) Those warned about mall abductions may assume that law enforce-ment is involved to some degree—but only enough to help send out these warnings, with the implicit message: watch out, because you are basically on your own.

As cultural artifacts, the earthly and otherworldly stories of abduction share some characteristics too. Dean (p. 18) found no particular demo-graphic aberrations from the general population in her study of alien and UFO subculture members, and remarks that this corroborates earlier research. Alien/UFO culture, too, has spilled beyond believers and debunkers. Likewise in the present study, participants appear not to deviate dramati-cally from the demographic characteristics of other Internet users, although "believers" in mall abduction per se do not form a coherent subculture.

Like Dean's assessment of alien culture, the world of crime legends returns constantly to the theme of unstable truths (Dean, 22) where the basis on which fact is separated from fiction is increasingly crumbling, and in the wake of this uncertainty, the vicissitudes of subjective experience become paramount. A world of multiple, contradictory, but "equally valid" truths emerges which are honored on the basis of perceived sincerity. Dean suggests that for those who claim to have seen flying saucers or to have been abducted by aliens, the role of personal testimony and the life project of "getting a hearing" are central. (P. 107) By contrast, the promulgators of the mall abduction legend value the information for its intent—which is to warn against a supposed danger—and also derives its perceived validity from its trusted "friend of a friend" origins. Finally, Dean's analysis of the role of alien culture suggests another similarity to the "cultural work" of crime legends, which is to fight against disenchantment in the Weberian sense: specifically, against the knowability of the world in principle, if not in a totality of known facts. (P. 149) Following their differing motifs, though, alien abduction culture revives the mystery of the universe, while crime legends in practice reinforce the idea that the world and even the society we live in are unknowable, bifurcated between the surface world and an underground world of criminality beyond the reaches of any witness or guardian.

Finally, alien and mall/theme park abduction tales are different in that no portion of the mall legend appears to present the abduction of a woman or child as a good thing. There are no stories about abductees being taken to wonderful places, being shown munificent truths, or being warned about some impending collective disaster and then released to spread the word. In some parts of alien abduction culture, abductees (who thus prefer the term "encounter" to "abduction") see their experiences as enlightening and positive rather than violent and traumatic, and often embark on a career of testimony for the benefit of humanity. Given the recent upsurge in fascination with the supernatural and the New Age movement's inroads into the mainstream of Western culture (concurrent with the rise in anti-government sentiment) it is no wonder that alien abduction may currently hold a greater unconscious attraction at the present time. Mall abductions have the disadvantage of not providing any transcendent truths, but also have fewer vociferous, organized, and specifically focused skeptics.

CONCLUSION: RESILIENCE OF THE LEGEND

Yet if, in this sense, the legend is a classic cautionary tale, what practice his being warned against? Unlike the snuff film and body parts theft legends, where some degree of victim culpability is implied, here the victims are children and have merely left their homes to go shopping. But perhaps the child serves as a kind of proxy victim, where the agent who is deemed partially culpable through misbehavior is the mother, who looks away for "only a moment." The children pay for the errors of parents. Specifically, they pay for the errors in attention of their mothers.

One of the West's oldest child abduction legends, that of the Pied Piper of Hamelin, has a cautionary tale as its basis. Through greed, manifested as their failure to pay the piper his due, the adults lose their children. Does the same fear animate the modern abduction legends? Do the shopping mall and Disney theme parks represent the soft life or rampant debt-fueled consumerism? It is often noted by raconteurs of the modern legend that one need only turn one's head a moment or two—perhaps with eyes lured by some glittering object?—for one's child to disappear. Nearly every narrative or discussion of the narrative's plausibility seems to require this phrase to appear, by way of explanation, and simultaneously to indict and absolve the distracted mother.

Shopping malls and Disney World, respectively, have a legion of urban legends attached to them, many of which are about crimes committed against unsuspecting patrons. Perhaps we can attribute this to the increasing centrality of shopping malls to the American consumption experience, as opposed to the folksy values associated with shopping on Main Street. When downtown was the place where one shopped, there were from time to time rumors attached to Main Street shopping.[16] Shopping malls, as Brunvand points out, are becoming a kind of cultural crossroads. Everyone's money is green in a mall: white, black, poor, rich, elderly, teens. Do mall rumors also reflect a submerged guilt about excessive materialism and consumption? Turner (1993: 174—178) suggests that commercial rumors popular among African-Americans, alleging ownership of fashion, sneaker, or fast food companies by racist organizations or people may address this submerged guilt and alienation. Gary Alan Fine's study of "mercantile legends" suggests a similar context of salience for commerce related legends, a more general-ized alienation from large, impersonal economic institutions upon which we have become dependent (p. 133, 142–1 43, 158–159). Corporations that run fast-food restaurants and provide overpriced merchandise are nonethe-less made very profitable by high levels of consumption. Thus in certain cases, a below-the-surface critique makes sense given the simultaneous use and resentment of such institutions, and perhaps the alienation expressed in African-American rumor cycles about fast food restaurants and sneaker companies is only the most concentrated form of this recognition of depen-dence on consumer products, especially those associated with time-saving, convenience, and leisure.

Likewise Disney World is a favorite destination for American families, a totally immersing and seamlessly simulated experience, and a fairly expen-sive trip as well. Alternatively, one may speculate that what unites the modern shopping mall with the theme park, aside from their common status as points of consumption, is its broad consumer *polis* quality: anyone who can pay can be there. These places are not racially, culturally, or socially segregated anymore. Nor are they limited to one's local hometown neigh-bors. Shopping malls draw regional crowds, while theme parks can draw people from all around the world. Barbara and David Mikkelson, who run the Urban Legends Reference Pages and the Urban Legends listserv, speculate about the underlying fears about Disney that feed the legend:

> Several of these fears are expressed in this one legend alone: fear of crime and mistrust of strangers (you don't know everyone here; criminals could be anywhere in the crowds you encounter every day, blending in with the masses), lack of faith in the willingness and effectiveness of police protection (the police are "powerless" to recover the missing children and therefore don't even try), and distrust of powerful, monolithic corporations (Disney doesn't care about you or your children; they'll pay you off to make sure you don't ruin ... their carefully-cultivated image.... Even though most versions describe the kidnappers as being caught because of their carelessness, the story still serves its function of providing a vivid cautionary tale to drive home the message that you must carefully keep an eye on your children at *all* times while out in public: just a few moments' slip-up can lead to disaster.[17]

The assumptions, though, about parents being completely on their own in a modern setting, are really tacit ones. Believers pass along such tales without explicitly suggesting that the police would not help them, or that all strangers are potential predators. Furthermore, the conspiratorial angle (being paid off by Disney to keep quiet) is one seen only rarely; usually there is no attempt among raconteurs to account for the lack of mainstream media publicity, as this latter criteria is mainly a debunker's criteria for truth or plausibility. Brunvand (1984: 78–80) also notes that allegations of coverup only appears in a minority of cases.

Like the snuff film, stolen kidney, and a number of other crime legends, the abduction legend relies upon the idea of patterned, organized capture schemes. Even in the newest versions that attribute kidnapping to sexual predators, the implication is clear that some sort of sharing of predatory techniques is going on. Furthermore, the abductions share the tacit implication that formal protectors can do little but warn women and parents to be hypervigilant. In the past, such legends were attached to either mob behavior, racial suspicion, or organized moral panics. The connection now, between the modern abduction legends and collective behavior, is much more tenuous. While the child-snatching version may have some relationship to the "missing children" panic of the 1980s, the relationship is not direct.

The lack of a social commotion around the legend now is of interest, considering that the predominant victims now are children as opposed to women. In the past, skeptics might have said that grown women could take care of themselves and choose not to succumb to procurers, but now the targets are helpless children. If the supposed capture of women off the street or out of stores could provoke such behavior in the past, why does nothing come of such heinous rumors now? While proponents of the belief in alien abductions lobby to be heard and for the truth to come out, the cover-up exposed, those that believe that predators lurk in bathrooms with implements for the drugging and disguise of children do little more than pass along warnings. Thus it seems that here as with other modern crime legends, expectations of redress are low or non-existent. This is perhaps the greatest measure of the legend's evolution over the past century. No purity league will address the problem.

Unlike Morin's Orleans, this "panic" is highly internal and individualized. This individualization, too, may foster a different kind of "civic immaturity" than Morin claimed modern France was suffering from in 1969. For Morin, this immaturity enabled an ancient canard to be revived and to provoke a collective panic. In the present case, such immaturity takes a different form—a kind of impaired skepticism. Skepticism about specific claims of evil doings are associated with "not caring at all" about various social problems, or with naivete and foolhardiness, or worse yet, with insensitivity in a world where every subjective claim is equally valid. It is likely that this association is even stronger with child victims. To challenge the claims of a trusted source ("sent to me by a friend of a friend") is to create a situation of insult; a challenge of a person's "right" to their beliefs.

In the case of abduction legends, too, the easy transition made between "true event" and "symbolic truth" for believers and promulgators is probably productive in the long run of the legend's career. Perhaps because the victims are complete innocents (both the woman victim and the child victim are drugged and disguised, rather than misguided in their trust) the moral force behind the passing along of the tale trumps any concern about facts, as it is the underlying message that the sharer wishes to convey. What is that message? On the surface, merely that people should watch out for strangers who may prey upon you or your loved ones during a moment of distraction. Deeper still, though, is the sense that predatory danger is no longer compartmentalized. Danger may come from anywhere, and, as evidenced by the increasingly generic quality of the supposed abductor, from anyone. The legend identifies with the fallibility of each person's vigilance while subtly indicting their hubris for letting down their guard even a moment's length. As such, the longevity of the legend both in North America and Europe suggests that current remission and diversification may be temporary.

CHAPTER FIVE

Debunkers and their Orbit

This chapter will examine the role that debunkers of urban legends, particularly those who gravitate to debunker-friendly sites on the Internet, have played in shaping the social life of crime legends in the 1990s. It will attempt to understand why debunkers find their enterprise important, how they approach the problem of truth and fiction, and how the collective development of an on-line debunkers' culture ultimately fails to directly challenge a credulous and fearful culture that surrounds and provokes them. It is based upon my participation and observation during this time (1995–1999) in *alt.folklore.urban* and the *Urban Legends Listserv*.

Little has been written in social science to date on Internet news groups and listservs. (Wellman and Gulia, 1999: 180, 186–188)[1] They are little societies in their own right; many of the older groups represent a vestige of the Internet's early days where a highly formalized set of rules for participation reigned. (Donath 1999: 30–36) Nonetheless, the culture of news groups is changing rapidly and the urban folklore groups are no exception.

URBAN LEGENDS AND THEIR DEBUNKERS

Debunkers have always played an important role in shaping the social meaning of the urban legend, but their visibility and influence have increased considerably in the last twenty years. A history of popular debunking and of the term, "urban legends" begins with its popularization by Jan Harold Brunvand's work. Beginning with the publication of *The Vanishing Hitchhiker* in 1981, a popular audience for the urban legend began to build. By 1999, Brunvand could call his latest collection of tales a "colossal" book of urban legends, reflecting the increased level of interest. Both academic folklore circles, and later general audience readers of Brunvand's popular works, adopted the term "urban legends" despite the term's seeming narrow reference to cities. "Urban" is used in the sense of a modern and complex society; another variation used mainly among British folklorists is "contemporary legend" although the former still seems to dominate in academic folklore studies, likely due to its adoption by media sources who relied almost exclusively upon Brunvand as an expert up through the mid-1990s. Brunvand also wrote a weekly syndicated column on urban legends that was published in various newspapers in the United States from 1987 to 1992.

But the real boost in the term and concept's popularization came with the rapid growth of the Internet. Since the medium enabled the dissemination of hoaxes of one sort or another, debunkers on the Internet gained a higher profile; and in turn, the idea of "urban legends" as an ongoing verbal narrative practice emerged in popular culture. Inherently a skeptical concept, "urban legends" are now so popular that the less-skeptical are also attracted to discussions of them. Word-of-mouth narratives, or those sent via e-mail, are now commonly considered for the category of urban legend when they are outlandish, audacious, or unusually clever tales that purport to be real.

Debunking as an organized cultural force gained a great deal of visibility and prestige with the rise of the Internet. Before the Internet was widely used, Brunvand himself served as a hub for correspondence about urban legends. The growth of the Internet then enabled the area of legend debunking to expand and diversify. Drawing strength in numbers for the first time, debunkers were able to develop a consistent set of ideas, archives and facts and make them available for would-be hometown skeptics. It is this function that slowly made *alt.folklore.urban* an authoritative group of people to consult about truth and fiction found in other news groups and e-mail lists.

While the Internet has served to increase the velocity and volume with which urban legends circulate[2], it has also enhanced debunking practices and the relative cultural power of debunkers to believers and promulgators. Since believers and promulgators pass on these stories with, for the most part, sincere belief that they are true, they are usually not prepared for debate in the way that debunkers are. They are not, by and large, socially organized as debunkers are, having no logical natural affinity to one another from their own disparate viewpoints. The only exception concerns those with fervent beliefs in things that are broadly assumed to be urban legends, and fervent believers are relatively small in number compared to casual believers.[3] By definition, believers in urban legends can only be defined as such from the skeptical outside. Since urban legend debunkers are a self defined grouping whose members actively seek each other out, they are to be contrasted for the purposes of this study with people who merely adopt a skeptical attitude toward such tales on an ad-hoc basis, or what will be termed "hometown skeptics." Some organized debunkers may find themselves in the role of hometown skeptic, but the reverse is not usually true: most skeptics are not part of the debunking community per se.

THE SOCIAL ORGANIZATION OF DEBUNKING

Through the development of an organized interest group of legend debunkers, several sites of intended expertise have formed on and off the Internet. Brunvand has been consulted by media sources and the lay public alike as an expert on urban legends since the early 1980s. The journal *Skeptical Inquirer*, originally begun to criticize the growth of belief in the paranormal, has taken a greater interest in the topic in recent years.[4]

But most of all, a consistent cluster of expertise and interest has emerged on the topic on the Internet. First, on Usenet, the news group *alt.folklore.urban* (AFU) emerged in the early 1990s as the place for correspondents from other news groups to check up on suspected misinformation. As the Internet grew, so did the volume of messages on *alt.folklore.urban*. In 1995, the estimated number of posts was under 23,000.[5] In 1996, the total was 69,671 and grew to 70,993 by 1998. *Alt.folklore.urban* is among the oldest and one of the most popular groups, with over 200,000 messages posted since 1995.[6] Group co-founder Joel Furr estimated that the group's readership had exceeded 100,000 by early 1995. (Furr, 1995) Most, then, merely read, rather than posted.

This surge reflects three trends: a large increase in the number of Internet users, the emergence of Deja.com and other search engines which provided an on-line interface that made it easier to access Usenet public news groups than previous software provided, and the increasing popularity of the "urban legends" genre.

The latter can be seen in the prevalence of the phrase "urban legends" in news group postings. Keeping in mind that conversations about urban legends do not necessarily utilize that particular phrase in each posting, especially in *alt.folklore.urban* where the topic is so central that it is assumed without statement, a pattern can still be seen. (Table 1.)

Table 1. Appearance of term "urban legend(s)," in all news groups

1996: 108
1997: 189
1998: 189

*Appearance of term "urban legend(s)," **excluding** those in alt.folklore.urban*

1996: 32
1997: 53
1998: 30

The term has a consistent presence both in and outside *alt.folklore.urban*, suggesting that at least for the available years in news group settings, the term had a steady although not dramatic presence. Although the appearance of the phrase is only one limited measure of the concept's popularity, the frequencies described above suggest that most references to it remain within *alt.folklore.urban* rather than other news groups, although some diffusion has taken place. Thus the topic, so labeled, has tended to center around the major debunking news group.

The group built an archive (a FAQ, or set of "Frequently Asked Questions") now housed at www.urbanlegends.com. Additionally, there is the *Urban Legends Reference Pages* website, which also has its own catalog of urban legends. The founders of this site, Barbara and David Mikkelson, also moderate a listserv, *The Urban Legends Digest*, which, in 1999, has a membership of 571. Also, the Mining Company website, now known as About.com, has maintained a wholly separate urban legends website. All of these sites are looked upon as authoritative by debunkers, as are Brunvand's books. Debunkers often use Brunvand's names for various urban legends as shorthand (e.g. "The Attempted Abduction" "Lights Out!" "The Kidney Heist")

THE ON-LINE DEBUNKING COMMUNITY

The urban legend debunking community itself underwent a rapid transformation as a result of both new levels of interest in urban legends in general and the explosive growth of the Internet. Both factors have brought new people into the debunkers' orbit. This process of expansion has been visible in the news group and listserv, with several notable qualitative effects. Those with a long term interest look askance at newcomers ("newbies"). These numerous newcomers perhaps threaten the intimacy and greater singularity of purpose that characterized the earlier, smaller groups. This situation creates a predictable set of mutual resentments that accompanies the increasing popularity of an activity previously exclusive to a well-defined group. The newcomers often display a more superficial understanding of the problem and may come to the enterprise with a variety of purposes, while the long term members attempt to retain the existing set of mores, tones, and practices and demand that newcomers abide by their rules.[7] It is in enforcing these boundaries that long term members often discover differences amongst themselves, such as those of epistemology, philosophy, politics, and religion.

The debunking community, though, while displaying some characteristics of a subculture, more closely resembles a social grouping based upon skill or highly-specific knowledge. They resemble a subculture in the sense that they regard all other serious debunkers as allies, and in as much as they see themselves as distinct from, and opposing, a culture that is increasingly credulous, not just toward urban legends but towards irrationalisms in general. But their form of social exchange and organization deviates from the subcultural model in that members display very little lifestyle convergence. While their meeting sites are characterized by friendliness and particular humor (*Monty Python's Flying Circus* and *Mystery Science Theater 3000* are common sources of jokes) their social convergence is basically problem-oriented rather than broadly encompassing of the life-activities of the individual. Wellman and Gulia (1999) suggest that Wireman's (1984) term "intimate secondary relationships" best characterizes the kinds of ties that individuals form in news groups. These are, as Wellman and Gulia describe them, "informal, frequent, and supportive community ties that nevertheless operate only in one specialized domain." (p. 181)

"Subculture," in recent years, has probably become too restrictive a term for the case of this news group, although earlier definitions were broader. Theodorson and Theodorson's (1969: 424) definition describes a subgroup within an existing culture that merely shares values. Since that time, the term has taken on a set of connotations that do not apply in the present case: a group with a common style of self-presentation that consciously differs from cultural norms, and that associates on that basis with a great deal of involvement of the individual's sense of personal identity. (Hebdige, 1979: 3, 17).

Nonetheless, debunkers do seek each other out for more than instrumental reasons. Debunkers gravitate to debunker sites in part out of their frustration with believers, to whom they do not wish to be impolite or mean. This perhaps helps explain the vociferous tone that characterizes some group members: it is compensatory for having to hold one's tongue in ordinary life. Among like-minded individuals, the depth of anger and frustration towards believers can finally be expressed.

To say that the urban legend debunkers more closely resemble the "intimate secondary" group model than the subcultural one is not to say that the group coheres in the complete absence of other similarities amongst its members. While the groups try to avoid long digressions on politics or religion, it is fair to say that there is a liberal or libertarian, and individualistic, consensus on both matters. Group members span the political spectrum, but lean leftward on social issues and issues of personal conscience (reproductive rights, civil liberties, gay and lesbian rights, multiculturalism, secularism and ecumenicism) and more center-right (but with greater diversity of opinion) on matters fiscal and economic. Most rarely discuss politics or religion at all, but those who do approach those topics with ideas that are highly developed and fairly consistent. Anecdotes with political overtones sometimes make their way onto the groups, mostly as demonstrations of public irrationality "out there." Unusually humorous instances of so-called "political correctness" are posted, but so are excerpts from articles taken from *Extra!*, a monthly media criticism magazine published by the left-leaning Fairness and Accuracy in Reporting. Camaraderie among the like-minded people gathered here adds to what Durkheim might call the "effervescence" of the debunking community, but "subculture" is probably a term which implies too much coherence and involvement.

Generally speaking, seasoned participants in debunking news groups and websites tend to be interested in the study of urban legends—their history, evolution, and innovation—and are more often amused rather than aggravated when a legend fails to fall in the face of repeated debunking. Newer members, like recent religious converts, tend to police the borders of the exchange environment for any whiff of credulity toward urban legends, often leaping angrily upon anyone who ventures some ideas about the persistence of urban legends.

In some ways, the urban legend groups' strict adherence to certain rules of engagement reflect the more generalized insistence in on-line discussion groups of the observance of "netiquette." Aside from the oft-repeated dictum, "Read the FAQ before posting" ("consult the archives before contributing your information or viewpoint to the ongoing discussion here") several social conventions, which most realize cannot be enforced but must be insisted upon nonetheless, are relics of the early days of the Internet, with a largely academy and research sciences set of users. Just as it is a breach in classroom etiquette to hold forth on a reading without having read it, it is also considered poor form to proffer opinions on the weight of certain facts and legends currently under consideration by the group without having reviewed the FAQ and recent "threads" (topical discussions). Just as the established etiquette in a classroom does not prevent students from holding forth on a skipped reading, though, newcomers routinely ignore the ethic of preparedness for on-line discussion.

This breach is attributed by peeved group members to be an artifact of the new access to the Internet of people who pursue on-line discussions primarily for fun rather than edification. The failure to follow a thread of conversation or consult the FAQ before bursting right in to offer an opinion is seen as rude, but also reflective of a lack of attention to detail, as in not being able to follow simple instructions. It usually does not occur to group members, at least in terms of what they have voiced publicly in the group, that the difference in practical ethics between newcomers—some of whom approach news groups expecting to be entertained or expecting a friendly audience ready to support any contribution of opinion without question—and themselves may be something more than the inattentiveness of the new wired masses. Donash (1999: 36) suggests that the derision aimed at users with e-mail addresses from the big, commercial, user-friendly providers such as AOL, CompuServe, and Prodigy has not only to do with elitism and resentment, but also with genuine and important differences in the expectations of old and new users. Old users, Donash notes, believe news group posts should be content–laden and constructive, offering the group, and thereby the news group reading public, some additional information or a well-reasoned argument, a guideline that is often not considered important by newcomers.

As the Internet grows and its users begin to reflect American (and eventually Western) society at large, the broad suspicion of expertise and the high cultural premium on self-expression becomes more a part of Internet life, as well. These values are in direct conflict with the evidence-and-argument values of many on-line topical discussion groups, particularly those hatched in the early days of Usenet like AFU. In other words, what debunkers see as inattentiveness may really be sheer defiance or rejection of these informal limits on Internet speech. The high cultural premium on self-expression does not necessarily include a high premium on being well-informed about the issues addressed, and news groups are no longer a refuge from this general problem.

Dealing With "Newbies" or the Rise of "Permanent September"

September each year has in the past meant an onslaught of new Internet users, as college students, staff, and faculty accessed their own Internet accounts for perhaps the first time. In turn, many would begin to visit the urban legends websites and participate in the listserv and news group, and inevitable conflicts between debunkers of long standing and "newbies" would ensue. The annual surge in electronic mail access that would occur every September meant that "net legends" and "e-hoaxes" would circulate around the country. Legends that had been thoroughly debunked and discussed reappeared in verbatim form, or perhaps with additional pseudo-documentation, or with a plea not to delete, "Attention! This is not an urban legend ..." No amount of notoriety directed toward the on-line debunking community and its work could prevent these legends from presenting themselves as virgin news every autumn.

In the past two years or so, as the country in general becomes wired and plugged into Internet culture, a situation that one UL-listserv member calls "a permanent September" has emerged. Settled matters are never settled anymore; instead a constant flow of legends circulating on the Internet comes into the debunkers' community, as do curious newbies. Many seem to the group members to be "clueless newbies" and there seems to be an emerging consensus that the ease with which new Internetters can access the Net through easy-to-use services like America On-Line (AOL) and WebTV means that most of the cluelessness will come into the group from these directions now rather than over-eager college students. Notes Barbara, one of the group moderators:

> WebTV has had more than its fair share of n'idiots [Net idiots], but I don't think any provider will ever take that crown from AOL. AOL markets itself as "get on the Internet fast!" with the consequence of new subscribers being thrust out here without any real notion of coming into a new culture with its own crazy way of doing things. Far too often you'll see a newcomer from one of those providers launch himself out onto the Net, flounder about, making enemies of everyone he comes in contact with, and all because he doesn't know not to post IN ALL CAPS!!!!,[8] let alone what a news group is.
>
> Newbies from any provider do eventually catch on, but I have to tell you I think AOL at least could be doing a much better job of preparing them for the culture they're about to toss them to the wolves in. A little less of this "get on the Internet fast!" and a little more of "hey, you're joining an established culture—here's how to look like you fit in until you've your feet under you" would go a long way towards making everyone—shouted-at newcomer and pissed-over veteran alike—a lot happier.

There is a legitimate question, though, whether such an "established culture" will remain at all with the democratization of the net. Perhaps the news groups will remain a holdout against the "message board" ethos that has characterized recent experiments in the interactive aspects of the Web. [9]

Still, striking is Barbara's emphasis on the offense she took about netiquette breaches. Barbara assumes that the problem is that "fools rush in" because they are new to the Internet and overstimulated from the flashier aspects of the digital age. It is true that those new to the news group setting tend to act as if they are shouting a cheer (or jeer) in a crowded stadium. By contrast, the news group feels to the long-term member, ideally, more like an animated, but much quieter and directed, discussion in someone's living room. Thus it is difficult to think that such breaches might be willful rather than stemming from ignorance.

Content is really at issue, though, too. New members often simply value their own contributions as expressive moments rather than as invitations to further discussion. These are two very different models of interactivity, but they stem from two different sets of ideas about the importance and purpose of expressing one's beliefs in an open setting. As for the specific setting of the *alt.folklore.urban* news group, the newcomer from one of those flashier sites like AOL may simply not value the received wisdom of the accumulating AFU archive or its emphasis on referenced sources. This archive is a form of authority on knowledge and as such it will be challenged wherever suspicion of expertise exists. Further, the specific topic of urban legends is *particularly* likely to attract newcomers who disdain the very idea of expertise on such a topic. All folklore is by definition vernacular, and the recent surge in interest in this type of folklore means that not all discussion will be disinterested or even analytic. Since the urban legend is currently enjoying a surge in popular culture interest, the spots where debunkers gather also attract those who simply like the stories and like passing them along, and care little whether they are true or not. As we have seen in the previously discussed case studies, basis in fact is only part of the appeal of promulgating or believing an urban legend.

Debunkers and the Social Meanings of the Urban Legend

Debunkers contribute to the overall social interpretation of urban legends first and foremost by being the only consistently organized interested party to them. As noted above, believers by definition do not see themselves as naturally aligned with one another, as they think that they are simply passing on a true story as one might pass along any other true story, opinion of a news story, or a joke. Debunkers, while increasingly aligned collectively due to the growth of the Internet, rarely face *organized* or *consistent* opposition. Instead, believers often enter into debate as single individuals concerned with single topics or specific stories, and engage debunkers in a diversity of arguments. Although these diverse arguments do display consistent cultural themes as discussed in the previous three case study chapters, they do not manage, as a whole, to cohere their proponents socially. Believers more often than not find themselves intimidated by debunkers' level of organization and documentation, rather than disabused of their belief in a given tale. Believers generally drift off rather than converting or conceding defeat. Others will take their place; the debate will then begin anew.

Furthermore, most believers are less fervent about their belief in the tale's veracity than debunkers are about its falsity. Believers are generally more interested in what the tale suggests symbolically about the world in which we live: depraved and atavistic, without guardianship or clear authority. The belief that the concerned incident actually happened, while important and defended based upon their trust of their sources, is often secondary in importance to that of the narrative's message. In fact, debunkers as a group spend curiously little time examining what the resonance of a particular tale might be to its believers, or on the tales' symbolisms. Instead, the larger interpretive context that mainly concerns debunkers is the culture of gullibility. In contrast to the myriad and dramatic interpretations of the world we live in offered by the crime legend and its believers, debunkers offer no counternarrative. In fact, the social conditions that make the crime legends plausible to the believer are often conceded without deep engagement on these issues. Snuff films are plausible to the believer because high levels of violence against women exist; debunkers do not demand a discussion on the nature of that violence. They simply say, "this thing never happened, and here's why ..." For this reason these legends will always have some life in them even after one million well-organized and highly-documented debunkings.[10]

Debunkers also add to the meaning of the tales by 1) stabilizing them through archiving and 2) upping the ante—forcing believers to fortify their promulgations and thus in turn affecting the language of new cycles of legends. New iterations of urban legends, particularly those that serve as warnings like crime legends, carry noticeable battle scars from previous encounters with debunking, and thus often take on a tone not only of urgency but a sense of purveying iconoclasm as well. These iterations, at least in written form and now commonly passed on electronically, make it sound as if the citizens of the United States (or Canada or Australia) are foolhardy and carefree individuals concerned too little about the threat of crime and the safety of their children and must be set right through the current example. The texts themselves have a moral righteousness and a direct challenge to skepticism that real-life believers, engaged in debate, often do not.

That is not to say that believers are never morally self-righteous. When they feel as if their sharing of what turns out to be an urban legend comes out of their own solidaristic motivations, they are liable to lash out at even the most diplomatic of debunkers. This response reinforces the desire of the debunker for relief, sympathy and camaraderie at the debunker's sites, and makes the frustration that debunkers express somewhat understandable.

It is not uncommon for group members to ask each other advice about

how to "handle" a believer at work or school. Jim, an active Urban-Legends
listserv regular, described his attempt to debunk a persistent urban legend
about a child dying of cancer whose treatment will be aided financially by the
forwarding of mass electronic mail. The legend takes the form of an e-mail,
describing the girl's plight and plea, in chain letter fashion.

> On another e-mail list, the latest version of the "American Cancer Society"
> chain letter hoax showed up. I made the foolish mistake of sending a post
> debunking it. My message was fairly matter of fact, and included nothing
> which could be construed as sarcastic or mean-spirited. You would not
> believe the hate mail I received in response!
>
> The person who forwarded the original hoax letter wrote that she felt
> that I had posted a "viscious [sic] personal attack" on her (actually I did not
> even mention her name in my reply), and that she would never allow herself
> to ever be "fed to the wolves on this list again!"
>
> In my post, I quoted Barbara's [Mikkelson, co-author of the Urban
> Legends Reference Pages] remark about this fraudulent chain letter that
> "common sense alone should show this up for the hoax it is."
> (http://www.snopes.com/spoons/faxlore/mydek.htm)
>
> In response, I received the following comment from someone who
> snipped the quote from Barbara, and then said:
>
> "I'm sorry, but I find this very offensive! It is one thing if you want to let
> us know that this chain letter is a hoax, but it is another thing altogether,
> for you to sit there and add insult to injury!! Please grab some manners, or
> don't bother writing."
>
> Sheesh! And this is only a sample of the nasty responses I received. The
> only other time I have ever gotten such hate mail was once, on another list,
> when I sent a post debunking the rumors pertaining to the alleged hidden
> naughty words and images in recent Disney cartoons.
>
> My hunch is that these hostile replies came from people who may have
> wasted several hours of their time forwarding the hoax e-mail to others,
> who then felt foolish when they discovered it was a fraud. After all, my
> post contained no negative personal remarks about _anyone_! (I purposely
> wrote it solely as a hoax warning, and nothing else.)
>
> Oh, well. As the old saying says: "No good deed goes unpunished." (Jim,
> UL listserv, November 30, 1998)

Jim's experience is not unusual, judging from similar remarks made by listserv and news group members. Perhaps it would have been wise for him to
avoid indirectly insinuating that the promulgator had no "common sense"
but this does not seem to explain in full the hostile response he received. He
assumes that the remainder of the offense taken stems from a submerged
embarrassment. One of the offended parties regarded Jim's debunking as
"adding insult to injury", suggesting that even had he not made this slight,

offense still would have been taken. Jim's frustration with the situation is no doubt enhanced by the sense that he was trying to do a "good deed." But he does not assert this intention (or frustration) to the list in question; he goes to the UL list for support instead. (To the other list, he later noted, he sent a general and vague apology to anyone who might have been offended.) Jim's experience reflects the sense of futility in debunking as an activity in the outside world; some debunkers have said that they no longer bother at all. The appearance and growth of debunker-friendly sites has likely enhanced both tendencies: given the assertive debunkers greater ammunition to challenge the veracity of legends when posing as hometown skeptics, while having also given the reticent debunkers a place to compare notes, develop ideas, gain support, and perhaps retreat from a real-world battle with promulgators.

What is the purpose of a debunking group?

The conviction that the ultimate purpose of the AFU news group or the UL listserv is to stamp out urban legends is a subject of recurrent controversy, despite the fact that it is a background assumption for a number of group participants at any given time. While there exists a general consensus among group members that propagators of urban legends should be told the truth about their tales, the idea that "stomping out legends" as a public service is the main purpose of the group is held only by a minority of group regulars, albeit a vocal one. This conviction, or sense of aggressive mission, is often revealed in the frequent arguments about what does and does not belong on the group. [11] Recently someone suggested that AFU itself might inadvertently act as a vector for urban legends. A newbie participant named Fruity launched a debate on May 27, 1999 by noting, "It occurred to me that this news group could actually serve to propagate urban legends rather than debunk them."

What followed was one group member's defensive reaction, and the rest of the group's attempt to mediate by examining the purpose of debunking. Henry assumed that Fruity was accusing the group of perpetrating a social problem (the spread of urban legends) that it was intended to "curb." After some volleying back and forth where Fruity tried out some inadvertent dissemination scenarios, Henry finally responded:

> Of course I agree some stupid git reading the ng [news group] and then going bananas believing that glass flows [a science legend] . Same thing can be applied to innumerable websites and news groups. Yes, it happens, so what? Some schoolkid made 10 questions in a *soc.culture* news group once and boy if she ever wrote down those answers she surely got a wild report. . . "Main product of Iceland are red herrings". So we should ban Usenet, is that what you are saying: kill them all, let g-d sort them out !?

Don concurred with Henry's sense of mission.

> Blaming afu for spread of an urban legend is like blaming radio for music,
> except that a better argument could be made for radio based on the billions
> exposed. We discuss what we hear about. If someone reading this discussion
> repeats what they read as "real" that is hardly the fault of afu.

To Henry and Don, the main problem is the spread of urban legends. Their
expectation is that AFU could be a tool to remove them from public
discourse through debunking. Fruity's post clearly angered them; they took
it as an accusation. Mike, who has been a group regular for several years,
defends Fruity's inquiry as appropriate to the mission of the news group
against Henry's attack.

> Did you need to be that rude? It may not be exactly the most stunning obser-
> vation that if people post ULs in AFU, even with the intention of debunking
> them, and some clueless people read them and pass them on, AFU has acci-
> dentally been a vector of ULs. It happens when people mishear broadcast
> news, or don't notice the "by the way, this isn't true" qualifiers in printed
> media, and if AFU is Usenet's UL Central, it is inevitable that some people
> will take from AFU precisely what we are trying to warn them against. But
> fruity was polite, reasonable, and was making a point which may not have
> occurred to some of the less experienced readers of AFU, or those who may
> just be passing by.

To group members of some longevity like Mike, AFU's mission is broader. It
is not unusual for newer, enthusiastic group members to be reined in by older
members, using a plea for civility as an entree to a larger discussion of
purpose.[12] While AFU has developed a reputation for being relatively "tough
on newbies" this has less to do with cliquishness than it does with the
tendency of some newcomers who are attracted to the topic of "urban
legends" not to read the group's famous and lengthy "Frequently Asked
Questions" (FAQ) guide, or to misconstrue the purpose of the group discussions altogether[13] Given the fact-and-evidence orientation of the group, this
omission on the part of a newbie is taken with great offense, and the resulting
ethic is that any newbie who hasn't paid homage to the FAQ is fair game.
Any newbie, though, like Fruity, may become ensnared. Madeline, a long-
time regular, defends Fruity in the name of both civility and broad group
purpose.

> Fruity seems like a clueful [smart] newcomber [sic], and doesn't know your
> [Henry's] style. To a stranger, this post might well look over the top and
> offensive. Looks a *bit* like that to a regular who knows your posting

habits. Ease up on the whack-the-newbie bit, and save the venom for the true vermin.

Later (5/31/99) Mike addressed the issue of purpose directly.

> I don't see where this is really alleging fault and apportioning blame. It is a observation about the paradoxical nature of a public, unmoderated news-froup's [news group's] attempting to play Debunk Central [...]
> Some people post here and imply that dispelling confusion and propagating enlightenment is the primary purpose of AFU, or at least a substantial secondary purpose. Measured against that criterion, if a lot of people read AFU and simply pick up bits of nonsense and go on to vector them, then AFU fails quite often.
> But a lot of ULs originate from people misreading or mishearing things. Some stories, for instance, undergo a phase-transition: once a skit in a stand-up comedy routine, now a piece of "common knowledge."

Notice than even in Mike's attempt to broaden the examination of purpose, the identification of the "problem" as the dissemination of urban legends remains. This stance is less explicitly stated in on-line exchanges as it is evident from the ongoing life of the group: its grappling with new and old legends, some group members' exasperation with the recurrence of the same, unaltered versions of legends over and over again, and the sense of mission among debunkers as evidenced by discussions of how best to debunk an urban legend "in the wild" while maintaining some level of decorum. The non-existence of a "counter-narrative" is likely to be deeply tied to this basic "problem orientation."

"Sounds Like" An Urban Legend

On the 17th of November, 1998, an active AFU group member posted an email that he said his wife had received at work.

> Dear Friends,
> I live in San Diego County, this past Saturday something horrible happened in another San Diego County town, a child was murdered. This random act of violence happened while a child was in a situation that most of us wouldn't think twice about being in.
> Matthew was 9 years old. His family was visiting from Northern California, they went to a campground near the ocean. He needed to use the restroom, an Aunt walks with him and sends him into the men's restroom as she waits outside, while she is waiting another young person seeming to be between the ages of 15–17 walks in, she thinks nothing until the stranger

runs out of the restroom, she goes in to check on him and there he lays in a pool of his own blood, his throat slit from ear to ear and bleeding from many stab wounds. The child died in his Aunt's arms. There is no reason for this crime, there was no motive. And worse yet, the suspect got away.

Today is Monday and thank the dear Lord above the suspect was caught in Hollywood, he was robbing a woman and stabbing her in the head. He was apprehended by bystanders and held for police. It seems that the evidence is showing he is the man that killed poor Matthew. He is a 20 year old transient from another state.

I have a son that is 9 years old, it brings tears to my eyes when I watch the news or when I read the paper, I can't imagine what this family is going through. I pray that the Lord brings them peace someday. I think of all the times I have sent my 9 year old into the restroom as I waited outside for him, never thinking he wouldn't return. You think that you've covered all your bases when protecting your children and another incident opens your eyes, Matthew's Dad said it best, "Protect your children to the point of being paranoid, the world is full of predators."

I pray the suspect gets what is coming to him and that justice is served. Please remember this family in your prayers. They will need many to ever find peace.

Please copy this letter and send it to everyone you know online, share the warning with them, share the fact that someone needs there prayers most desperately now.

Jim posted the message and asked the group whether they thought it was true. Tom, a group regular, explained why he thought it had the feel of an urban legend: its maudlin quality and its explicit hortatory for a stance of paranoia, its sketchy details. But several members confirmed that they had seen it or read it in the news and filled in some of the details which were left out, without remarking upon Tom's undue skepticism.[14] Other group members also confirmed the random and sad nature of the crime. Meghan complained about Tom's previous skepticism, suggesting that any on-line search engine would have turned up the story as "widely publicized" real news, and basically questioning why he didn't check if he was so suspicious.

Tom responded angrily:

Given the lack of detail in the story, what keywords would one search for? Matthew's last name, the city of Oceanside, the killer's name all were missing from the story. Dejanews turned up nothing. A hotbot [commercial search engine] search for "Matthew, killed, restroom" (the only real details in the story) turned up nothing.

Whether or not the original post is based on a true story, the tone is particularly disturbing to me. Because of a random act of violence, we are supposed to be convinced that "the world is full of predators." If we are to give creedence to this story, which turns out to be true, it would be nice if the author didn't end up writing a letter which read almost word for word like a typical UL.

Lisa agreed that the story seemed like an urban legend to her too:

> I realize I'm not saying anything most of you don't already know, but this basic concept is such a large aspect of why many ULs continue to circulate that I thought it was worth noting again. I was also ready to believe that the original post was a UL, or at least a once-true story whose kernel of truth had been lost over time and circulation, because of its form. That it came out in practically letter-perfect UL form so soon after it actually occurred says a lot about both human unconcern for details, and the power of the net in circulating such things.
> —Lisa

But Meghan countered, after noting that she suggested the "obvious" search-engine solution because she turned up the real news wire stories on the Cecchi murder herself, that the message with its common sense warning, was not to blame:

> it's just called "watching out for your kids." murders such as this one may be unavoidable, but the message still sent is to be careful. not a bad message, in my opinion. i was a victim many times as a child, some of it could have been avoided by paying attention to stories like this. that is, of course, the role of many ULs . . . and the lesson of many true stories.
>
> it's not the author's fault she/he isn't up-to-date on how to avoid wording something like an UL. it's up to the people who research whether or not these things are true to do thorough searches.

Notice here again the importance of finding "fault" on the issue of truth or falsity—so central, in fact, that the issue of legitimate fear contained in the message is eclipsed for some members. But for others, the oversensitivity of debunkers to the pernicious, rather than merely annoying false, nature of crime legends comes through. James comments:

> One incident, however ghoulish or tragic, is still by far a statistical exception—the vast majority of nine-year-olds are not going to meet their grisly demise in a public restroom, murdered by evil transients. Kiss your children, remind them to be cautious, take stock of your awareness of possible danger—and then live your life out of the constant shadow of fear.
>
> However true or not true, I don't really think stories like this, told in the heat of passion with as many trumped-up details as the author can summon, help people much.

After someone asks what details, as compared with the real event, were "trumped up" Tom responds:

> The "trumped up details" in the original story include the lines about the child's Aunt going into the restroom, thinking nothing was wrong. In fact, the child's mother was in the womens restroom, and heard screaming, but thought the boy might have been stung by a wasp. Also, the line about dying in his Aunt's arms. I have not seen this mentioned in any reports. In fact, no mention of anyone but the parents. The whole melodramatic nature of the letter could also be considered misleading. (18 Nov 1998)

Here, even the emotional hyperbole of the story is seen to be erroneous, or "misleading." This echoes earlier examples of the debunkers' tendency to regard promulgators and believers as "unschooled" or "mistaken" in their behavior rather than having a difference in purpose for the story and the information it contains. Here, the sensationalistic presentation and melodramatic tone of the recounting of the story seems to outweigh the story's basis in fact, usually a central focus of debunking. Snopes, one of the group moderators, adds that, "If it takes a brutal murder to make you realize you should be paying attention to your child's safety, haven't you already demonstrated yourself to be an unfit parent?" Thus Tom's expansive debunking looks for a means to show the real to be symbolically false, in a sort of mirror to the procedure of those who promulgate legends based upon their symbolic, rather than empirical, truth. Snopes seeks to undermine the "lesson" seeming inherent in the frightening story by questioning the competence of the would-be learner as a parent.

Debunkers are unique in this respect: that they regard the promulgation of such scare legends as dangerous themselves through the excessive fear that it promotes. This reveals that more than factuality is really at stake in urban legend debunking, although these issues are rarely addressed at length. The very idea of deriving meaning from a maudlin tale, true or false, seems under scrutiny as well. Meghan doesn't think that crime legends are any more likely to promote paranoia than any other bit of information about crime.

> there are some people who are going to be paranoid without these messages. but there are also those who read this stuff and simply decide to be a bit more cautious. where's the harm in that?

Pointing back to the legitimate portion of the symbolic value of the story is an unusual move for a member of a debunker's group. This represents one of the ongoing splits among members: pure debunking versus analysis of the underlying messages. Meghan and some other group members didn't find the warning particularly out of line with real life threats, probably here bolstered by the story's basis in fact. The confusion in the group is that the Cecchi incident revealed an ambiguity in debunking; a conflict between debunking's technical or instrumental method, and its expressive element which is often submerged beneath the former.

The submerging of the debunkers' expressive element is shown here in almost existential musings about the sorting of sensible caution from paranoia. These ideas are less elaborated, however, compared with the surfeit of expressive elements in crime legends, in their promulgators, or in the Cecchi warning. Debunkers seem reluctant to draw meaning from stories in general, and although it was initially the facts about the Cecchi case that were questioned, more was really at stake for them.

This hesitancy to derive meaning may be related to the individualistic and rationalistic ethos of debunkers. While the hyperbolic crime legends act as generalized warnings and express definite ideas about the disintegrative nature of contemporary society, the counter-view, warning of the dangers of paranoia, is not highly developed. The narrow fact orientation of parts of the debunking community seems to discourage the expression of highly-developed claims about modern society, such as the factors in gullibility or the reasons for the paranoid mindset reflected in hundreds of urban legends. Thus, their anger and frustration with believers often seems unfocused and dismissive: the believers' world view is never addressed on its own terms, even though it is clear that group members have definite ideas about it.

Reaction to Satires of Urban Legends

In 1999, the usual round of e-mail and Internet hoaxes, chain letters, and urban legends were followed quickly by a number of urban legend satire messages, and distributed nearly as widely. While there is no evidence that these anonymous satire messages were authored by regulars at the usual debunking sites, they were certainly popular there. The satires generally pointed towards the role of widespread gullibility in the circulation of urban legends on the Internet. For example, the following message appeared in January 1999 and was circulated widely.

> I know this guy whose neighbor, a young man, was home recovering from having been served a rat in his bucket of Kentucky Fried Chicken. So anyway, one day he went to sleep and when he awoke he was in his bathtub and it was full of ice and he was sore all over. When he got out of the tub he realized that HIS KIDNEYS HAD BEEN STOLEN and he saw a note on his mirror that said "Call 911!" But he was afraid to use his phone because it was connected to his computer, and there was a virus on his computer that would destroy his hard drive if he opened an e-mail entitled "Join the crew!" [...] So anyway the poor guy tried to drive himself to the hospital, but on the way he noticed another car driving along without its lights on. To be helpful, he flashed his lights at him and was promptly shot as part of a gang initiation.
> STOP THE INSANITY! NO URBAN LEGEND EMAIL STRINGS IN 1999![15]

The satire recapitulates most of the crime and other urban legends that have enjoyed wide circulation in the last decade. A number of Internet users enjoyed this satire not so much because they were active debunkers but because all manner of warnings, chain letters, and top-ten lists fill up electronic mailboxes much as junk mail does in a real mailbox.[16] This static also finds its way onto listservs and news groups, where it is resented for being "off-topic" even when it is not actively debunked. So debunkers do have some allies in the campaign to "stamp out" net legends, but with different and more practical motivations. Not all satires are as gentle.

> Hello, my name is Alfonso Merkin. I am suffering from rare and deadly diseases, poor scores on final exams, lack of sexual activity, fear of being kidnapped and executed by anal electrocution, and guilt for not sending out 50 billion f*cking forwards sent to me by people who actually believe that if you send them, that poor 6 year old girl in Arkansas with lung cancer brought on by second-hand smoke from the cigarettes smoked by the big bad men who kidnapped her and took pornographic pictures of her for use on their child pornography web site [. . .] If you're going to forward something, at least send something mildly amusing. I've seen all the "send this to 50 of your closest friends, and this poor, wretched excuse for a human being will somehow receive a nickel from some omniscient being" forwards about 90 times. I don't f*cking care. [. . .]

With this example, as well, there is no evidence that the message was authored by a regular at the debunking sites, and when it was forwarded onto the UL listserv in early September 1999, many said they had seen it for the first time. The message also attacks the content as well as the annoying persistence of net legends; there is a harshness that would be present here even without the crudity and profanity. While the sentiment expressed likely appealed to some in the debunkers' circles, others were put off, and put off in a way that revealed some serious lack of consensus about the "problem" of urban legends and why people feel compelled to pass them along. Jim's echoing of Barbara's description of the dying-child legend, as a defiance of "common sense" certainly did not represent the analysis of many other active debunkers. On the same day that the above message was passed along on the UL listserv, several responses were also posted. When one debunker on the list claimed that she sent one of these spoofs along to anyone who had ever sent her an electronic hoax, Tom, another list regular asked:

> Out of curiosity, do you send this to your friends? I for one would not go so far as to call everyone who has fallen for a UL or email hoax "f*cking stupid." I dare say everyone on this list has fallen for at least one of these in their life (in fact, that's probably what drew us here) but we're hardly "f*cking stupid." It's only after we discover that there are these things called "Urban Legends" that we begin to look at everything with skepticism. I'd

bet money that if you took a person of average intelligence, whose education did not include a specialized study of folklore, myth, or hoaxes, you could give them a true/false test on every story at snopes' website, and they'd fail miserably. [...] Of course, nowadays, more and more people are beginning to realize that many of the messages they get are hoaxes, but only thanks to researchers like Barbara and snopes, and a healthy dose of skepticism. The fact that I've read a dozen or so books about hoaxes and legends, memorized the AFU FAQ and snopes doesn't make me "smarter." I didn't figure any of these out on my own. True, I've been able to debunk (or at least determine untruth in) some stories myself, but I'm still very much dependent on what others say to determine my own concept of the "truth." [...]. About all I can fault them for is not doing enough fact checking or second guessing on their own. But that's up to one's personal nature, not their intelligence level.

Becky, the original poster, responded:

Sorry Tom, did not mean to offend anyone. In fact I put a little warning in my post that it was offensive. No I do not consider everyone who believes e-mail hoaxes stupid. It was my mistake not looking at that part of the e-mail so literally. In fact it is sort of ironic that the point of that statement is people are not checking into these hoaxes before believing and forwarding the e-mails. [...] Yes I did send it to friends. My friends understand me and my sense of humor, they know I am a very sarcastic person and that e-mail is about as sarcastic as they come. [...] No stupidity does not enter into it, but the point of the e-mail (granted again the line was uncalled for) is to stop believing everything you hear. Have common sense, all these e-mails do is create paranoia. I am not a highly educated woman, but I do use common sense, is it too much to ask of the people around me to do the same?? So again, I should have deleted the line, but please don't make me out to be some arrogant ass who feels she is superior to anyone and everyone who falls for a hoax. [...]

James, who concurred with Tom about the overreach of the spoof into viciousness, wrote:

I've always had far better luck with polite, reasoned responses to people who forward ULs and other netsam [Internet flotsam and jetsam], rather than blisteringly sarcastic rejoinders. And I'm generally a sarcastic person— I just don't think it's the right tool for every occasion.

Becky capitulated in an interesting way:

I am sincere in saying I do not assess other people's intelligence, in the last e-mail I should have replaced the word intelligence in your referenced state-

ment with the word common sense. So there it is and I'm done explaining to
the group and I'm sure they're tired of hearin it, so if anyone else would like
to voice their disapproval perhaps you can send it directly to me, not the list.

She still wishes to make a blanket assessment of the reasons for believers'
credulity, but is willing to consider a "lesser charge" of lacking common
sense rather than being unintelligent. Certainly Jim and Barbara think such
language should not bring offense and are surprised when it does. Yet in
some ways, being accused of lacking common sense can perhaps be seen as
more offensive than being accused of stupidity. From Tom's post it is also not
clear that common sense or a skeptical mindset is necessarily the basis for
disbelief. He has in this case simply transferred his trust to the "old hat"
debunkers, or been driven out of his previous tendency to believe by an
onslaught of gathered facts. Here we can see why believers are assumed to
be "mistaken" as opposed to simply "taken" with the stories, their meanings,
and their morals.

Debunkers do what they do differently than people not well connected to
the Urban Legend debunking community. They seem to have a more unitary
mission than that of hometown skeptics, who do not have the advantage of
common culture. However, the debunkers are also sensitive to the inherent
social difficulties produced by their endeavors. Many found the aggressive
satires, which appear to have come from outside organized debunking circles,
to be a bit too offensive and dismissive.

CONCLUSION

The issue of haughtiness, rudeness, and sensitivity notwithstanding, it is clear
that debunkers do not have a clear idea about why people believe urban
legends, that would help them to form a counter-narrative, even though
several seeds are mentioned in passing—paranoia, information overload,
fundamentalism, and short attention spans. Debunkers are deeply connected
to the "old hat" culture of the Usenet that erodes more and more everyday.

At one point in 1998, the regulars at *alt.folklore.urban* placed themselves
on a strict one-week program of politeness. "Nice week" was a response to
a kind of sheepish self-critique of the group regulars with regards to their
impatient behavior toward outsiders who didn't know, or care to know, the
rules of engagement. It's not as if fervent believers in the truth of a certain
legend jumped on line to defend their beliefs. Rather, out of curiosity, a
variety of people wandered in and lurked silently, reading post about
hundreds of tales until one jumped out at them that they just *knew* was true.
Alt.folklore.urban regulars become, by their own account, tired and grumpy
over newcomers ("newbies") who would demand personalized, repeated
debunkings; or who insist that a tale was true without presenting any credible references or make inferential claims ("well, it could be true...").
Newbies may have already been inclined to see debunkers as arrogant and

self-satisfied, but some weren't quite expecting the ridicule and sarcasm characteristic of *alt.folklore.urban's* more prickly regulars.

The group vowed to be nice for one week and politely dispatch newbies with an array of facts, citations, and references—and most important, a plea for the newbie to read the FAQ archive before simply holding forth in the news group. Currently, when regulars feel that one among them has been too mean to a newbie, they threaten to reimpose "nice week."

This episode illustrates an intrinsic social tension between truth and kindness that operates at both the micro and macro level concerning crime legends and their meaning. The tension replays wherever believers and skeptics meet or speak. Yet the rudeness is not only stemming from debunkers. Fervent believers can be equally cantankerous. However, debunkers often express more guilt and conciliation when they engage a believer, perhaps in cowed response to believers' often more morally self-righteous tone. The "right" of parents to warn other parents of dangerous kidnappers in shopping malls is defended by some believers, for example, not on the basis of the warning's basis in fact, but rather upon the perceived social good that such an action is thought to produce. Debunkers often wish to validate (some might say *condescend to*) the underlying moral distress that the believer feels about the crime tale. Yes, people in third world countries are drawn into selling an organ for an unfair price because they are desperately poor. Yes, women are subject to a variety of violent acts and threats in this self-described civilized country. Debunkers are often repeatedly apologizing for their disbelief in a specific crime legend. As well, when believers are confronted with demands for proof, they can feel backed into a corner and humiliated. Busting faith is a hostile thing, and one does not like to think of oneself as someone who was taken in.

The presence of organized debunkers on the Internet will continue to influence the general perception of the urban legend genre. What it is unlikely to do, however, is slow down the circulation of and belief in urban legends, crime legends included. As more believers join the Internet world, their voices will be amplified. The legends themselves have proved resilient over years, decades, and in some cases, centuries. Debunkers also have not seriously addressed the underlying impulses and perceptions that feed the crime legend. While debunkers favor an "ignorance" attribution for the persistence and promulgation of urban legends, the inherent challenge to knowability and the value of the fact and fiction distinction often present in believer's investments with the legends in contemporary times may be more central in explaining it.

For this reason, believers and promulgators will always be at an expressive advantage. Uninhibited about presenting a given legend as a cautionary tale regardless of its truth status, the promulgator has a range of expressive and symbolic options that debunkers tend to eschew. While the research and archive building done by debunkers will no doubt aid hometown skeptics as the Internet grows, the believers' view of contemporary society is much more highly elaborated and generative than that of the reactive response of debunkers to the meanings of the stories at issue.

The changing character of debunking influences the discussions that take place about the substance of crime legends. This process is part of a larger trend which could be called the mainstreaming of the urban legend as a form. Both on and off the Net, more people know what an urban legend is. They are more likely to be chastised by their associates for telling an incredible tale without having any references. They are more likely to preface stories they believe are *or might be* true with either a positive assertion like: "this is true—not an urban legend!" or with a hedging disclaimer, "I don't know whether this is true or not, but we should all be careful." Movies and television shows include urban legends, and incorporate the vital issue of belief and disbelief into their narratives. However, while the mainstreaming of the concept of the urban legend would seem to promote skepticism, it has also gained currency at a time when the criteria for truth, in general, have become more subjective. This situation in itself is likely part of the reason why the themes of social breakdown, loss of authority, and epistemological ambiguity are so prominent in informal speech settings about crime, as they are in the current study.

CHAPTER SIX

Crime Legends
and the Role of Belief

Why are people invested in urban legends? What explains the persistence of this thematically modernized, but ancient genre amidst a wholly mass mediated society with relatively high levels, historically and globally, of formal and higher education? If social marginality does not explain it, what does?

The purpose of this chapter is to place the current study in the context of contemporary discussions about the social and cultural nature of belief, with particular reference to the United States but with peripheral reference to Canada, Great Britain and Australia. These ongoing discussions include the role of so-called "information overload" in producing a socially conditioned environment in which the evaluation of the worth of information becomes more difficult. Alongside this issue is the possible influence of postmodernism and of radical relativism, and widespread distrust of traditional sources of authoritative information. Also to be considered is the supposed "culture of irrationality" which consciously resists attempts to develop systematic knowledge of the world through the powers of observation, empirical research, and analysis. Included in the latter are shifts towards a therapeutic ethos and changes in spiritual life.

The specific case of the crime legend will be considered by first examining some common themes emerging from this study, in particular those which reflect upon ways of speaking about the belief or disbelief of authorless texts. Themes emerging from this study which concern the sense of lost guardianship, social disintegration, and the politics of crime and fear will be considered in a separate chapter.

Sociological research into rumor and hoax between 1940 and 1975 focused heavily upon the role that such collective behavior plays in times of crisis, whether due to natural disaster, war, or civil unrest. Shibutani's work (1966) summed up this era of rumor scholarship best: rumor was understood as a problem-solving activity by groups of people who are deprived of adequate information; thus they produce "improvised news" through a "collective transaction." After a decline of interest in such research in the discipline of sociology by the 1970s, the paradigm of "urban legend" or "contemporary legend" emerged with the popularized works of folklorist Jan Harold Brunvand, who emphasized the recurrent nature of many such rumors and saw them as expressive reactions to the strictures of modernity.

The legend concept, adopted by the social sciences, has added a new sensibility to the study of such behavior. It is now seen less as an appendage to ephemeral crisis conditions than a symptom, or collective expression, of more enduring social anxieties. However, thus far the study of the social meaning of urban legends has tended to focus mainly upon analysis of the folk texts themselves: their narrative progressions, motifs, and cultural symbolisms. Linda Dégh (1971: 55) suggested that the use of informants engaged in using folk texts in naturalistic settings might provide a way to understand folklore as a part of a larger "public conversation." Dégh put this idea forth as a suggested means of modernizing folklore study for an age of transience, multiculturalism, rapid technological change, and mass media saturation. For this generation of folklorists, it is no longer accurate to neatly attach a relatively static folk text or set of folk motifs to one ethnic or geographic enclave and view the folklore as a nostalgic "holdout" from an assimilated world.

Here in the current study, newsgroup interlocutors provide a glimpse into how contemporary folklore is used to make sense of crime, safety, and danger and also of how culturally available repertoires are drawn upon to create styles of belief and disbelief. The crime legend, as in Shibutani's model, is a creative, if unintentional, collective enterprise. However, no specific crisis of social order is seen to exist; rather a chronic state of anxiety about crime, conditioned both by real increases in crime rates since World War II and greater mass media sensitization in post-industrial societies, exists. This process of folklore creation and maintenance takes place in a world saturated with information, both in general and about crime specifically. It takes place in what are often a set of contrarian exchanges about the truth status of these tales; where debunkers are important to the overall shape of the social context of these legends, both in situ in newsgroup discussion and in popular culture treatment of crime legends. Finally, crime legends, and the belief and disbelief surrounding them, are examined as a part of a larger sociological concern: how do contemporary cultural influences affect how we relate to our own view of the social world, and how do we attempt to be understood in an environment of ambiguity and loss of authority?

From this study of crime legends, it is hoped that several concepts about the ways in which people believe and disbelieve in an epistemologically contested environment can be inductively generated and supported. By such an environment I mean both the local one of the newsgroup and the broad one of cultural influences. The former represents a hothouse atmosphere where evidence and logic processes are scrutinized and debated. The latter is the broader society, which is characterized by a surfeit of information and a radical individualist culture. The goal is modest: to produce "portable" concepts about belief styles, which could be deployed outside the specific case of crime legends.

First it is necessary to summarize some of the strategies or styles of belief and skepticism that characterize the talk that has surrounded crime legend case studies here. This chapter will focus upon these strategies and the cultural context of contemporary belief that surrounds them. These are: the use of expansive definition (used exclusively by casual believers, never by fervent ones, or in mass media fiction); protective uncertainty, or the importance of not knowing; inferential belief (such as the inference that stories are likely to be true given the capacity for evil); symbolic truth and curative belief, the use of insider knowledge, and pseudo-occultist and supernatural strategies, the latter used exclusively by fictional mass media treatments of legends.

INSTRUMENTAL PROMULGATION AND CASUAL BELIEF

While the folk texts themselves may take an affirmative, confident and polemical tone, those who passed them along or believed them often did so in a highly conditional manner. As opposed to fervent and highly polemical dissemination, more common is instrumental promulgation and casual belief of these legends. Where the truth status of such a text is contested, as it often is in newsgroup settings, believers focus upon the *salience* of the content of the tale. That is, the moral or the message is held to be important regardless of the story's truth. Attached to this instrumental approach is an overall set of ideas about social life that holds the story to be "realistic."

In the case of the body-parts theft legends, fervent believers who "advocate" for the truth of the story, are almost wholly absent and the legend is sustained completely by instrumental approaches. For shopping mall and theme park abduction legends, casual belief is also dominant. Fervent belief has a much higher profile in the case of the snuff film legend, although the work of fervent believers is rarely cited among the more casual believers in this study. Indeed, only debunkers and skeptics seem familiar with prominent believers such as Catherine Mackinnon and Yaron Svoray. Casual believers of the snuff film legend also often rely upon expanded definitions of the snuff film in order to maintain belief, as opposed to fervent believers who espouse the cognate version only.

Often when examining urban legend texts in isolation, with particular emphasis on their ability to reflect contemporary anxieties, one may lose sight of the apparent fact that a synergy between styles of belief exists, producing a perennial fertile ground for tales repeatedly debunked. In some ways, fervent belief (such as that of moral entrepreneurs) may be the least powerful part of the explanation. Fervent believers are easier to study: they are articulate and consistent (or confidently perceive themselves as such) and may commit their beliefs to print. An excessive focus upon fervent believers, however, has led many in the past and present to the desire to affix blame for the spread of a particular tale—the assumption being that actors who are especially engaged in and insistent upon a given tale are the primary actors in keeping a tale alive. The three case studies presented here suggest that the opposite may be the case; that the crime legend sustains itself in the face of repeated debunking through casual belief, where the truth status of the legend plays a role secondary to the resonance of its message for those that wish to pass it on. As noted earlier in the chapter on debunking, the vitality of urban legends probably depends more upon believers who are "taken" with, rather than "mistaken" about, the crime legend.

To say that many believers are casual believers is not to imply that they are not emotionally engaged in the folk text, but rather to say that their interest in and commitment to the literal, empirical truth of the story is dramatically smaller than that of a moral entrepreneur or fervent believer. Even in the case of the snuff film market legend, where small, agenda-driven groups of fervent believers in the cognate version do exist, and where the legend enjoys support from popular film and television treatment, the strategies of expansive definition, inferential belief and symbolic belief outpace that of belief in the "cognate version" at least in the current research context.

Expansive Definition

The use of expansive definition takes place when a debate about the factual quality of a given story prompts supporters to bring in examples of events or practices that do exist, which share some superficial themes with elements of the legend, to lend support to the original story; or where a problem once defined as such pulls more and more objects into its fold.

The term "snuff film" will have supporters trying to include hardcore, violent (but fictional) pornography, film and video recordings of any death, for instance the freely available "Faces of Death" series and "Mondo Cane", and privately held tapes taken by victimizers of their victims (but not circulated). News media sources will sometimes use the phrase "snuff film" to mean any recorded scene of death. Fervent believers, and fictionalized treatments of the issue, though, *never* do this.[1] This operates almost like a two-pronged strategy of legend support, although there is no evidence that any intentional orchestration exists. In fact these belief styles operate separately but may nonetheless have a synergistic supporting effect. Debunkers try to debunk the cognate version. Casual believers are taken with the concept and are experimenting with ideas about how to pull other, better documented practices under its rubric. In some cases the argument is both expansive and inferential: Snuff films are thought to exist because other things which are disturbing, like violent pornography or amateur "crush" videos of the violent killing of animals, do exist.

In the case of the abduction legends, prostitution rings for which women and children are captured can be transformed into rings of pedophiles without fundamentally altering the narrative in which abductees are disguised and drugged in order to be kidnapped right under the noses of their parents or companions. Thus while the snuff film's definition is often continually redefined to make it plausible to the believer, the abduction legend retains its narrative integrity by simply replacing one set of villains for another, or by allowing the motivations for the captors to remain open-ended or a matter of speculation for tellers and hearers.

One may believe either the loose or the strict definition; in a passing reference of the phrase "snuff film" one may have either in mind or may even assume it is being used metaphorically. In this way the compelling nature of this particular legend is sustained through its very diversity. Diversity of versions, though, does not mean that infinite numbers of possible versions exist—the stories do remain clustered around the idea of a specific idea or event. The point is that several definitions may be held at once by different interlocutors, and that, as such, this state of affairs actually serves to reinforce the strength of the *cognate* version.

Inferential Belief

Since life-sustaining organs are in great demand, why would they not be stolen from a hapless healthy person? The inferential believer does not fully rely upon their own knowledge to lend support to the likelihood of a story being true, rather he or she relies on a grey area of events for which no evidence exists. Inferential belief is characterized by a commitment to an open-ended social reality which is thought to be ultimately unknowable, and depends upon the undeniable truth that anything is possible. This claim of the "unknowability of the totality" is to be distinguished from a similar one in post-structural thought, which disavows possible knowledge of the totality due to the incommensurability of standpoints or the final determinations of language. The current claim is less epistemologically suspicious: it suggests instead that social totality cannot be perceived due to the cloaking mechanisms of those who engage in secret criminal behavior, and thus exist in a hidden world synchronous with the known one.

Specific evil is inferred from the more general. Since terrible things do happen to women, why suppose that the snuff film and the store abductions have not happened? Here inference from existing conditions provides the support: if people are cruel and will do anything for money, then any supposed event containing such actors and victims may be occurring. Therefore, any given story *could* be true, and can be treated as true in order to make sense of the dangerous world in which we live. Zodiac, the interlocutor who insisted that the real-life Bernardo-Homolka murder case had generated snuff films, says it well, but his words are only the most vehement of the examples in this study: if people slow down to look at accidents, and we know about other prurient interests that they may have, then why are people saying that snuff films don't exist? And while author Yaron Svoray uses an empirical approach to his investigation of snuff films in Europe and the United States, his ultimate explanation for the disbelief of debunkers, or the reticence of law enforcement officials to pursue further investigations, comes down to an attribution of naïveté. He feels that they simply cannot countenance the evil that exists in this world, and so enter a state of psychological denial. He does not ask them why they disbelieve, but rather infers in their resistance that they cannot deal with the truth. Thus the main motivator keeping the story at play is its possibility.

Symbolic Belief and Curative Belief

These two styles of belief, curative belief being a special case of symbolic belief, are instrumental in the sense that the value of the story in explaining the world in which we live is made logically distinct from its truth status in real or similar events. In traditional folklore we colloquially say that there is "a moral to a story" or a lesson to be learned. Casual believers use this approach, often when challenged on the factual elements of the story. (This is a different epistemological stance than that of the inferential believer. Here the difference between what is known and what can be known is granted, but the truth status of the story is demoted in relative overall importance. In contrast, inferential belief weights the *possible* truth of the story quite heavily.) This symbolic belief, alleging a greater truth amid possible false-hoods, may or may not be accompanied by the idea (a "curative" element) that passing along such a story is valuable in its own right regardless of truth status. (Where curative elements are absent, symbolic belief simply means that the person considering the legend finds the story consistent with his or her ideas about how the world operates.) It bears repeating that believers are less invested in a tale's veracity than debunkers are about its falsehood. The underlying message about danger in the world is taken to heart by believers, and while the specific narrative passed along or believed is important to them, its truth status is of little importance compared with its metaphoric illustration of a perceived real set of conditions.

In curative belief, specifically, the primacy of the lesson learned is taken a step further. Here the teller believes it is important, that it is good and kind, to pass the tale along regardless of how true it is. The promulgator is invested in what the legend will do, rather than what real-life events the story might be based upon. Where curative belief is present, the solidarity-promoting qualities of the crime legend are more prominent. The end justifies the means: perhaps this exact thing never happened, but similar things could, and the tale is being passed along with the hearer's safety in mind. Kellie, Val and others who passed along warnings about theme park and shopping mall abductions quite emphatically stated that the alternative to not heeding the accompanying warnings was to "not care at all." Thus skepticism about the specific tale is linked to a foolhardy obliviousness to danger in general. Cura-tive and symbolic beliefs are the clearest instances of a believer's exercise of conscious choice in the matter of truth.

Curative belief is here especially strong in the case of abduction legends that describe both women and children being at risk. By contrast, it is rela-tively weak in the body parts theft legends—at least the first-world version, with humor playing an undercutting element—except as cautionary tale. It is almost wholly absent in the snuff film legend. That is not to say that in the latter case there is no "cautionary tale" element within the text of the tale itself, but rather that interlocutors discussing the tale do not concern themselves with the relative instrumental merit of passing the tale along. The snuff film legend does not generally present itself as a warning, and thus perhaps is unlikely to be a narrative tool. This is perhaps because the supposed victim in the snuff film legend is more socially marginal (thus beyond potential warning or help) than the mall abductee or the man seduced out of a kidney. In the case of abduction legends, the role of legend dissemination in encouraging cautious behavior in others is a prominent discussion in its own right.

Curative belief, while exhibiting some solidaristic elements, reveals a larger social pessimism: heed this warning because no authority will protect or warn you. Solidaristic elements usually accompany the giving and getting of such narratives in warning form: 1) there is no broader solidarity, in the form of guardianship or civil society to rely upon 2) the promulgator is offering sometimes anonymous, localized solidarity by sending along what is thought to be safety promoting information, 3) it is implied that criminals maintain such solidaristic networks, so potential victims should, too.

Curative belief and promulgation may be objectionable to debunkers, but it is extremely common even outside the current study. It is often associated with claims to "a greater truth" amidst defenses of lies, hoaxes, and half-truths. From what Leon Trotsky called the "Stalin school of falsification" (Arendt, 1973: 342) to Ronald Reagan's tendency to "misspeak," (Hertsgaard 1988: 136–151) from the testimonials on behalf of Tawana Brawley (Kaminer, 1992: 153, 156) to most recently, stories about would-be Columbine martyr Cassie Bernall (Besze, 1999: A1, Janofsky, 1999: 14), numerous public actors in modern Western culture demand that we believe things are literally true and merely symbolically true at the same time.[2] The transcendent quality of mythology and metaphor has all but disappeared; to admit that one's speech is figurative is somehow to concede defeat. Therefore empirical truth is still the prize that counts; it must simply be redefined instrumentally for higher purposes.

For the snuff film legend, at least, symbolic and expansive elements sometimes blend. More common in the case of the snuff film is use of expansive definition, but again, only by passive believers, not fervent. To the anti-porn movement, the snuff film encompasses all claims about the harm of pornography and about a culture of woman-hating. But also non-feminists may use it to illustrate how depraved people are and how money can buy anything, such as Zodiac and Bob Martin quoted in the chapter on the snuff film. Even skeptics may support this viewpoint.

Vicky Lou, a regular participant on the Urban Legends listserv, links a possible snuff film market directly to the process of social, and therefore moral dissipation, although she also doubts that previous reports are true. Kenneth Lanning, debunker of the snuff film legend on behalf of the FBI, also nonetheless suspects that one soon might surface. In other words, the non-appearance of an actual snuff film is provisional for some skeptics. It is not linked per se to a more optimistic view of one's neighbors and public guardians as whistleblowers. In the arena of symbolic resonance, skeptics are often as compelled as believers are about what the snuff film means about the world in which we live.

The idea that a crime legend's message is valuable and represents a greater truth regardless of how well it reflects actual events was surprisingly prominent among believers. Debunkers also often concede the basic accuracy of the brutality of the world for women before attempting to debunk legends in which the victim is female. A counter narrative that suggests that ordinary dangers, although they may be banal, are more likely to place women at risk is rarely attempted. This means that claims to symbolic truth are often strong in the face of factual debunking, as with the more polemical examples above. These are the embers that remain, not so much a cognitive dissatisfaction with the empirical claims of debunkers but an affective or expressive one.

Protective Uncertainty, or The Importance of Not Knowing

This practice occurs where believers insist that neither they, nor anyone else, have the ability to know whether certain claims are true or false. Finding out is specifically guarded against. A believer might suggest that the extreme depravity of the described acts leave the supposed set of crimes beyond the scope of law enforcement. For Brett, the snuff film is "so illegal, that you would have a very difficult time finding a copy."[3] The key distinction here is not Brett's distance from a copy, but ours that he imputes to the situation. Bob, who was "haunted for weeks" in the 1970s by what appeared to be a snuff film shown at a wild party he attended, nonetheless still does not know whether he saw the real thing or not. Since his overall goal in the discussion was to denounce violent imagery in pornography in general, he had not identified his own lack of information, one way or the other, as a priority. Yet perhaps more disconcerting, a widely-cited national expert on violence against women, Diana Russell, feels she cannot know the extent of the snuff film underground, either—what she describes in 1993 (p. 163) as a "new cottage industry."

The clear function of this constructed non-clarity, whether intentional or not, is to protect the area of scrutiny from would-be skeptics. Some of this protective reticence towards evidence of a snuff film underground is a natural consequence of the endemic suspicion of expertise, especially about crime and safety. Thus, there is likely to be some resistance to being told that a scary and depraved practice like snuff film manufacturing probably does not exist, especially when being told this by self-appointed experts at the urban legend debunking sites. Yet more than that, the use of protective uncertainty actively maintains an atmosphere of ambiguity that helps preserve the "lesson" or meaning for the believer. Part of the tragedy, then, is not just the snuff film industry but also never knowing the extent to which it victimizes.

Not knowing, ultimately, is an intrinsic part of the appeal and spread of legends. It is a part of believing, not a counter-weight to it. By declaring some things simply unknowable, the casual believer makes room for the crime legend of any specific sort to be true. The protective uncertainty approach seems to be relatively strong in the case of the snuff film, perhaps because its supporters are so wide-ranging: from serial killers to some prominent feminists; from underground films to popular movie treatments. This strategy is actually a protective move towards the object of scrutiny and against interlopers (equivalent to protecting one's own experience as unique and impenetrable to outsiders)—protecting the object of scrutiny not only from others but also from oneself. For this reason there's a hint of reënchantment activity: preserving the mystery, for oneself and others. If no one's knowledge can be greater than anyone else's, then the possibility that a story is true is just as likely as that it is false. Debunkers are rarely accused of falling for a cover-up on the part of the police, the media, or the Walt Disney corporation, but their ability to build a convincing wall of skepticism through an accumulation of negative evidence about a given tale is challenged epistemologically.

Inasmuch as crime legends are authorless and of vague origins, and thus are not subject to the extrinsic discipline of the facts of any given really-existing case, they are not only open to narrative evolutions but also subject to any number of imputed unknowns.[4] Unknowns imputed by promulgators can be seen as potentially as meaningful as that which the interlocutor feels he or she does understand. Unknowns are often broader in their claims-making than an interlocutor admitting their own ignorance about the subject. Instead, the "knowability" of the social world itself, which, if it could be known, would shed more light on the truth status of a given legend, is itself challenged *generally,* for oneself and for others.

"Scorched Earth" Skepticism: A Special Case of Protective Uncertainty

Debunking as an activity may also unintentionally enhance this uncertainty for casual believers. If something that one has heard from what one considers a reliable source, is being challenged in its truthfulness, and there is thought to be no greater authority of reference in such matters, then what can one believe? Debunking and skepticism that challenges these stories encourages believers to elaborate ideas about what no one can know.

In the 1999 horror film *Urban Legend* a folklore class is convened and a fateful section of it is devoted to contemporary legends. Sensitized now to the duty to disbelieve, the students are then unable to evaluate any claims whatsoever about any crimes on campus, past or present. Skepticism turns into "scorched earth skepticism" where the very basis of evaluation has been undermined by the introduction of skepticism. Real events, such as the real mass murder that happened on the fictional campus twenty-five years earlier, are viewed with the same suspicion as that of the "pop rocks combined with a carbonated drink will make you explode" legend trotted out in the lecture hall. This scorched earth skepticism is a kind of believer's view of debunking, or its inevitable effects.

This sort of extreme cynicism is actually a pretext for arbitrary belief, as Arendt (1973: 382) suggests. If nothing may be believed, then anything may. Kaminer (1992: 156) takes this to mean that the relative importance of one's belief *preferences* are enhanced in such settings; that there is less inhibition to simply believe what one wishes to believe. Mass propaganda, which Arendt (p. 341–342) distinguishes from the totalitarian indoctrination sort, only operates in relatively open, constitutional settings and is decidedly *not* aimed at elites, on the one hand, or the *lumpen* "mob" on the other, but rather to the disaffected middle.[5]

The existence of organized debunking may, for some casual believers, create a relatively open cognitive space where nothing at all can be known for certain. The stated goal of debunking communities, to sort truth from fiction, is thus seen as the folly and hubris of those who trust in their own information sorting abilities.

The Occultist or Supernatural Strategy

With the possible exception of believers who think that debunkers are in a state of disbelief because they are ignorant of true evil, this occultist, or "psychic peril" strategy seems to be limited to the world of fictional drama: books, films, and television. In the current study few of the interlocutors or folk texts exhibited this approach to the legend material; rather they either assigned plausibility to a legend or refused to—the beliefs of others were not thought to place them in danger particularly. The film *Urban Legend* (1999) provides an excellent example of how a skeptical attitude about crime legends can create its own dangers, when the skepticism engendered by the folklore class leaves new victims off their guard and thus in danger's way. This approach to belief has in this study been called a "occultist" or "supernatural" one because a given actor's disbelief *itself* spawns a narrative in which believers are proven right from the start, and there are subtle implications that esoteric forces enable this process to unfold. In *Candyman* (1986) a graduate student's skeptical interest in housing-project urban legends drives her directly into a protagonist's role in restoring the tale to truth, through the work of a ghost.

Sometimes, the "coming true" of what were thought to be urban legends by the main protagonist in fictionalized treatments relies upon actual supernatural *deus ex machina*, such as the episode of FOX-TV's *Millennium* where the skeptical investigator, Frank, finds that real murders, with motifs resembling urban legends in the immediate environs of a mental hospital are "explained" by a homicidal patient that can transmigrate his will onto someone on the outside. The film *Candyman* also heavily relied upon a ghost intent on claiming the skeptical protagonist for his bride. In such cases, secular, worldly guardianship is of little help.

Yet even where avowedly supernatural elements are absent, initiation into the world of crime, depravity, and evil necessitates a falling away from original skepticism. In order for the wayward fathers of both *Hard Core* and *8mm* (discussed in the snuff film chapter) to return their rightful place as avengers of young women lured to the streets, veils of illusion must first be lifted. In the case of *8mm*'s Tom Welles, the status of the snuff film as an "urban myth" must be overcome; only then can the sincerity of the victim's pain be seen. Billie, the protagonist of *Mute Witness*, is placed in greater danger every time her dramatic tale of witnessing a snuff film is met with skepticism. Lenny of *Strange Days* must see past his own jaded eyes so used to fictionalized violence in order to avenge the snuff film murder of Iris, and gain the affection of Faith. These transformations take place as a result of initial skepticism—the hero's conversion to faith is only possible where disbelief precedes.

None of these examples involve supernaturalism, but the omniscient narrative moves forward, drawing the skeptic deeper and deeper into belief. These protagonists seem to psychically attract the crimes described in the crime legend by their original state of "innocent" skepticism.

Insider Knowledge

Knowledge available at the moment is often relied upon. *Within* the folk texts themselves, insider knowledge is often claimed. Various versions of the stolen kidney legend cite second-hand medical insider knowledge, such as being a hospital staff member or having a husband who is a firefighter and thus privy to the emergency-personnel grapevine. Fans of pornography or underground film infer that snuff films exist because of their own experiences with other strange, jarring images; in a conversation, this is presented as a kind of insider knowledge to which other interlocutors do not have ready access.[6] Mall and theme park abduction warnings use bogus, but decidedly non-insider knowledge, such as newspapers or local police department reports.

However, citing insider knowledge was rarely used as a strategy in newsgroup debate about a crime legend. Personal connections were generally *not* cited to add ammunition to a believer's case. This is not the case in a number of early studies of rumor, where promulgators would often claim to know someone who knew someone on the "inside" that had access to better information than everyone else did. (Hart 1916; LaPierre 1938; Knapp 1944; Peterson and Gist 1951). In these cases claims of having an inside track were used to enhance the promulgator's prestige and believability. There are at least a few reasons why insider knowledge was not a very robust element of building a case for the salience of a crime legend in the current study. First, it is possible that insider knowledge's comparatively important role in early rumor studies appeared because they were important to crisis-bound rumors, such as those of wartime. It is also possible that the current study's middle-class, highly educated demographic pool is also characterized by a reluctance to argue a case in this particular way. Finally, it is possible that insider knowledge may no longer carry prestige for its claimants, and the projected authority of an insider figure with good information may have receded in importance compared to more egocentric interpretations, that is, "one's own beliefs." Insider knowledge also may be more deeply tied to the pursuit of empirical truth, and thus would be less important in the case of crime legends, where expansive definition and symbolic truth strategies obviate the insider's verification role in a casual belief context.

Interestingly, personal experience was cited on occasion by *debunkers*. Mike H. used his proximity, a transplant surgery center's work, to help debunk the stolen kidney legend, although this citation of scientific authority was also mixed in with an understanding and promulgation of the technical implausibilities of organ theft for transplant. Yet even where specific expertise was not present, debunkers sometimes relied upon their own experiences, and people they knew with specialized knowledge, to reinforce the sense that there was a lack of evidence where rightly there should be some, if the crime were real. J. McC. based his dismissal of the snuff film legend upon his personal lack of experience, since neither he nor anyone he knows has seen one. He mixes this with the more typical argument that no police department or fervent believer has ever produced one as evidence. The fact that in this very local case of the current study, debunkers are actually more inclined to use insider knowledge in a conversational context than are believers is curious. This seems to support the earlier-discussed speculation that assertions of certainty, of which insider knowledge might be a logical part, is of weak importance to the believing interlocutor—although not for the folk text itself, where insider knowledge becomes a source of outside authority, nor for the debunker, who is less epistemologically conflicted.

BROADER CULTURAL CONTEXTS

None of the above belief style attributes takes place in a social vacuum. To what extent do these styles reflect contemporary cultural influences upon our way of using social knowledge? Below several possible contemporary contexts will be examined for their shaping of the reception and promulgation of crime legends. The fit of "legend" type information within the modern information environment is examined in the remainder of the chapter.

Information Overload

"I see people developing a more blasé attitude toward the unthinkable as our information overload increases," Barbara, the co-moderator of the UL-listserv told a *Seattle Times* reporter when asked why people seem not to be shocked by outlandish stories. (Lacitis 1999) That is, the ability of individuals to decide based upon content or source what is likely true, false, or exaggerated is also conditioned by the amount of other information that they must process and glean for pertinent knowledge.

The idea or hypothesis of information overload has empirically been the most well researched idea in the area of marketing. Although there has been some speculation in the social sciences as early as 1970 (Lipowski 1970; Wright 1975) that post-industrial Western societies were bombarding individuals with so many discrete messages that cognitive limits would soon be reached, the bulk of research has been conducted more recently (Jacoby 1984; Malthotra 1984). Jacoby was the first to develop an experimental model for testing information overload, with hoped-for applicability to market settings.

The "problem" as advertisers and marketing interests understood it was that the recall of information that consumers gleaned from advertising was declining. As a result the tangible results of advertising expenditures were becoming increasingly unclear. (Landler 1991) Using the experimental method to operationalize conditions of information overload in the marketplace, consumer research fairly uniformly finds that there is indeed some "tipping point" at which individuals may have too much information to make decisions in line with their self-described preferences. It also seems likely that in non-experimental settings cognitive overload is even greater, or at least more diverse. In the experimental settings, all available information is about a particular hypothetical product and the independent variables are merely manipulated in the quantity of standardized "bits." Indeed Jacoby has expressed some doubt as to whether the research has applicability beyond advertising, such as in areas like public policy and health and wellness campaigns, into which the concern about information overload has also been imported. (Jacoby 1984)

Debate exists, however, as to what people do when they reach a cognitive limit. Does information overload result in the individual employing cognitive self-limiting strategies, as Jacoby suggests? "The key finding [which may be applicable to more general contexts than the experimental setting] to emerge is that consumers stop far short of overloading themselves. They tend to examine only small proportions of the brand and attribute information that is available." Jacoby (1984) also notes that practical access to "critical" information may be lost in such overload situations. However, Malthotra (1984: 438) who also finds empirical evidence of information tipping points in experimental settings, provides a contrasting account of cognitive strategies:

> Although consumers develop mechanisms for limiting their intake of information, their limited processing capacity can become cognitively overloaded if they attempt to process 'too much' information in a limited time, and can result in confusion, cognitive strain, and other dysfunctional consequences.

Malthotra also believes that Jacoby's pessimism about the applicability of the information overload model to other public cognition situations is unfounded. In any case there is a consensus that too much information creates, at the very least, cognitive distortions, whether such an effect is produced by the jettisoning of excess information or the ineffective attempt to process all available information. It is mainly this research, though, that influenced large advertising purchasers in the early 1990s to move away from mass marketing campaigns based on product attributes towards on the one hand, mass ad campaigns more tied to the setting of mood than the conveyance of product information, and on the other hand, to niche and direct marketing. (Landler 1991)

The information overload idea, though, has been too attractive to cultural critics to remain in applied settings. Shenk (1997: 30) suggests that in this increasingly "message-dense" society a deep fragmentation is the necessary result when ordinary cognitive sorting mechanisms become overloaded. As a strategy to manage such overflow, he suggests, people now seek out information communities which are "self-reinforcing." So much information exists, in other words, that it is entirely possible now to build a world-view based upon the volitional selection of information sources. Niche marketing and the Internet will only exacerbate this tendency. Shenk notes that "the Net encourages a cultural splitting that can render physical communities much less relevant and free people from having to climb outside their own biases, assumptions, inherited ways of thought." (p. 125) The novel point here is not that people and groups live inside their inherited biases, as they have done for centuries, as a practical result of provincial life-circumstances, but rather that in the modern world these sets of thought parameters are chosen and constructed amid myriad and overwhelming options, and the authority and discipline of outside knowledge is increasingly optional.

The relationship between what could be called a "volitional information economy" and the dismantling of public goods and services in these same post-industrial countries, especially the United States and Britain, may be mutually reinforcing: both help build societies with an ethos of privatism, where notions of collectively-understood truth and the production of the public good are under constant strain. The rise of the Internet itself seems to fit comfortably into this environment. Grossman (1997), who studied the interactive elements of the Internet during the years 1993 to 1996, included a discussion of the libertarian politics of the Net and its institution builders.

[John Perry] Barlow talks about the Net's leading to the death of the nation-state, a common idea in diplomatic circles, too. Is this likely to happen tomorrow? Will most people cheer if it does, if it means paying directly for schools, garbage collection, law enforcement, and emergency services and removes any safety net that might help people who, for reasons of poverty, unemployment, or disability, can't pay their way? (Grossman: 195)

Shenk concurs:

> To the great detriment of society, this [information] technology will help
> libertarian Republicans create the world they've been wanting to create for
> a long, long time: a more fragmented, asynchronous, decentralized 'free
> market' culture where the public good is sacrificed for the sake of increased
> opportunity for certain individuals. (Shenk: 174)

In other words, the niche market follows the niche society: it is chosen yet it
is self-reinforcing, highly personalized, and challenging ideas are kept to a
minimum. Not surprisingly, such a society bears more than a passing resemblance to the monadic, guardianless one referenced by the interlocutors and
the contemporary folk texts in this current study. One may not rely upon
strangers either for the truth or for safety and protection.

Crime legends, being authorless and arriving often as friendly warnings,
create ambiguity and fear. However, at the same time, information is sought,
processed, acted upon, passed along, and negotiated with others—here, in a
cognitive context overlaid with ambiguity and anxiety about the safety of
oneself and one's children. The underlying message or moral received—or
more accurately, developed or gleaned by the believer—is often one that
favors a view of danger in the world operating in ways that are not accessible
to ordinary information seekers or newspaper readers: conspiratorially,
without opposition, and often without a trace. In an 'information overload'
context, the solidaristic elements of crime legend promulgation become
clearer. A promulgator may not know whether a hearer might know about
the crime story being passed along, but he or she isolates this tale amidst all
stories about crime for emphasis. A consciousness of the hearer's information
overload is likely involved—the promulgation wishes to warn others above
the din.

The theory of information overload developed here may also help explain
the perceived lack of need to cite authorities, religious, scientific, or otherwise, to bolster one's claims. In a setting where empirical claims are casually
juxtaposed with personal beliefs and the two are often confused with one
another, the discipline of objective references is moot. It should be reiterated
again that most often these claims are not fully relativistic, but rather are
ones in which outside authority plays a waning role in the assertion of truth,
or at least of what might as well be true.

Internet Context and the *Polis*

To some extent, the above-describe tendencies reflect the fact that the current
study has been centered upon on-line social interaction during the birth of
this new medium. Internet culture, so far, has concentrated those qualities
favoring niche-shaped and preferential knowledge. The Internet creates

"microcultures" (Shenk: 127) with good and bad effects. News groups, websites, and electronic chatrooms have enabled millions to connect with others far away over shared values, interests, and problems. A sense of community for those dissatisfied with their physical communities can be provided. The urban-legend debunkers community is thoroughly a creature of the Internet itself.

The fractious quality of discussions within the news groups studied here are not unique. Other commentators have described the vociferousness of debate in Internet settings, even creating the phase "flame wars" to describe them. Curtis (1996) attributes this tendency to a lowered set of inhibitions among on-line participants, where bolder behavior cannot escalate into physical consequences and where virtual consequences can be avoided in a number of ways, too. On-line, unlike in face to face disputes, one has unlimited chances to re-explain oneself, to take on a new virtual identity, or more than one, or simply move to a new area of conquest in cyberspace.

One of the most popular metaphors for the projected structure of social life on-line is the virtual *polis*, where the only barrier to a truly wired democracy is the limited access that traditionally disenfranchised populations have experienced. In reality, even universal access would not be able to overcome some of the barriers, both social and technological, that prevent the Internet from serving this function. Probably a better metaphor for the really existing Internet would be a wired post-society, or perhaps a private libertarian utopia, where no particular moment of *polis* is assumed or even strived for. Even if the increasing commercialization of the Net did not pose a threat of the information-overload sort, the custom-niche quality of the on-line experience means that no one need pay any particular mind to anyone else. Ludlow (1996) notes that in Internet settings:

> Contrary to these myths ... in cyberspace you quickly fade into the background. Even the words that you leave there, if not ignored completely, will quickly mutate into some new form, expressing new thoughts quite different from what you originally intended to say. Indeed, rather than carving out some identity for yourself, you are much more likely to be erased." (Ludlow 1996: 313–316)

Thus even after one finds one's voice on-line, one may find only silence as a response. This situation in itself may explain the often contentious quality of discussion—the ante must be upped. News groups that are highly organized also routinely post instructions for new or occasional participants on how to filter out messages that they do not wish to read, and also caution each other about not falling for "trolls."[7] A troll is where someone intentionally posts to a news group, chatroom, or message board with the intent to provoke the group into heated argument. The troll poster may not even believe what they are saying—they merely wish to stir things up. As the perpetrators of mini-hoaxes, trolls are often successful in getting the reaction they want—posting messages about the sanctity of the fetus in a pro-choice group or insisting that a brand of bubble gum really is made from spider eggs in *alt.folklore.urban*. Is a given poster serious about their absurd position, or is he or she just trying to be provocative? How real is the Internet experience? These are questions that a newcomer might legitimately ask. The confusion of boundaries between the virtual and the real presents itself in on-line social settings constantly, enhancing or complicating the truth versus fiction element of crime legend discussions on-line in a way that may not have been true before the Internet. Dibbell (1996) describes a widely publicized incident in which a "virtual rape" took place in an on-line meeting place (called a MUD or a MOO).[8] Dibbell explains that while some participants regarded the environment as a virtual extension of their really existing consciousness and assumed that other participants were doing the same, others regarded this same environment as an extension of "merely" their own consciousness, that is, harmless, without impact, and ultimately without responsibility or repercussion. As such, the latter group included one, Mr. Bungle, who enacted a rape fantasy and was surprised to find that the community chose to hold him accountable. A furious debate ensued as to who had the authority to do what, if anything, to Mr. Bungle. Dibbell was among those that favored sanctioning Mr. Bungle through exclusion (a technical process whereby no one would receive the data that he sent.)

> The more seriously I took the notion of virtual rape, the less seriously I was able to take the notion of freedom of speech, with its tidy division of the world into the symbolic and the real. (Dibbell 1996: 393)

The very experience of being in news group, MUD, or chatroom settings throws the boundaries between real and fake into disarray, and Internet communities are intrinsically bound to a conflict over who speaks and exercises authority on behalf of that community—who can speak on what topic and what it means to ignore someone or challenge them. This situation perhaps explains why urban legends flourish there while also giving rise to a strong and coherent debunking community. The impetus for the growth of this community has to do with the more general problem of verification of all information on-line, where the truth and even the terms of debate are constantly problematized. In a situation where everyone has an equal voice yet one is most often ignored, and where information and belief communities are driven by preference and are self-reinforcing, the model of collective speech is less *polis* than multiple nodes of information partisanship.

The user-driven process characteristic of on-line information-seeking accelerates a process of customized information delivery in the current media environment in general. In an age of plentiful information, the choice of information available is increasingly democratized and yet preferential—one may choose both CNN and the offbeat newsletter from a new evangelical church and the Libertarian Party as one's ideas of "reliable sources." This is unlike previous media eras where folklore filled in the broad absence of available information or countered the untrustworthy mouthpieces of elites.

Postmodernity

Is the contemporary crime legend a postmodern genre? Crime legends may indeed be *about* a world without convincing "grand narratives" in Lyotard's (1985) words. But is the cheeky playfulness of the boundaries between truth and fiction, as illustrated by the above strategies, indicative of a postmodern condition of knowledge? It does little good to claim, with Best and Kellner (1997), that Jacques Derrida or any other major poststructuralist figure never made a complete epistemological break with a really-existing world outside particular language options and that post-structuralists are not complete idealists. This claim implies that such authors have or should have maintained authorial control over the interpretation of their work. The point—at least for the current case and for any study incorporating the influence of postmodern thought on culture—is that a popular radical relativism, and a radical belief in personal truth, have made gains into the culture as can be seen in styles of argumentation.[9] This is not to say that any of the interlocutors in the study thought of themselves as post-modernists or post-structuralists. In fact, all seemed to assume that some finite truth about the legend was out there. Further, their investments in particular kinds of empirical details (one can purchase a snuff film for ten dollars, or fifty thousand dollars) suggests that the radical relativism I speak of is limited to the style of argument, rather than to more abstract epistemological uncertainty.

To the extent that postmodernism is a set of ideas attached to highbrow arts and academy trends, it is unlikely that it has much influence on the everyday life of people outside those orbits, inaccessible and self-referential as much of the language that describes those ideas is. But postmodernism is more than that, really a kind of zeitgeist, or as Lyotard would have it, a condition, with a set of popularized, simplified ideas that are drawn upon by everyday culture –including the instability of contexts for symbols and signs, and their vulnerability to the effects of power and social hierarchy; pastiche and ironic reference as forms of intentional destabilizations of meaning, uncertainty; and the deprivileging of outside, collective referents for truth. To the extent that knowledge is commodified it is also subject to the shifting demands of exchange value. And to the extent that consumer markets are increasingly nichified, preferential knowledge too can become a source of constant self-flattery and identity reinforcement to the same, perhaps even greater, extent than objects of consumption. Truth and belief become wrapped up in selling and public relations models, and in the niche preferences of consumers. Commodity and labor substitutibility, on the one hand, and constant destruction, obsolescence, and innovation on the other, all contribute to the sense that signs increasingly have arbitrary referents. As such, as Arendt suggested, when nothing is to be believed than any particular thing believed can be a matter of choice.

Postmodern themes in this study are perhaps the most visible in the strategy of protective uncertainty and scorched-earth skepticism, where what is often challenged is the ability to know about the structure of society in which we live. Crime legends thrive upon an age of post-certainty, although in another fashion, so does the debunking of such legends. While skeptics and debunkers may display more confidence in their ability to sort truth from fiction than do believers, they also would likely not have developed such a coherent project had Western culture not experienced drastic cultural shifts during the 1960s and 1970s, which included a seemingly sudden and broad distrust of traditional authority. The challenges to the infallible authority of law and the state, church and cultural tradition, gender organization, the regulation of sexuality, and corporate rule that characterized that era enabled the flourishing in post-structural thought and post-modern cultural expression. That which was thought to be a congerie of ancient certainties flew apart. An interest in the paranormal, the "unknown" and in cults resurged as had not been seen since the 1880s. Art shocked again, rather than remaining inaccessible to many. That is, the everyday order of post-war affluent modern life came under strain. For debunkers, this break enabled a suspicion of "local" authority with its idle talk, superstition, hateful canards, and fear of outsiders and of youth. For believers, it made truth more slippery, especially if it came from on high.

A postmodern context for an explanation of the vitality of the crime legend amidst corporate mass media consolidation and commercial saturation suggests a more willful model of belief than does the information overload context, although they are not mutually exclusive possibilities. There is an element of information overload theory that sees belief in urban legends as a kind of happenstance mistake of cognitive overload. For Barbara and other high-profile debunkers to adopt this explanation is, in some ways, kind. My own assessment is that a great deal more willfulness is involved.

One important distinction should be made, however, between the seemingly relativist expressions of belief seen in this study and the polemical arguments with relativist or idealist overtones in more formal settings, such as academe and social movements. In the current study, no one interrogated the very idea of truth existing on a shared basis. Instead, participants often relied upon a highly subjective sense of truth and a series of imputed and affirmative unknowns—more towards the aim of destabilizing the perceived certitude of others, often debunkers. While the current post-modern condition might influence the sorts of strategies employed by interlocutors, it clearly did not result in a complete abandonment of empirical assertion. Empirical assertions of truth, while often being conflated versions of figurative and literal truth, were merely bolstered by subjective and broadly inferential elements.

In some sense, this drive towards the expansion of the empirical and rational, and how one arrives at it, is highly modern rather than postmodern. The empirical and rational being so highly prized while the assertions of subjective truth being so compelling, myth and parable no longer suffice. In a highly rationalized society, the story must be really true as well as figuratively true in order to bring its meaning out to hearer and teller.

Therapeutic Culture and the Style of Argument

Both postmodern and therapeutic culture rely heavily upon the cult of self-esteem, where being right is everything because being wrong hurts one's feelings. It has been suggested by some cultural critics that the rise of self-help, recovery and related therapeutic cultures in the 1970s and 1980s has influenced the format of public debate. In *I'm Dysfunctional, You're Dysfunctional*, Kaminer (1992) describes, among other things, the effect that this therapeutic ethos in both social and personal problems has had on the ability to make significant distinctions in the course of public conversations.[10] Of specific relevance to analysis in the current study is, first, the idea that "all suffering is relative" and second, that the lack of an individual's avowal of addictions or victimizations in most cases constitutes denial rather than the absence of a problem. (Kaminer: 3, 26, 28)[11]

In the "all suffering is relative" model, the otherwise cogent observation that one's subjective sense of loss and pain are relative to one's initial or developed expectations in life, is reframed in a way that differences in the quality or degree of suffering are erased in public settings. In commenting on the spate of "toxic parents" literature, which became popular in the 1980s, Kaminer writes, "when the minor mistakes that every parent makes are dramatized, or melodramatized, the terrible misconduct of some is trivialized." (p. 26) Moving to a broader level, then, the tendency of believers of the snuff film legend to conflate real deaths of women with faked or depicted deaths of women begins to demonstrate a similar logic. Since corrupted forms of desire are at the root of both, it is claimed by casual and fervent believer alike that this distinction, which is insisted upon by all variety of skeptics, is a kind of hairsplitting difference. Likewise in the case of mall and theme park abductions, the warning that is linked to a specific narrative of an abduction is taken to be important to heed regardless of whether it actually happened. Yet the tale does not consciously present itself as a parable, but rather tries to hold simultaneously the claim to being a cautionary tale and being real news (hence, in the latter manifestation, the importance of detail such as disguise and drugging, the attribution to specific locations, and so forth.) Subjective claims of worry cannot be challenged without allegations of "denial" of danger ensuing. The abduction legend, like the snuff film legend, is able to straddle such contradiction through the unitary legitimacy of any parent's fear. All warnings are relative, in a sense—here the "right" to be scared of real abductions and non-existent ones is a unified right. Variances in the salience of fear material, as in the case of toxic parents, are overlooked.

The erasure of degrees of suffering and fear in both cases of the snuff film and the mall abduction appears to take place through the tendency towards expansive definition and symbolic truth, for the conflation is notably absent in the case of the kidney theft, even though real-life organ trafficking practices would seem to offer material for such a blurring. Given that many poor people in the Third World, particularly India, part with their organs under very unfavorable terms and are often swindled out of them through underpayment, it would seem likely that such practices would be commonly used as bolstering evidence of the market in stolen first-world kidneys, given the broader availability of accompanying transplant technology. Yet such claims were absent, even though texts included sympathy for the victim. The kidneyless man's fate was not linked to a larger context of victimization, even though logically it could have been. Thus expansive definition and symbolic truth practices may be linked with an ethos of "all suffering is relative" and for the desire for maximal inclusion in the category of objective victimization.

Perhaps expansive definition and symbolic truth accompany contemporary folk texts that depict a woman or child victimized as opposed to a man. Indeed the social context of the use of the kidney theft legend was often accompanied by humor by interlocutors, and in the commonly circulated email text itself, entitled "Reason Not to Party Anymore." A gender-specific interpretation of victimhood in these cases makes sense given women's greater interest in self-help literature and television talk shows, which showcase therapeutic and personalistic interpretations of social and political problems. The cultural association between women and greater altruism and emotional warmth means on some level that imputed women victims are perhaps more willing to share the victimization spotlight with almost-victims.

The second aspect of therapeutic culture that applies here is the tendency of recovery and self-help converts to regard others as "in denial." Kaminer found that it was not uncommon for recovery authors and group participants to claim that everyone not in the recovery orbit was in denial of some sort. While it is not out of the ordinary for converts to any new coherent set of beliefs to regard non-adherents as less enlightened than themselves, it is notable that this particular claim references high levels of suffering, evil, and victimization which are unknown to large portions of the population; which includes large numbers of people unaware of such suffering in their personal selves. It is more or less a claim of mass delusion, where a broad reality exists despite a similarly broad perception otherwise. As compared to the claims in the current case studies, it has an uncanny resemblance to the claim by believers that skeptics disbelieve because they cannot countenance the existence of powerful evil in the world. Skeptics are in a sense "in denial" about that which they do not share with the believers.

There is a distinction to be made here between this sort of claim and one that might be made on a religious or spiritual level: what is at stake here are supposed earthly facts and not the nature of God, soul, salvation, or any other intangible. Thus to be in denial about earthly evil is not the same as to deny Satan his due, as in the traditional mode. Believers see themselves as more aware of danger than debunkers. In a number of ways, believers must maintain a similar "denial" analysis of their social contexts. The very act of promulgating a crime legend, particularly one shaped as a warning to others, is a testimony to a world that has suppressed certain realities, or at the very least has buried them in its frantic modern rush. Intrinsic to the promulgation process is a kind of protest against complacency and an expectation that the message being sent along to others will serve as news. It is meant as news in the sense that the recipient is expected not to know this story beforehand, and also news that has managed not to be reported in conventional news outlets.

Finally, the therapeutic ethos makes the moment-to-moment subjective stances of individuals sacrosanct. When collective reality is in negotiation then, difficult and epistemologically strained arguments must take place. "You can't argue with a testimonial, you can only counter it with a testimonial of your own." (Kaminer: 40–41) The situation of multiple monadic testimonials, she notes, has influenced not only the talk show circuit and popular self-help literature but journalism and academia as well.

Nonetheless, the crime legend does claim to be true or revealing of a truth, one that is true in a world in which the promulgator and hearer both live. This imputed commonality is the only thing that makes the conversation possible. Indeed while various forms of reversion to subjective relativism do take place in these legend-talk contexts, the ability to define social reality is not a pursuit that anyone involved wishes to relinquish. The brass ring is still truth—whether it is an empirical one or a symbolic one.

Kaminer notes this ambivalence about traditional rationalism and science in sectors of the New Age and self-help segments. "Packaged as science, any wishes, speculations, and the wackiest systems' for success and salvation, through the alchemy of the marketplace, into established, objective truths. . . . That a disdain for rationalism can coexist with an attraction to science is one of the wonders of personal development in America." (Kaminer: 113) Carl Sagan (1996: 58) sees a similar tension in UFO culture, where the authority of science is used to make claims about alien contact while skeptical scientists are disdained for their narrow positivistic thinking.

Fundamentalism and Other Spiritual Shifts

It is important to consider, as well, the influence of religious and spiritual shifts in the United States in the last twenty years. However, this change seems to represent a less direct connection to creating an atmosphere of uncertainty and ambiguity, except perhaps as a defense against it. First, fundamentalism uses literalism as the basic critical inroad to meaning in textual interpretation. As with the symbolic truth approach to the urban legend, it must be literally true as well as figuratively true in order to speak meaningfully as a story. This requirement was decidedly not true in previous decades where liberalism in religious life was ascendant. Liberalism also co-existed more easily with scientific and naturalistic explanations of events than does orthodoxy. Most social attitude surveys suggest that an orthodoxy versus progressivism scale is much more predictive of public issue stances than denomination. (Rubin 1996: 162)

Fundamentalism has also brought (to be fair, perhaps incidentally to its logic) a paranoid mindset and a sense of constant threat that is posed by modernity itself. Since the crime legend speaks to a world of sinister forces unbound by secular indifference, it seems to confirm the already existing objections of the more religiously orthodox to a decadent world. Likewise the anti-science bent of much fundamentalism likely means an equal suspicion of the debunker's tools such as verification through sources and documents, assessments of plausibility, and definitional strictness.

Another significant change in spiritual life is the resurgence of interest in a reenchanted world replete with helpful angels, alien life forms with multiple motives, and spells and affirmations. Such interests are decidedly not fundamentalist in their orientation or worldly existence but are often aimed at enhancing a sense of universal belonging in a world that is seen to be sterile, technocratic, and otherwise overly rational and detached. As such, though, this more "new age" version of subjectivism can share in the over-emphasis on personal truth and experience. Decidedly more ecumenical and secular than fundamentalism, it is nonetheless part of a desire for reenchantment where mystery is restored to its central place, but where individual volition replaces the infallible word of a powerful god. Close to the assumptions of the therapeutic ethos, it raises the importance of self-expression in public contexts at the expense of systemic knowledge or collective dialogue.

What makes the crime legend comfortable in all of these cultural settings is its liminal status between myth and news; its confusion of boundaries between figurative and literal truth. To gain a life lesson from a parable story is no longer enough. Lacking supernatural elements, the story must also be "true" or "real" in order to reveal. Thus both modern empiricism and post-modern subjectivism are employed at the same time.

CONCLUSION

There are a number of cultural contexts influencing the shape which belief and disbelief take in talk surrounding the contemporary crime legend. These are consistently appearing mechanisms of understanding that appear at the contested line between truth and fiction. These mechanisms, or styles, seem to be not so much characteristic of different groups of individuals as they are a set of available repertoires that can be and are used, *ad hoc*.

Why has mass society failed to obviate folklore as predicted? Why do those who have remarkable access to both higher education, and on a minute-to-minute basis, fingertip access to dozens of points of mass mediated information, at times continue to prefer information that arrives via unofficial sources? What continued hold does the crime legend hold amidst a world of crime news, real-life reality crime shows, crime drama in television, film, and books, and political pronouncements about lawlessness?

The crime legend has distinctive qualities. Its authorlessness, far from increasing suspicion of the material contained within it, enhances its credibility *precisely* through its unverifiability for some believers and promulgators. Its liminal status between cautionary tale or parable on the one hand, and real-world news on the other, enables it to take on the compelling qualities of each genre. The crime legend is also something that is enacted—passed along often with solidaristic intent, whereas mass media treatments of crime do not necessarily do so. Mass media treatments of crime are also inextricably bound up with the "official" version of events, while the crime legend seems to offer several open-ended options of interpretation. The text of the kidney theft legend, for instance, takes the receiver through several theories about how the victim could have been lured to his fate. The snuff film's definition expands and contracts depending upon the context. Here, Shibutani's understanding of the rumor as a collective transaction and a problem-solving activity is most vivid. Folklore, therefore, serves a unique purpose and is unlikely to be fully trampled under foot by the mass media at any time soon. Debunking only serves to disprove the specifics of a given tale; rarely does it go so far as to challenge the symbolic claims being made about how crime operates in the world. Since symbolization and the crystallization of meaning in narratives is a nearly universal if not inherent characteristic of cultural development, folklore will always be present as a counterpoint both to the perceived absence of information and to cold, analytical skepticism.

Is the sense of collective dissensus on the means and importance of sorting truth from fiction an artifact of social decline and disintegration? Is crime itself implicated in this sense of dislocation in the current era? In the next chapter, the role of the crime legend in shaping our understanding of the nature of social life and its dangers in the modern world will be examined.

CHAPTER SEVEN

Crime Legends, Protection, and Fear

The purpose of this chapter is to review the dominant themes of the crime legends studied here, and to place these themes in the context of existing literature about crime, generalized social anxiety, and fear of crime. The dominant themes in these legends include: 1) a strong sense of social disintegration and the decline of civil society, 2) a sense of lost guardianship, and 3) comparatively high levels of organization and systematic activity among criminals and predators.

A related theme woven through those described above concerns the interruption of modern pleasure and leisure by a sophisticated form of victimization. I will explore in this chapter the contrast between expectations of leisure, affluence, and relative security in late modern or post-industrial societies and the persistence of crime, particularly violent crime. Also, the role of the crime legend in relation to the politics of crime control will be examined by drawing on recent literature in criminology linking Anthony Giddens' "ontological anxiety" and Ulrich Beck's "reflexive modernity" to an increasingly alienated relationship between the state as an "official guardian" and the individual citizen.

Social disintegration and lost guardianship have an obvious connection to one another; the third theme of organized criminality, however, also testifies to the generalized sense of a world without protection. This sense of chaos and an absence of socially sustained protection exists alongside a decidedly modern and entitled sense of order, affluence, and leisure. These discordant conditions provide a stark contrast with those expressed in traditional folklore, where personal security expectations are low, and where supernatural and earthly powers are capricious in their distribution of fortune. (Darnton 1984: 38, 55–57)

I will also argue that while the crime legends explored in the current study may be concretely implausible and may, as the debunkers suggest, promote an unwarranted social paranoia, they also express fears of a kind of postmodern social drift which can be intelligibly, if speculatively, linked to certain real-world conditions. First, however, dominant themes regarding crime, fear, and victimization, which consistently appear in talk surrounding the crime legends, will be reviewed.

157

DOMINANT THEMES IN CRIME LEGENDS

Who is the Criminal?

In these narratives, how central is the criminal him or herself? In these crime legends the identity of the criminal is strangely decentered. Unlike as with other media preoccupations, little attention is paid to the non-instrumental, expressive motives of criminals. Here the criminal is a shrewd actor and his or her sophistication stems from this sober state. The criminal seems to have nothing against his or her victims personally; opportunity and instrumental motives drive the victim and the offender towards one another.

To this end, the notion of a predatory syndicate of offenders is necessary, but rarely in the foreground. In these case study legends, an existing syndicate explains the replication of crime practices across time and space. This enables raconteurs and believers to share knowledge and warnings about these criminal practices. While some variations upon the mall abduction and stolen body parts legends cite racial or ethnic differences between predators and prey, most versions referred to in Internet newsgroup settings contained no information about the people involved. Differences between them were made generic. The victims were normal and the victimizers were shrewd amoral actors. In the case of the snuff film legend, the victim is wayward and female, but otherwise unremarkable. In the stolen kidneys legend, the Texas student and the New Orleans businessman fall dangerously astray, but the attached warning sees their victimization as something that could happen to anyone. Children abducted from theme parks and shopping malls may have mothers whose attention has been drawn away by some distraction, but warnings indicate that the hearer's children could be next—snatched out of the temples of consumption and leisure. In each case, the predator punishes enjoyment.

In the current version of the mall abduction legend, for instance, the motifs of drugging and disguise remain (brought forward from the similar stories associated with the white slavery panics) while the predator's motives are obscured and his characteristics, prominent in previous versions, are unspecific. And even though the predator's motives are ominous but obscured, the conspiratorial element remains as well—predators are alleged to share certain highly specified techniques of capture.

The crime legend suggests meaningfulness and instrumentality in crime, an attempt to restore sense to the senseless reality, albeit by means of stories which are apocryphal. In a tale like the kidney theft legend, the victim faces a knife for an instrumental reason. It is a violent crime with a sensible, if amoral, face. None of the crimes presented here as urban legends are "senseless."[1] Their apocryphal nature leaves much unanswered, restores a mysterious element, and yet enables practical answers to emerge. The modern version of the abduction legend, for instance, enables the teller and hearer to impute motives. The popular University of Texas version of the kidney theft legend also includes a section where guesswork is included. (Was the party "a sham?" Was the seductress part of the larger scheme?) In real life, and often on television, we must be satisfied with the conclusion that victimizers are deeply disturbed and vicious, either by organic psychological deficit, sociopathy, or by the nightmarish environments in which they come to maturity. For whatever varied truth value there is in these explanations, they place the problem outside rational control, thus undergirding the general pessimism of recent decades. In this sense, the sensible, profit-focused quality of the criminals in crime legends imbues the fear-provoking situation with hope.

This is not to say that the expressive element of crime is absent in these tales. Every kidney thief, snuff film maker, or shopping mall procurer of children must first be depraved enough to choose profit over moral inhibition.[2] But the point is that he or she responds to incentives and deterrents. The predator is thought to respect the hypervigilance promoted by the warning. The way to protect against the alleged crime is wholly an individual matter. Debunkers also express individualist responsibility for self-protection, emphasizing the importance of watching out for yourself and your loved ones and using common sense—implying that victims of crime like the real-life Matthew Cecchi (discussed in the chapter on the culture of debunkers) were really victims of poor parental judgement. More than one *Urban Legend Listserv* member stated such directly.

In a sense the attribution of calculating sobriety is in some ways an identification with, if only on a cognitive rather than fully emotional level, the predator. Elsewhere I have argued (Donovan, 1998; Chancer and Donovan 1994) as has Duncan (1998) that the contemporary politics of crime are overlaid with the public's unconscious identification with criminals. Offenders are spoken about in mass media treatments of crime in ways that seem to reflect jealousy over their supposed lack of inhibitions, alleged coddling and sympathetic treatment by judges, and imagined jailhouse luxuries. In the present case of crime legends, the underground solidarity among these criminals necessary to sustain these illicit markets is implied although rarely addressed directly. The removal of "foreign" attributes of the predator in some, but not all versions of these tales, also reflects signs of the desire to pull the mysterious stranger closer. It is hard to say in the case of crime legends, though, whether this better reflects a subliminal identification with the aggressor or the generalization of social anxiety such that anyone can now be a predator. In both the abduction and stolen kidney legends, the level of detail offered in electronic texts about the crime itself, the location, and the reaction of victims is very high, compared with the relative paucity of information about the criminal.

In fact, what we do know about the predator in the stolen body parts legend seems to be double-valenced. On the one hand, this kidney thief enacts a brutal and gory violation in order to profit from a ghoulish market in organs. On the other hand, the thief takes care to sew the victim up carefully, pack them into a tub of ice, and provide them with instructions on

how to get help. For a crime that on the surface seems to be a wanton mutilation, the thief is as gentlemanly as possible—or in this case, gentlewomanly.
Again the purely profit-oriented motivations of the criminal actor are prominent in the care that the narrative takes to assure the reader that the thief
retains a modicum of decency. This narrative choice both tames the
Promethean terror implicit in the tale to one understood in purely market
terms and tames the criminal into an instrumental rather than expressive or
thrill-seeking predator.

The nature of the criminal—who he or she is, and what he is doing seems
very vague in these recountings. In all three case studies, the dominant
versions of the legends indict remote individuals who are part of shadowy
syndicates without being identified as part of any specific social group. All
of this suggests a leveling and "cleansing" of legends of their previous scapegoating qualities. It is unclear, in this current study, whether this shows a set
of narrative transformations in recent decades which typifies a generic
predator, or whether this account reflects the overwhelmingly middle-class,
largely college-educated group studied here. Since most accounts in earlier
decades used a folkloric approach which concentrated concern upon genre
rather than social context, it is hard to tell whether a white, largely professional middle class cohort in the past would have presented a generic
predator or not. A third contextual factor is the Internet setting, which may
also encourage a generic predator, adaptable to the unknown recipient in
cyberspace. Pernicious, xenophobic versions may mingle still among the
more generic versions; however they were almost completely absent in this
study.

In fact it is *debunkers* who are more inclined to recall (and in some case
impute, as a covert feature, to the present version) pernicious versions that
blame Jews, Arabs, racial minorities, homosexuals or some other social
bogeyman. For this reason, debunkers are able to counter the self-righteousness of worried mothers with a sense of anger over potential
scapegoating, even if current versions have generic predators.

The debunkers' tendency to impute a more pernicious predator, that is,
involving a predator that has a specific stigmatized racial, ethnic, or sexual
identity, enables the debunker to then have a moral basis to denounce the
legend. The need to do so is revealing. Perhaps the debunker feels that her
skepticism erodes her moral standing. From an interactionist viewpoint, the
raising of the older, scapegoating versions seems to be an attempt by the
debunker to mend a breach inherent in the very act of exhibiting skepticism
towards an offered narrative of warning and caution. However it is a
combative sort of mending rather than a cooperative one. By failing to identify with the victims in the narratives, or simply by the act of vocally
disbelieving the story, the debunker has a problem of moral credibility, even
if factual credibility is intact. This is a interlocutory problem that can be
"solved" by the debunker's cross-accusation of canard perpetuation on the
part of the raconteurs and believers.

Goska's (1997) analysis of the tropical-tourist version of the kidney-theft legend, in which white tourists are victimized by locals (black or brown), as a projective inversion of real-world political, social, and economic power relations, depends on a degree of specificity in victim and predator in order to apply. But this analysis is made problematic by the generic predator. Projective inversion as an explanation depends upon a disconnection or inversion between the accusations in the tale and the really-existing balance of social power in which it circulates. When both predator and victim may be anyone, projective inversion necessarily becomes a less animating force in the sustenance of the tale. Perhaps in the specific case of the North American kidney-theft legend, the portrayal of the victim as a seduced, symbolically castrated man and the predator as a *femme fatale* would qualify as an inverted version of reality given the nature of crimes involving mutilation. However a contradiction between the use of "projective inversion" and "reflection of a greater symbolic truth" (which sees a direct, or metonymic, relation between folk text and reality) as interpretations emerges. It would be difficult to say that both are true at the same time, but it is the case that modern folklorists often rely upon both interpretations. [3]

I am arguing instead that the crime legend more consistently reflects broader themes of lost guardianship and social anonymity that erodes solidarity. The anonymity is reflected in the lack of details about both predator and victim, while the sense of eroded solidarity is reflected (and to a limited extent, "fixed" or "resolved") in the warning-like quality of promulgation. The sense of lost guardianship is reflected in the overall absence of police and mass media concern about the supposed crimes implied by the folk texts. Mainly this absence is constructed by omission, but on occasion, with claims of intentional law enforcement disengagement (such as in Svoray's 1997 book on snuff films and some versions of the Disney theme-park kidnapping tales).

One thing we do seem to know about predators from these tales, though, is that their level of organization and coordination, characteristic of all three cases presented here, appears to exceed ours.

Who is the Victim?

The promulgator's imputed social distance from the victim in these tales varies. In the case of the snuff film, the distance is perhaps greatest. A wayward girl or "throwaway" child is sacrificed into the maw of depraved spectacle. An intermediate victim is that of the businessman or college student who has lost his kidney in a seduction. He has paid dearly for a common but ill-fated bout of decadence. Yet the warnings attached to this legend imply that "you" might be next, that is, you are not so socially marginal as to be so besieged by threats as to have this one be redundant. Often entitled, "Reason Not to Party Anymore" the warning both engages the recipient or hearer as a potential victim and subtly ridicules him at the same time. The undercutting element of humor associated with this tale was highly consistent. In the case of theme park and shopping mall abductions, the victims appear to display the least social distance from the teller.

How sympathetic are the victims in these crime legends? The current study suggests that the tale and the tellers both display anger and fear on behalf of the victim while also holding them somewhat responsible for their own victimization. This outcome is consistent to some extent with the "just world" thesis advanced by Lerner and Miller (1978). The authors explain the common appearance of victim derogation among research subjects as a correlate of the "need to believe that they live in a world where people generally get what they deserve. The belief that the world is just enables the individual to confront his physical and social environment as though they were stable and orderly." (p.1030)

The ability to derogate a victim in order to produce a symbolically stable cognitive environment is complicated in the current instance by the generic predator, the sense of lost guardianship, and the continuing relevance of an elite criminal syndicate. All of these imputed social factors would logically tend to mitigate against the victim's ability to resist his or her victimization. Yet Lerner and Miller, in their review of existing experimental-method studies which explored "just-world" issues specifically in relation to criminal victimization ("attribution studies"), also found that derogation patterns seemed to deviate from conventional expectations. Subjects tended to direct greater derogation towards victims who displayed the least possible "complicity" with their attacker; that is, people attacked by strangers in experimental scenarios of stabbing attacks or rape. (Aderman et al, 1974; McDonald 1972) Even the biographical characteristics of the portrayed victims seemed to provoke unexpected patterns of derogation. In Jones and Aronson's 1973 study of rape-fault attribution, subjects tended to hold a divorcee least responsible and a virgin the most responsible for her victimization.

Lerner and Miller offer an explanation how this pattern is actually consistent with "just-world" views. There is a need to direct greater derogation towards victims who, perhaps like the subject, do not engage in any apparent provocation of or proximity to the victimizer. The idea that someone "like" themselves could be victimized in such a scenario is so psychically threatening to the subjects that in many cases it cannot be countenanced and the victim must be blamed. Commenting on several studies of attribution that seem to confirm this tendency outside the specific case of criminal victimization, they note, "Even the act of randomly drawing an unlucky slip from a bowl seems sufficient for observers to infer [victim] responsibility." (p. 1041) By contrast, the authors surmise, the subject risks little psychically by being sympathetic to a victim they perceive to be *unlike* themselves, or unlike socially favored persons like the 1973 virgin over divorcee, in biography or behavior.

This goes some way perhaps in explaining the greater attention paid to the faulty behavior of the mother who loses her child in a mall or theme park, even though by most conventional criteria she is non-marginal and enacting a highly favored social role. Greater outrage on behalf of the snuff film victim and a noted absence of specific scrutiny of her behavior is thus explained by the lack of psychic risk that such sympathy involves. The already-understood-as-marginal snuff film victim, and, to a somewhat lesser extent, the kidney-theft victim are people whose fates are what Lerner and Miller would call "transgression-compliant." (p. 1041)

This double-edged attitude towards the victim (or the victim's parent) is especially poignant in the mall abduction legend. The mother's attention is drawn away for only a moment but with tragic consequences. In both the mall and theme park versions of this tale, and in the original white-slavery abduction tale, which centered around the candy-shops, it is the dual streams of the independent woman and the bright lights of an affluent and leisure-enhancing society which provides the opportunity for victimization. At the same time, this seductive world is fraught with danger from every angle and is without consistent guardianship. Thus applying the basic insights of just-world/attribution research we can more easily see why identification with the victim in these tales is often of a mixed, push-pull nature. To fully acknowledge these fears is to admit them into one's own orbit of possibility, and if some residual work-ethic guilt remains it is not surprising that the victims in these tales are taken out of places of leisure and pleasure—never from schools, homes or workplaces, where we are in real life, much more likely to be victimized, but where we are, psychologically speaking "morally" safe.[4]

Indeed there is also a thematic consistency in these tales with the sociological literature on the routine-activities approach to understanding the post-war boom in crime rates, up to the 1990s. This suggests that much of the increase in crime beginning after World War II can be explained by affluence, an increased global market in consumer goods and currency, greater labor-market participation, and increased leisure-site opportunities, all of which have provided vastly greater opportunity for crime. Cohen and Felson (1979) link crime to modern "routine activities" which result in social, particularly neighborhood-level, anonymity and guardianlessness. Paradoxically, this disorganization stems from a robust economy and greater labor-force participation (particularly for women). Spatial decentralization and an increase in single-adult households characteristic of the period 1947—1974 also play a role. Both per capita property and violent crimes increased[5], because crimes are dependent upon legitimate activities in order to be enacted. The greater and more mobile the number of legitimate activities and transactions, whether of a work or leisure related nature, the greater opportunity for crime. Specifically, Cohen and Felson cite a large increase in "nonhousehold activities involving nonhousehold members" thus logically enhancing the portion of crimes, which are non-home centered.[6] Routine activity theory, the authors note:

may prove useful in explaining why the criminal justice system, the community, and the family have appeared so ineffective in exerting social control
since 1960. Substantial increases in the opportunity to carry out predatory
violations may have undermined society's mechanisms for social control ...
Rather than assuming that predatory crime is simply an indicator of social
breakdown, one might take it as a by-product of freedom and prosperity as
they manifest themselves in the routine activities of everyday life. (Cohen
and Felson, 604–605)

There are more opportunities nowadays to become a victim precisely because
of some positive changes in Western societies. The greater numbers of choices
about activities for both work and leisure for women, means that greater
opportunity is mixed with greater danger. To the extent that high expectations of safety and order (associated in general with modernity) are combined
with lower levels of informal guardianship (people around the household
and around the neighborhood who provide informal surveillance and social
control) and formal guardianship, a sense of uncontrollable threat and subsequent resentment may have developed. There is a sense of solidarity being
lost, in both the sense of increased criminal threat, and also in what
Durkheim suggested were the anomic effects of economic prosperity and
intensity, such as not really knowing one's neighbors and relatively higher
numbers of impersonal, instrumental social interactions throughout the
course of the day.

    This sense of resentment of criminal threat amidst freedom of movement,
affluence, and increased leisure activities is strikingly reflected in the crime
legends' narratives of interrupted pleasure.

BETWEEN TEXT AND TALK

Urban legends, and crime legends in particular, are more than symbolic
carriers of diffuse anxieties about risk and fear in modern life. When examined as texts in a social context, they are, by definition, a practice. In this
study the crime legend clearly serves several interlocutory purposes: warning,
revelation of the raconteur's fear and revulsion and the solicitation of the
same in hearers, and finally, in most recently collected forms, a frontal assault
on skepticism itself. When one considers the crime legend as a *practice*, we
see that it has both aggressive and solidaristic features. The practice of
sharing crime legends is aggressive in the sense that believers wish to disrupt
the hearers' sense of safety or confidence in the protection currently provided
by law enforcement agencies. There is also clearly a desire to challenge their
confidence in the adequacy of conventional forms of "crime news" such as
that purveyed in great volume and sensation in the mass media. The practice
is solidaristic in the sense that the crime legend is offered as warning and a
gesture of protection; as a practice it can be seen as an attempt to restore a

form of collective bond that has been thought lost, and a desire to be heard "above the din." Thus in both senses, crime legends are a problem-solving activity.

Moral Panics and Crime Legends

Specifically, crime legends are a problem-solving activity on a protean level. I do not believe that there is good evidence that they are the product of any significant organized activity, although, as in the case of the snuff film, they may be amplified by well-placed moral entrepreneurs. In recent years, a considerable literature has been built up in the social construction of social problems field on so-called "moral panics" which have periodically struck the United States and the United Kingdom. To what extent are crime legends, particularly the case studies considered here, connected with moral panics?

Originally elaborated by Cohen (1972: 9) to describe swelling public fear about British youth subcultures of the 1960s, especially "Mods" and "Rockers," the term moral panic has come to mean an historically distinctive, overactive public concern with an ongoing behavior which is nonetheless identified as a new threat. The implication by those who deploy the term is that the public reaction is either out of proportion to the true size of the threat, or that its cause is attributed incorrectly.

According to Cohen's definition of a moral panic, certain elements must be present. These are: media overemphasis, the rise of group action for redress, law enforcement escalations, the appointment of "folk devils," and the onset of a "disaster mentality." Specific incidents often help catalyze the panic, but underlying anxieties drive it. In some interpretations of the moral panic model, for instance Hall et al (1978), underlying anxieties are manipulated by elite interests.

The moral panic, as a concept, must be distinguished from certain contributing, but distinct ideas. First, it understands public reaction as a multi-causal process in which manipulation by moral entrepreneurs (Becker, 1963), organized interest groups (Gusfield, 1963), and status defenses (Zurcher and Kirkpatrick, 1976) play only a partial role. The moral panic model joins these institutional accounts with an attribution of a more freefloating social anxiety associated with collective behavior accounts. Institutional interests during times of moral panic are not always clear cut; populist elements may even challenge them.

Although urban legends about crime may contribute to moral panics, they are not synonymous with them. Crime legends lack demands for redress, law enforcement expansion, and media overemphasis. In fact, they seem to have a somewhat limited sense of urgency that has more to do with "being aware" of supposed danger than taking collective steps to eliminate or mitigate it. Moral panics often explicitly attribute social problems to specific social trends such as irreligiosity, secularism, or profiteering, while crime legends do so only obliquely or not at all. Overall, moral panics carry within them more points of thematic coherence than do crime legends; in other words, they are less flexible and more "constructed." Crime legends may serve contradictory public claims: is the story of the man who lost his kidney to a seductress about the greed and amorality that drives the modern market-place, or a story about how dangerous women really are, or a story about the wages of sin, or a bravado story about lucky and unlucky men of adventure in a brave new world?

Nonetheless crime legends and moral panics often share some themes and may, in this sense, overlap. Best (1990) shows how urban legends, such as shopping mall abductions and tainted Halloween treats, can be seen as a part of the mounting moral panic in the United States, particularly in the 1980s, about "threatened children." But crime legends such as these can precede and outlast panics to which they become attached, and can be deployed by people and groups trying to illustrate different points.

Yet crime legends may only be integral to the growth of specific moral panics to the same extent that specific real incidents are; their function as "news" dominates here. For instance, the shopping mall abduction legend no doubt adds quasi-evidence to the concern about strangers kidnapping, abusing, and killing children. During the height of moral panic in this regard, outrageous claims of the numbers of children affected by this threat gained public currency. Real crimes of this sort also served an illustrative purpose; the fact that they were not truly typical of what had befallen "missing chil-dren" whose faces appeared on milk cartons did not delegitimize them as examples. The missing children panic involved organized activity—from the formation of new government databases to parents purchasing fingerprinting kits for their children—while the abduction legend puts no such trust in collective safety practices and may even see the dissemination of the story-as-warning as an end in itself.

The Risk Society

The story-as-warning as an end in itself is made all the easier by widespread social distrust. The identified problems to which crime legends are deployed and used as a solution stem from endemic conditions of late or reflexive modernity. Beck (1992: 20) describes this phase as one where the distribu-tion of risk joins the distribution of wealth in characterizing basic global and intra-societal inequality. It is "reflexive" in the sense that the risks stem from modernity itself (from such factors as industrialization and previous capital accumulation structures) rather than from a technocratic inability to master and control traditional risks (for example, subsistence crop failure). Crime, or danger coming from other persons, is increasingly seen as a part of reflexive modernity.

In a similar vein, Giddens (1990) sees this phase as one in which people in already industrialized countries have high expectations of security and risk control without any reliable democratic mechanism for assuring that security. In a later section of this chapter, I will address the issue of how personal safety is being transformed and somewhat politicized in this oncoming risk society, but at this point I wish to focus upon the communication implications of it. To Giddens' assessment, I would add that an authoritative knowledge base upon which to make informed decisions about individual and social risk seems increasingly more difficult to obtain for the ordinary information seeker. Sensual clues are contradictory. Continuous reminders of the threat of crime, such as electronic fortifications, enhance uncertainty about the safety of one's surroundings. As Lianos and Douglas suggest (2000: 113–114):

> Instead of experiencing victimization or learning about it, thus perceiving it inevitably as exceptional, the user is individually experiencing the omnipresent probability of victimization. This is the case with all visible measures of crime prevention: they are reminders of dangerousness.

These authors speak specifically of fortified and access-controlled physical environments, but the same can be said of the mass mediated environment. Reminders of crime risk are enhanced by the widening of the information net. As security consultant Gavin de Becker (1999: 99) writes, "All of us will have to experience calamities in our own lives; that's unavoidable. In the satellite age, however, we experience the calamities in everyone's lives—and that is avoidable." Two generations ago, perhaps, someone living on the East Coast of the United States might never have learned about the death of Polly Klass in California or even an incident with multiple murder victims, such as Columbine. Far from displacing less formal knowledge about crime, the current risk environment may, in fact, enhance its value. Folk knowledge and word-of-mouth information may take on more value for some than it might have in previous decades when expertise and authority garnered greater respect and trust (whether legitimately earned or not) and exuded confidence in the eradication of social problems through "enlightened" policies. Urban legends in general, and crime legends in particular, reflect this sense of uncertainty and insecurity over the issue of safety in the physical and cognitive environment.

Here, though, a thematic divergence between the crime legend texts *qua* texts and the talk *about* the texts investigated in this study emerges. Texts seem to emphasize some themes, while the talk about the texts reflect others. I will discuss these interpretive frameworks in more detail below.

Post-Social: Themes of Social Disintegration and Breakdown

First, there is the overall sense of the post-social, where the expectations of collective provision of the common good are under siege. Second, there is the related theme of post-guardianship; the sense that formal guardians and civil society can no longer guard against certain crimes and may only be able to warn beforehand and comfort after. Self-protection redounds to the individual. Woven through these post-social and post-guardianship frameworks are some elements of conspiratorialism and post-patriarchy. Collective social inattention, it is suggested, has allowed underground networks of coordinated criminality to flourish. Predators are able to share crime-making information with one another unimpeded. Profiteers upon the post-social era need not fear these absent guardians.

The case studies of crime legends investigated here most clearly and consistently show a sense that social life in the post-industrial west provides no longer any "safety in numbers." These tales suggest that criminal conspiracies are able to flourish in the absence of obstacles such as law enforcement personnel, media attention, and various nodes of civil society such as health care practitioners and witness bystanders. Hence the use of the term, "post-social" throughout the case study chapters, but especially with reference to the snuff film legend. Leisure, pleasure, and entertainment activities are constantly threatened by violent predators, such as those who kill porn actresses on screen, seduce and drug people for their kidneys, and steal children from theme parks and shopping malls. Thus the very affluence and social freedom that has come to characterize the contemporary life of the professional middle class comes with an apparently great price. In contrast to what official statistics suggest, the crime legend tells us that home, school, and work are zones of safety whereas public places in which leisure is emphasized are not. This might be attributed to a residual work-ethic, or a moralistic sense of guilt and punishment for transgression. However, the specifics of the legends themselves suggest the social distrust runs deeper, or perhaps broader.

The theme of social disintegration has several manifestations in these legends: first, a sense that the social structure as it stands now is without resources to respond to serious crimes, second, that criminal enterprises are often seen as collective, conspiratorial, or at least exhibiting internal "underworld" organization as against the law-abiding public, and finally, that individuals must rely upon themselves for precaution and must accept that we cannot know the nature of threats within our society with any precision.

The additional fact that debunkers as well as believers expressed themes of social disintegration suggests that most interlocutors sorting out truth, fiction, and meaning in relation to the crime legend share the basic assumption that some previous sense of social centrality and consensus has broken down. The contrast here with most media depictions in recent years is striking. Real-life crime shows such as *America's Most Wanted* and *COPS* (Donovan, 1998) and news presentations about crime still assume the ability and desire of the state and legal apparatus to intervene. Loader (1997: 3–6) argues that in Britain the authority inherent in policing has come into crisis as the juxtaposition of a scaled-down state clashes with the traditionally exalted image of police officers—an image that has a "high fantasy component" which desired their omnipotence.

Media frameworks affirm the state's role, competence, and expertise in assuring public safety while crime legends do not. This orientation of news media is accomplished in a number of ways. First, the media relies upon state agencies for basic information and they are able to provide such information in formats that are easily appropriated in a newsroom environment. From the point of view of newsmaking, then, frameworks provided by state agencies reinforce the idea that the state's role is both proper and functioning. The practical outcome of this routine practice is that state actors have a disproportionate ability to help media actors in selecting and transforming events into "news." (Fishman 1980: 139–143) Second, journalists often favor experts who share their belief in objectivity, thus reinforcing the distinction between authorized and non-authorized speakers, which tends also to be social class-bound. (Gans, 1979; Tuchman 1978). Finally, sources who are able to seemingly provide simplicity and certainty ("soundbites") amidst ambiguity are likely to be favored in news media reports of social problems, regardless of the content of the claims being offered. (Altheide 1997: 655–656) Each of these bases of authority in official news media claims are undermined in the crime legend genre. Neither competent authorities, objective truth, nor certainty amidst ambiguity are routinely sought or expected in the talk surrounding the crime legend.

In television crime-drama treatments of crime legend, the affirmation of law enforcement competence is also emphasized, in contrast to the folk text. This is accomplished mainly through narrative resolutions of implausibilities existing in the folk text. Almost all fictional treatments of body parts theft, for instance, resolve the technical problems of the tale by developing an additional narrative of corruption within existing medical facilities. While this move erases some of the technical implausibility, it retains the social implausibility—ignoring the broad chain of command and control that oversees organ transplant, for instance. Ultimately corrupters and underground syndicates are too sophisticated for the ordinary citizen, but not the police.[7]

In contrast, both believers' and debunkers' accounts of the social context of snuff film legends, as well as film treatments of the subject such as *8mm* and *Strange Days*, make a scathing indictment of society's moral status. In all of these arenas, the notion is that an increasingly indulged cache of depraved desire produces, or will soon produce, its own demand for snuff films. This ominous outcome depends heavily on the idea that no one cares any more, enough to intervene. This "no one" includes law enforcement agencies. This is the apathy against which the fictional heroes Welles (*8mm*) and Lenny (*Strange Days*), and the real-life moral entrepreneurs including Yaron Svoray (1997), must counter in their journeys.

Post-Guardianship: A World without Intervention

Let us consider the snuff film first. Here a violent and decadent form of entertainment is produced, sold, and consumed without leaving a viable trace. Since rumors of the existence of the snuff film market date back to 1969, this means that such a secretive practice has sustained itself for thirty years without exposure despite investigation, and despite the number of second- and third- hand claims to the contrary. By contrast, other illegal markets, such as those of the drug trade, of the smuggling and exploitation of illegal immigrants, and of child pornography, have resulted in constant arrests and convictions. These latter markets, and reports about them in the mass media, still seem to suggest that "intact" and morally mandated governments, and law enforcement agencies in particular, continue to address themselves to impeding these markets, however much they may be effective in doing so or not. Yet the unimpeded snuff film market suggests otherwise: that beneath the surface impression that we have, another world of knowledge exists— essentially a very big, very well kept secret. Both the content of the legends and their form or genre, a word-of-mouth process that travels along personalistic lines, testify to the privately networked nature of social life. Perhaps in a mediated, scientifically and commercially saturated world the idea of both an underworld and an exclusive network of curious above-ground interlocutors seems appealing or romantic. Certainly, the strategy of using "affirmative unknowns," a technique for preserving a sense of mystery about the legend, (described in the last chapter) enhances this view.

But more likely, the permeable nature of the boundary between above and below, between the decadent and vicious underworld and the everyday manifestations of modern society, is being considered. The snuff film legend really asks how much social distance there is between order and barbarism. Who were all those millions of Internet web surfers anxious to see the next girl die in "The Mikado" episode of *Millennium*? How did they find out about it? Why did they allow it to continue, while the two conscientious boys at the beginning of the episode, frightened and convinced by what they saw, contacted the police? Why did the police (and our protagonist, Frank Black) not have access to the knowledge that the millions of web surfers did? The implication, of course, is that barbarism may begin at one's front door despite outward signs otherwise. Black remarks that in a better world, he would hold these millions responsible as accomplices. Despite outward appearances of order and progress (specifically, technological progress), the show portrays a society already too morally degraded to hold violent criminals responsible, and also one to watch raptly and tip others off to the show.

The cognate version of the snuff film legend, which flourished during the 1970s, is not much different in its assumptions about the world around it. The market in snuff films is thought to operate with perfect enough secrecy to not generate evidence, yet also with enough porousness to generate a thirty year whispering campaign about its alleged existence. The examination in this current study of the talk around the snuff film in public Internet news groups shows that believers and skeptics alike worry that social life in the West might very well, if not now, then very soon might be socially devolved enough to allow a market with such characteristics to flourish.[8] This conception of social structure suggests several assumptions about the role of crime in general.

The snuff film legend suggests a decline in moral outrage and a decline in the watchdog quality of civil society, which ties directly into loss of guardianship. (In this latter sense, it is probably more than narrative convention that ties wayward daughters and fathers who need redeeming to cinematic treatment of the snuff film.) In both *Hard Core* and *8mm* the protagonists not only pursue rescue and/or revenge on behalf of wayward daughters, but also battle a world that simply doesn't care enough to prevent the market in snuff films from developing. The apathy of conventional law enforcement agencies, in these media accounts and folk texts surrounding the snuff film legend, speaks directly to the need for heroic outsiders who will on their own attempt to restore a moral and retributive-legal order where it is supposed that one no longer exists.

With regards to the perceived weakness of civil society to address crime, two divergent accounts of snuff film availability seem to converge. One version, which is among moral entrepreneurs the most dominant, describes the enabling of the market in snuff films by an elite conspiracy. Variously described as an exclusive practice of decadent Hollywood elites, a profit center for international organized crime outfits, and a secretive wing of the above-ground domestic pornography industry, the snuff film industry supposedly operates "above" and "beyond" the reach of the law, the media, and advocacy investigators like Svoray.

The second version, the "democratic" version, holds that far from being a province and practice of elites for elites, the snuff film is readily available to the ordinary aficionado if he or she has been given proper information on how to obtain one. (Lovelace 1986; Morgan 1992) Amateur snuff film makers are thought to operate as easily in such an underground market as elites would. Interlocutors in news groups held one or the other view of the flourishing of the snuff film market, but rarely were such ideas explicitly conspiratorial. In both versions, "elite" and "democratic" we can see a convergence of the idea that both law and civil society are disinterested in, or functionally incapable of, detecting and interfering with this market. The renewed moral center, where it exists, rests only in an exceptional individual seeking to interfere. Movies with a snuff film component generally underscore this point by employing the independent investigator-protagonist to fight not only the snuff-makers, but broad indifference all around him, as well.

A sense of lost guardianship characterizes the other two legend case studies as well. A ring of kidney thieves steal body parts and traffic in them, again without attracting attention. This time, an even wider net of potentially outraged witnesses has gone missing in action, and likewise the secret-keepers must be larger in number as well. Unlike the victim in the snuff film legend, the victim of the kidney theft does not live on the margins of society. He is a student or a businessman. The underground activity of organ theft is peopled by a network of individuals with very high levels of medical technical expertise. Everyone in this scenario must have some means of keeping this trade a secret. This is made all the more easy if no one witnesses these activities or if these witnesses simply do not care or are uniformly bribed or threatened. These potential witnesses include 911 dispatchers, hotel personnel, hospital personnel, vendors of medical equipment, law enforcement personnel, the victim and his loved ones, as well as the organ recipient's. In a world without intervention, where everyone minds their own business, this scenario does make sense.

A similar set of tacit assumptions about social life makes the abduction-into-bondage of women and children from shopping malls and theme parks plausible to its believers. Again a broad and diverse group of potential interveners must be convinced to look the other way. Or perhaps it is assumed that they are already disposed to do so. In all three cases, the relative inattention of the news media to these particular crimes can be explained by the endemic chaos that is assumed to characterize everywhere but close to home. The best the police can do, as suggested by most versions of the abduction text, is to send out these warnings via the electronic mail grapevine. It seems that area malls will not be watched over to combat this "new" criminal practice; it is instead up to individuals to guard against this danger.

Likewise these warnings passed along have not produced any incipient panic as in earlier incarnations, such as with the white-slavery panics and Morin's (1970) Orleans episode. This absence of panic, while being good news for the usual scapegoats, itself speaks to a certain dispersal of civic responsibility. The current warning is thus shifted not only from woman to child as prey, but also into a highly individualized urge to precaution. Morin claimed modern France was suffering from a "civic immaturity" which was not strong enough to deflect the spread of an ancient canard and subsequent panic. In the present case though such immaturity takes a different form, with the same impaired skepticism but also with a consigning of the threat to the level of an everyday condition. Notably, believers do not look upon the words of debunkers with relief, with the desire for the threat to be extinguished by it "being merely an urban legend." Instead, debunkers were viewed as either hostile, naive, or both.

A media cover-up is rarely alleged. Instead, the media is mostly irrelevant in the story, as are the police and courts. The contest of wills, thus, to maintain safety for oneself and one's loved ones, is a poorly balanced match between potential victim and victimizer, without a referee or audience. The victimizer's social network and criminal skills are described as advanced. By implication, those of the potential victim are not. He or she has only her own knowledge and precaution to rely upon; no help is forthcoming from law enforcement, except perhaps to fill out reports.

Responses to the fear of crime in the United States have always carried an extra-institutional quality, more so than the other Atlantic countries discussed here. Vigilantism, widespread gun ownership and accessibility, as well as a "do-it-yourself" ethic of local justice have all created an ambivalent relationship with official institutions of law and order. Folk texts of crime legends hold law enforcement to be a marginal force in the fight against the menace of crime; although they are generally also pessimistic about the ability of citizens to self-organize against criminal threats.

Mall security may close the exits to the mall, but it is the mother's powers of observation, now again hypervigilant, that actually foils the crime in the abduction legend. (In versions where no shoe recognition exists, the predator successfully leaves the premises with the child.) Such "attempted abductions" (Brunvand, 1984, 78–82) apparently are thought to happen so often that a security-force procedure exists, and so as hearers we are to understand that this is an ordinary crime.

In sum, the above-surface society seems to fare poorly in the area of mutual aid and solidarity, whereas the underworld network of criminals constitute and effective and mutually supporting network of money, materials, and skills.

Criminal Conspiracies

Only one element of modern society—the predatory element—is depicted in folk texts, film representations of these texts, and the talk about the texts as highly self-organized and internally solidaristic. While falling short of "conspiracy theory," crime legends nonetheless display certain traits of that form. Criminal conspiracies are rarely alleged here to flourish due to government or institutional complicity, but rather due to *indifference* on the part of these entities. There are rarely explicit accusations of cover-up, but, as news group interlocutor Brett said of snuff films, they are "so illegal" as to be out of the scope of anyone looking to foil one, although not, interestingly, out of reach to one who wished to consume one. These conspiracies, or criminal underground networks, do not conform to traditional, political conspiracy theories, by imputing to the motivation of conspirators the desire to quietly seize control of state powers, or insidiously impose a new social order.[9] Rather they emerge out of a synergistic effect of guardian indifference, money, and decadence taken to their limits in the current scene. The tacit assumption is that they are profiteers gaining their trade upon a contemporary breakdown of social order and law enforcement inefficacy or indifference. These conspirators are thought to quietly operate out of the reach of above-ground society, because they can, because no one cares.

Mr. Christian, the wealthy recluse in *8mm*, makes a snuff film because he can. Everyone in *Hard Core* and *Strange Days* assumes that the avenger or rescuer must have their own agenda, and imply that it is probably as corrupt as that of the snuff film makers. That is, the will and the means by themselves are enough to produce, as the jaded Los Angeles private detective tells Jake Van Dorn, a police force that's completely out of the loop and where "a lot of strange things are happening in this world. . . doors that shouldn't be opened." Such is the power of those who produce and profit from the snuff film, and the weakness of the compromised, postmodern patriarchs.

As I shall discuss below, this view of offenders as largely agents of criminal syndicates may be fanciful for most crime, but the sense that crime control is only marginally effective, and set against forces which are too powerful to combat, is much broader than that found in the word-of-mouth, idiosyncratic form of the crime legend text.

WHAT DOES THE FEAR OF CRIME REFLECT?

While debunkers accurately capture the 'culture of credulity' and some instances of social paranoia in their analysis of why crime legends are immortal, debunkers pay relatively little attention to the real material conditions which may give rise to an underlying sense that the world is indeed increasingly post-social and without reliable guardianship and recourse. Certain broad trends in United States, Canada, the United Kingdom and Australia are "intelligibly" if not directly linked with a legitimate sense that we increasingly do live with a great deal of disorganization in our social lives amidst great affluence. Likewise we can see the material possibility, and the political remoteness, of the end of scarcity. Garland (1996) describes it:

> Rates of property crime and violent crime which are historically unprecedented in the modern period have become an acknowledged and commonplace feature of social experience. So too have linked phenomena such as a widespread fear of crime, pervasive media and cultural representations of crime and the politicization of crime control. Despite the fact that crime has an uneven social distribution, and that high risk victimization is very much a pocketed, concentrated phenomenon, crime is widely experienced as a prominent fact of modern life. (p. 446)

The previous chapter suggests that diversity in the styles and degrees of belief help preserve the crime legend. Here it will be suggested that crime legends also tap fears that have not been well articulated in conventional news media and television's fictional images of crime. These fears may have some basis in social and political reality: that the world is increasingly without guardianship and does contain elements of social disintegration. Crime legends simplify this long-term and often contradictory process, in the same way that conspiracy theories simplify and personalize power structures and add elements of mystery or "imputed uncertainty" to what would otherwise be in plain sight.

Is There Something Realistic about the Fear of Crime?

The difficulty in sorting apart "rational" and "irrational" elements in the fear of crime in the post-industrial world also reflects emerging institutional interests on the part of governments. It will be argued that the transformation of many Western countries from redistributive and civic welfarist, modified capitalist states to minimalist and increasingly remote *laissez-faire* states which demand that individuals make it on their own socially and economically, are increasingly seeking to address crime "after the fact only" with expanded incarceration and incapacitation. This state strategy is matched in the popular media with ritualized moral outrage combined with little sense that conditions can (and in recent years, particularly in the United States, did) improve. That is, the optimistic, mid-century "high modern" view of crime control has decisively ended.

These shifts have not been widely accounted for in speculations as to why North Americans, Europeans, and Australians are "excessively" fearful of crime, and thus why folk practices like the crime legend may be found especially useful in problem-solving. Both real and depicted crime shapes a cognitive environment that sees little possibility of socially produced safety and raises general suspicion and fear.[10] The fear of crime has been investigated and discussed in a number of ways. Below, a set of discussions, selected for their focus upon the rationality-irrationality dichotomy in the fear of crime and in public discussion of it, will be considered, in order to paint a background to the current specific analysis of crime legends.

Since the 1980s, critical or 'left' criminologists and other social scientists have debated the role that social construction plays in popular accounts of crime in industrial and post-industrial western countries. In the United Kingdom, this debate has taken place primarily among left criminologists and has had direct political implications. The so-called 'left realist' debate concerns a critique advanced by Lea and Young (1984) that radical criminology had developed a tendency to criticize only those institutions involved with the control of crime and empowered to define it, including the state, the punishment apparatus, and the mass media, the latter often accused of exaggerating crime's threat. (Smith, 1986: 21)

In other words, the left seemed preoccupied with distortive and reactionary depictions of crime and the attendant rise of what Stuart Hall called "authoritarian populism" in Britain. In 1978 Hall et al. examined the emergent moral panic surrounding the supposed "crime wave" of muggings in London. Their argument rested philosophically upon an underlying contrasting empirical reality: "mugging" was a relatively new term for an old criminal practice which had spiked more dramatically in past decades without producing a panic. Hall et al's argument decidedly did *not* rest upon the idea that confrontational armed robberies in London were few and far between, but rather that an authoritarian populist response emerged which required explanation in its own right given the lack of evidence that mugging was really something new. Implicated was the onset of post-industrial decline and the attendant class conflict which left an embattled and weak British state besieged by popular demands which it could not meet; authoritarian populism against crime enabled the veneer of social consensus where there was very little. [11]

The work inspired a generation of left criminologists in Britain to look critically at the construction of crime as a social problem: what was defined as a crime, who was thought to be responsible for crime, and who benefitted from the expansion of surveillance and punishment resources. Nonetheless, left realists alleged, a subsequent "idealist" turn seemed to characterize left and critical treatments of representations of the fear of crime. (Matthews and Young, 1992) Relatively little attention was in turn paid to the real impact that crime had upon victims and the real destructive impact that crime has upon social solidarity, particularly in poor and working class communities which are disproportionately affected while also being poorly resourced to respond to it. Fear and anger about crime, both of which did in fact rise dramatically in Britain since the 1970s, Lea and Young argued, contained a "rational kernel" and could not be honestly seen as merely a baseless "moral panic."

Finally, the left's unwillingness to treat crime as a "real" problem, either because fear of it was thought to be irrational and reactionary (paranoid, racist, or perhaps merely authoritarian) or because, in some more orthodox Marxist formulations, crime was conceived as an inexorable element of capitalism and could not be addressed fruitfully unless capitalism was defeated, meant that there was from the criminologically-informed left, a defeatist and abstentionist stance toward the whole issue. In turn, the right was able to wholly own it in popular politics from the 1970s onward.

The case of the United States has similar polarizations, but not identical ones. The United States has always had one of the highest crime rates in the industrialized world, although compared to the spike in media attention since the 1970s, changes in rates of crime have not been so dramatic and have broadly declined in the 1990s. Criminology in the United States has had a fair number of policy progressives, but not enough critical left ones to sustain such a vociferous debate as in the UK. As for liberals and left-liberals in the United States, notes Currie (1986: 13–15) their greater suspicion of the state also manifested itself as a tendency to downplay the severity of the crime problem in the country and to dismiss the fear of crime as inherently reactionary. (Paradoxically, it was also liberals who claimed that poverty and inequality were criminogenic.) Radicals, though, like those on the British left, often tended to defer the issue of serious crime until some unspecified future when, like the state itself, crime too would wither away.

Challenges to this 'idealist' model on the left has also come from feminists, who argue that real (not imagined) levels of victimization, threat, intimidation and harassment both in and outside the home make women's fear (in relationship to their actual risk, statistically) less "irrational" than some have made it seem. Nonetheless crime prevention campaigns in the UK and elsewhere have individualized the problem. (Stanko, 1995) Crime legends also tend to reinforce the idea of individual actions for personal safety, and as frightening stories purported to be real, they seem to counter more "reassuring" viewpoints. Talk about the crime legends take place in a discursive atmosphere in which the "rationality" of fears are highly contested. As such they promote the importance of hypervigilance. As we shall see in the section to follow, such vigilance can take a psychic toll while producing on the whole little increased protection.

Crime Prevention Activities and the Fear of Crime

In the field of community psychology, the effects of local and individual crime prevention strategies upon anxiety, victimization, and fear of crime have been examined. These studies seem to overall suggest little positive effect stemming from such measures, as well as some indication of possible negative effect. (Norris and Kaniasty, 1992).[12] While such crime prevention pamphlets and local initiatives may help promote psychological coping adaptations to already-existing fear, they may also increase specific fear by implicitly blaming victims "by suggesting they were somehow responsible for their misfortune." (Norris and Kaniasty, 644) Individualization of risk is intensified by such approaches, as community and structural causes of crime are not addressed. Thus crime persists while the unsubtle message that protection is a personal matter is reinforced. Further, while the rewards of such voluntary measures are absent or at best unclear, they may also serve as constant reminders of insecurity and thus enhance specific fear. (Rosenbaum 1987; Reid et al, 1998)

Here the tension between the individualistic and solidaristic features of the crime legend finds a parallel. Promulgators of the legends, which often take the form of warnings, see themselves as performing a socially helpful act, regardless of whether they are deeply invested in the story's basis in real events. At the same time, the message of the legends themselves call for independent measures, which, as the community psychology literature suggests, may produce greater feelings of insecurity. Yet the crime legend differs in its "advice" to the hearer; arcane knowledge is favored over general caution and conspiratorial elements are more prominent. Why is this the case?

The question points to the intersubjective, rather than purely risk-based, nature of fear about crime. Again, the problem of information overload, raised in the previous chapter, is intertwined here with crime and fear. While the tenor of the times emphasizes personal responsibility for precaution, the cognitive environment for producing fear is increasingly collectivized as the net of media coverage broadens. Today, however, all of North America and perhaps even Europe and Australia might have access to news about specific crimes.[13] Crime legends, as a practice, have the advantage of being "idle talk," addressing fears without any real social action being required. It is relatively low-risk, socially, in this respect.

The "Risk-Fear Paradox"

Traditionally studies of the fear of crime have measured statistical risk against level of fear, finding that those less likely to be victimized (women, the elderly) were the most fearful. Thus a "risk-fear paradox" was identified. Some forms of fear of crime, then, were seen as irrational. Debate ensued as to what was actually being measured, however, with the implication that the paradox might be more apparent than real. The paradox while technically accurate, could not capture some rational cognitive processes that were likely to lead to increased fear. Both Skogan and Maxfield (1981) and Lea and Young (1984: 37) suggest that some of the "excess" fear among these groups could be explained by both real and perceived physical vulnerability in comparison with would-be attackers.[14] By contrast men of ordinary physical ability might, whether accurately or not, assume that they could defend themselves against attack. They may have higher rates of victimization and lower rates of fear because they do not take precautionary or evasive measures. Relatively low rates of victimization among women and the elderly may be an effect of greater precaution and self-restriction, rather than purely its cause.

Stanko (1995, 1997) has further suggested that many women's lives are filled with threatening situations, harassment, and outright threats that fall short of actions which provoke legal sanction against the aggressor but, nonetheless, shape their perception of the world's safety. Such a situation also undergirds the theme prominent in the current study of crime legends that guardianship is remote and means of recourse inconsistent at best. Fundamentally, the would-be victim's sense of social standing, connection, and place are at stake in the fear of crime. Since these matters are very much in flux in the current era for *everyone* in western postindustrial society, fear of crime may be a marker of a broader social anxiety.

Ultimately it may be difficult to disentangle elements of rationality and irrationality within the broader category "fear." While left realists such as Lea and Young (1984) and feminists such as Stanko correctly point to a whole level of realistic threat which is likely unaccounted for, the argument often still relies upon a specific set of ideas about how much fear and how much risk would be too much or too little. Realism, notes Sparks (1992) like other perspectives on the fear of crime which rely upon either existing risk data or imputed, undetected levels of risk, may be avoiding the basic issue of uncertainty as a key element of both specific fear and generalized social anxiety. "What from the point of view of an outside observer looks like actuarially accountable risk is, from the point of view of any individual (potential victim) more like a problem of uncertainty." (Sparks, 126–127) Stanko (1997) concurs that more is really at stake in the individual's management of fear than risk. As "situated" women, she notes, women who are the object of crime prevention educational campaigns:

> also worry about disrupted relations with colleagues; getting 'it' wrong (heightened risk or actual attack due to 'not thinking'); or being labeled a bad mother for not protecting children. Lurking in our safety talk is an acknowledgment of blame—both from the self as well as from the wider community—if (or when for some) they get it wrong. (p. 489)

Thus the fear of crime cannot easily be separated from, nor is it accurate to say it is a displacement of, overall social anxiety concerning the permanence and strengths of one's social standing. Victimization strains, and unfortunately often breaks, social bonds of the victim. In other words, there is ample evidence that stigmatization, disrupted personal relations, victim blaming, and even outright denial or disbelief on the part of others emerge in the wake of crime for the victim. In many cases as well, official claims that people are too fearful given their statistical risk (which is often based, problematically, upon reported crimes) slides quite quickly into victim-blaming. Where it is constantly reiterated that risk is low, those that are victimized are subtly judged as provocateurs.[15] In this same manner, the fears expressed in crime legends are difficult to separate from a profound sense of social decline. The existing literature on informal talk about crime, discussed in the first chapter, also found this to be the case.

The risk-fear paradox is a interesting but limited artifact in that it tends to individualize the problem of excess fear. Fear of crime must necessarily be a highly intersubjective, and in some cases, mass fear: otherwise crime news and fiction would compel much less of an audience than it does. It is unlikely that (mis)calculations of risk alone could explain fear of crime. Differential levels of altruism, identification, moral outrage, and scapegoating (particularly towards minorities and youth) complicate the calculus of fear even further. Yet part of the appeal of the risk-fear paradox to government officials is its underlying risk-rationality logic. Like *homo economus*, (O'Malley, 266) and the new *laissez-faire* subject of the post-Keynesian era, the rationally crime-calculating individual is expected by experts to make accurate and efficient decisions with perfect information and elastic material resources. If they miscalculate, or as Stanko put it, "get it wrong" they have only their own carelessness to blame. Thus it is easy to see how well the "responsibilist" (Garland) or "prudentialist" (O'Malley) strategy regarding public crime policy fits into larger ideological and political changes favoring neoclassical models as a basis of social policy.

Intersubjectivity as a factor in the individual's assessment of risk and of, on a somewhat distinct level, their own fear means that the victimization of others produces a reaction in the self—in a way that seems difficult to operationalize in a parsimonious fashion. To the extent that generalized anxiety, in the clinical or psychoanalytic sense often has its etiology in submerged anger, intersubjectivity becomes even more important. One may be anxious and outraged over the victimization of a loved one, a neighbor, or a stranger in the same way that one might feel any type of group feeling of wounded solidarity or basic human empathy. Levels of fear may also be enhanced by greater numbers of "others" victimized in one's cognitive orbit. "As social splintering occurs, there is a decrease in direct knowledge about crime, but, although the quality of information declines, the actual quantity increases." (Lea and Young, 263)

What ties these debates together for the purposes of this study is their common theme of uncertainty about the "realistic" nature of the fear of crime. With policymakers, the news media, and researchers unable to sort out what a realistic level of fear would be, it is not surprising that laypeople trying to evaluate word-of-mouth information would be wracked by the same uncertainty. The implications are vital for understanding the sustenance of crime legends. It will be argued here that crime legends might enable the management of fears related primarily to social disintegration and uncertainty, rather than representing a direct symptom of irrational or excess fearfulness. Yet this argument does not suggest that the fear of crime embodied in the tales is somehow a "substitute" for, or "displacement" of some other fear.

"Surplus Fear" Explanations

Glassner (1999) argues that specific kinds of collective contemporary fear should be understood in a larger context of a generally fear-laden society, in the case particularly of the United States. Most areas of daily life are fraught with menace, Glassner argues, if one judges from the evening television news. Not crime alone, but fear of accidents, natural disasters, germs, and disease as well make up a fearful landscape even for those with relative economic security. The level of overall fearfulness about these matters is historically high although most categories of threat posed more danger in previous decades.[16]

Glassner, however, relies upon an "art of misdirection" (Glassner, 1999: 88, 209) analysis of the mass media's role in producing and sustaining such fear. He argues that some legitimate fears are systematically displaced in popular discourse while others are exaggerated. Mass media frameworks provide a space for moral entrepreneurs—especially credentialed professionals who shepherd new threats into the light of public legitimacy. A constant trail of "scares" parades before the American public, from salmonella to stranger abductions of children to Internet pedophiles.[17] Meanwhile, other real dangers, such as the declining social wage, economic polarization, and environmental contamination, go unheralded.

Glassner relies upon the rarity of the crimes behind various over-emphasized "scares" to argue that fear of crime is *generally* unfounded, even as he includes a chapter about the real threats posed by ease of access to guns.[18]

This analysis has at least two problems. First, most Western countries are still experiencing historically high crime rates since World War II, and the United States still outpaces other all other industrialized countries dramatically, with the new exceptions of Russia and South Africa. Further, the risk of victimization, and the social erosion that it causes, has never been evenly distributed in any case. Class, race, and gender all contribute to the risks and fears of various crimes and to the level of long-lasting social damage that they cause. Finally, it is too soon to tell whether the various causes of crime's decline overall will prove persistent.[19] Some possible partial causes, such as mass incarceration and aggressive policing, may also be socially undesirable in a democracy.

I think it wise to avoid the use of such "displacement" arguments in an overly general manner. Clearly it is appropriate to say that the panic about the sexual abuse of children in day-care centers and by satanic cults might logically be a displacement of the more realistic, but psychically threatening fear, of abuse closer to home, to use one example. Yet it is a bit of an overreach, given current historical conditions, to dismiss the fear of crime as a manipulative diversion from economic insecurity, for instance. This is especially so if one understands crime and economic polarization to be deeply intertwined.

Taylor and Jamieson (1998) suggest that while citizens of Western countries fear crime with varying degrees of "accuracy" this fear also expresses simultaneously their fear of social dislocation through it. Citizens in the United Kingdom are both responding on some level "realistically" to historically high crime rates in Britain and also folding less easily articulated fears, associated with economic dislocation, into it, forming a kind of surplus panic. (Taylor and Jamieson, 161) In the United States they suggest that fear of crime in a time of declining rates (the 1990s) reflects, "a profound but suppressed recognition of the essentially violent and competitive character of American culture ... and the particular types of crime (especially involving firearms) which such a culture engenders." (Taylor and Jamieson, 151) Their assessment suggests that there is always a cumulative effect of fear in a society as well as in an individual.

Within a society where notions of common provision are under pervasive challenge, the crime legend is uniquely positioned to carry, tame, and reshape threats such that control can be asserted by individuals, rather than communities or state entities, over the threat of victimization. This goes well beyond overestimating the probability of attack by a stranger and underestimating one by an intimate or colleague; it instead places responsibility upon the potential victim for avoiding *any* possible threat and as such offers up threats that can be avoided through specific precautionary activities.

A striking example of this process is a crime legend which circulated broadly in the years 1993 and 1994 in the US called "Lights Out." (see examples in Brunvand, 1999: 393–395) As described in the introductory chapter, "Lights Out" comes in the form of a warning to motorists not to flash their headlights at night at a car which has failed to light theirs, for fear of being then chosen as the victim of a gang initiation rite. Here the whole problem of random youth violence is "magically" resolved by merely restraining from a simple activity. At the same time, the story suggests, it is now necessary to restrain from what would ordinarily be a collective safety-promoting action. The conscientious motorist is thus forced to choose between the safety of others and her own, again reinforcing the idea that precaution is an individual matter.[20]

While the stories themselves often rely upon implausible assumptions in their depictions of specific crime practices, and by all evidence are indeed apocryphal, the underlying themes of social breakdown that they reference may have a realistic core. They speak to fear of society unable to provide one of its most basic functions: common defense.

The End of "High Modern" Crime Control and The Risk Society

The dominant themes of dislocation and uncertainty regarding crime and fear in this study fit well with Giddens' discussion (1990, 1991) of "onto-logical anxiety" and Beck's 1992 analysis of the "risk society" which are characteristic of the current late modern or post-modern period. Several authors have sought to connect Beck's and Giddens' analysis with the specific case of crime and policing. They argue that specific paradigm shifts in really-existing law enforcement policy seem to confirm the legitimacy of some fears of social disintegration. These are the same fears that are broadly expressed by interlocutors in the current study.

An optimistic modern period in which governments 1) saw the preserva-tion of safety and order as a directive and a responsibility fundamental to the state's legitimacy and 2) engaged in discursive practices promoting general public trust in an ultimately positive outcome with respect to the former, has waned. Speaking about shifts in the US (Currie 1985: 13; Bayley and Shearing, 1996: 586–587), Australia (O'Malley, 1992: 264–265) and the United Kingdom (Garland, 1996; Stanko 1997), criminologists have pointed to the state's shift in its role vis a vis crime.

As part of the modern welfare state's loss of legitimacy, modernist (reha-bilitative and preventive) policy approaches to crime and its mitigation have been eroded. The state has sought to disinvest in the prevention of crime, to cease resisting competition from nongovernmental and commercial security forces, and focus mainly upon apprehension and incarceration of offenders. These shifts are part and parcel of the ascendancy of the anti-statist or *laissez-faire* Right. Thus the prominent theme, in this study, of a remote, inconsistent, and uncaring net of guardianship against crime is not without objective corroboration in certain governmental trends in these countries.

Within the risk society, then, victimization is increasingly an individualized risk that cannot be prevented, but only avenged, by the state. The dismantling of the welfare state, far from energizing local collective initiatives to address social problems, has instead moved our societies towards collections of atomized citizens who must rely upon incoherent market solutions.[21]

As safety, or freedom from victimization, as a public good travels down this road of individualized risk, cultural responses may be unpredictable. Governmental and media visibility on the problem of crime is quite strong and strident, while ground-level help is lacking. Garland and Sparks (2000: 16–17) suggest that:

> Citizens become crime-conscious, attuned to the crime problem, and many exhibit high levels of fear and anxiety. They are caught up in institutions and daily practices that require them to take on the identity of (actual or potential) crime victims, and to think, feel, and act accordingly. This enforced engagement with crime and crime prevention tends to produce an ambivalent reaction. On the one hand, a stoical adaptation that prompts the development of new habits of avoidance and crime prevention routines. On the other, a measure of irritation and frustration that prompts a more hostile response to the danger and nuisance that crime represents in daily life.

As O'Malley describes the shift in Australia, the destruction of the social wage is accompanied, in the area of crime control, by the "reinstate[ment of] the morally responsible individual and sets it against the collectivization inherent in the public risk-management techniques." (p. 259) In the United Kingdom, likewise, Garland suggests that the Home Office went through an "hysterical" period during the 1970s, when the persistence of historically high crime rates since the end of World War II—despite the expansion of policing—was finally faced head-on. Since that time, Garland argues, the state has sought to redefine (and Garland suggests, minimize) its role in the basic preservation of order and safety, instead redefining that basic social task as an individual- and neighborhood-level concern.[22] This shift is seen to be in tandem with the broader rollback of the state's emphasis on general social welfare and common provision and towards the privatization of previously public services.

The parallels with the United States are striking. Bayley and Shearing (1996) argue that tax revolts and continued frustration with exceptionally high rates of crime have encouraged the rapid growth of private security services, the privatization of social functions previously carried out in public space (e.g. the transition from Main Street shopping to large regional shopping malls, and private, gated neighborhoods), and the promotion of self-reliance in individuals and local, nongovernmental groups to prevent crime.

Risk societies are media message-dense and increasingly characterized by economic polarization and social distrust. The return of responsibility to the

individual to sort through this information and prevent their own victimization nonetheless leaves all but the wealthiest outside of the electronic
gates. As such, the sorts of arcane advice woven through crime legends, delivered along informal lines, is seen as "helpful" for people now reliant on their
own wits to negotiate this task. More conventional crime prevention advice
is seen as insufficient, as predators are now depicted as more organized and
less easily recognized by potential victims as predators.

Crime Control and the Rise of the New Right in the United States

From the 1980s to the mid-1990s, this general *laissez-faire* tendency became
enshrined as public policy. Under the direction of Reagan Administration
Attorney General William French Smith, the Department of Justice issued a
report in 1981, which announced the recession of the federal government in
all matters relating to the combat of violent crime—with the exception of
drug interdiction and increased block grant funds for incarceration facilities.[23] In the case of violent crime, the Attorney General's office reiterated its
view that public safety was primarily a local matter which did not warrant
federal intervention. While conceding that the Constitution includes the
imperative to "ensure domestic tranquility" the document nonetheless
begins, on page 1, with a clear statement that crime was a strictly local, and
perhaps even non-governmental matter.

> ... nowhere in that document [the Constitution] is there any provision for
> the federal government directly to police its citizens . . . . the people of this
> nation would have to display forbearance, show one another mutual
> respect, and build self-regulating neighborhoods and communities . . . . we
> are mindful of the risks of assuming that the government can solve what
> ever problem it addresses.

By contrast, drug traffic was just such a case that did warrant federal intervention.[24] At length the dangers to health and criminogenic qualities of illicit
drugs were reiterated throughout the document. Thus mutual respect and
self-regulation were not seen as adequate to the task of defeating the drug
trade, nor was it seen any longer as primarily a local matter.

In another important contrast to the persistence of federalism in crime
fighting, the document recommends a dramatic expansion in correctional
facilities nationwide. While these facilities were to be built under state and
local auspices, they would be funded with federal resources and heavy financial support for this project was recommended. It was hoped that this would
decrease crime.

> We think that the provision of more and higher quality correctional facili
> ties will ease the problems faced now by almost all states of dealing swiftly,
> certainly, and fairly with convicted offenders and that this, in turn, will help

deter some would be offenders and incapacitate other known offenders.
(U.S. Department of Justice, 2)

The document then reiterates that supposed previous leniency encouraged crime and that increased incarceration would help. Further, it reinforces the idea that little support could be expected for localities coping with greater crime-related challenges. State and local governments, and "private citizens" the document repeats, are primarily responsible for crime control. The pessimism which expressed itself in British policy documents was manifested as a decided withdrawal in the U.S. case; ideologically the latter was able to rely upon federalist principles, albeit inconsistently, to do so.

It is clear that the desire to redefine the role of the state away from one that served as a guarantor of public safety was manifest. Garland (1996) and Currie (1985) concur that governmental abstention followed larger pessimistic trends, including that of the academy. Despite the law-and-order politics associated with the conservative governments in this era, a decidedly minimalist and ex-post-facto (i.e., incarceration-focused) approach to crime quietly became the norm. Thus, notes Currie (1985: 10), "the passivity that began to infect scholarly thinking about crime during the seventies had become enshrined as a fundamental principle of government policy."[25]

Hence the case of the United States seems to confirm the increased association between a *laissez-faire* governing philosophy and a late or post-modern phase of crime control. The rapid expansion in incarceration during the 1980s and 1990s can be seen to support rather than contradict this trend, in two ways. First, many of the newly incarcerated are drug offenders. Secondly, the faith in punishment as the preferred, or often singular concern of the state (as explicitly stated in the Attorney General's report) reflects its pessimism as to its own role in guardianship. This admission of helplessness on the part of authorities, which coincided with conservative political ascendancies, helps explain the increase in the fear of crime and media sensitization to it. Changes in crime rates per se do not explain it very well. (Zimring, 1997) The post-World War II surge in crime rates across the board in industrialized countries, including a sharp increase in both violent and property crimes beginning in the 1950s (Gurr 1977: 44, 84), appears not to have provoked the same reaction earlier.

It could be argued either that a "natural" inclination to increased fear was suppressed during the 1950s and 1960s, or instead that the cultivation of fear in the 1980s and 1990s was artificially enhanced against a backdrop of relatively steady but historically high rates of crime. Were the latter explanation to be more compelling than the first, we might look perhaps to opportunistic politicians or media frameworks.

Yet some prior state of affairs must have enabled those respective crusades. That is, that the politics of authoritarian populism saw an opening—it emerged in a vacuum created by the end of confidence among crime control agencies. This populism is different from a simple, confident, and optimistic belief in the need for, and possibility of, law and order—a state of affairs which reigned among policymakers and the mass media in that early post-war period and which may have suppressed fear. Garland notes:

> A show of punitive force against individuals is used to repress any acknowl-
> edgment of the state's inability to control crime to acceptable levels. A
> willingness to deliver harsh punishments to convicted offenders magically
> compensates a failure to deliver security to the population at large (p. 460)

The rise of pessimism regarding crime control amidst the persistence of high crime rates, along with the hegemony of conservative political leadership, creates the optimal conditions for a fear of social breakdown with the fear of victimization as its lodestone. Conservative talk about crime purports toughness, but generally with regard to punishment only.[26] Explicitly it often regards crime prevention and control as a matter for people to handle privately.

CONCLUSION

These perceived conditions of social breakdown, loss of guardianship, and the strength of criminal syndicates in many Western countries create an ambivalent situation and a confusion over social roles with regards to personal safety. Debunkers of crime legends often fail to notice these loss-of-solidarity themes that are at the heart of the crime legend, focusing sometimes too much upon the falsehood of the tales. Seeing believers as representative of a larger trend towards self-righteous social paranoia, credulity, and even maliciousness, debunkers often fail to understand why a legend, once debunked, will rise and rise again.

Yet the post-modern world also makes a welcome host for the crime legend. Brunvand's understanding of the anxieties of a modern age that have sustained the genre—transience, mass society and anonymity, rapid techno-logical change—are even more characteristic of current times. Heroes in film depictions of crime legends tend to be underdogs and renegades while conventional, patriarchal authorities are seen as weak, corrupt, or indif-ferent. In conversations about these folk texts in news group settings, heroes are often absent altogether. People must rely on warnings passed along through idiosyncratic networks—a form of kismet and also local, particu-larized networks of trust—and on their own wits.

The crime legend is able to speak to losses in social life which are far from easily articulated, but do have some basis in political shifts during the 1980s and 1990s. The crime legend's authorlessness, and the informality of its routes of communication, seem to fit into a broader sense of uncertainty, public distrust in institutions, and anxiety which follow the end of the assertive and confident law-and-order modern era.

The image of the criminal in these tales seems to deviate from the one presented in a number of formal media settings (the young minority male, or the white, psychotic serial killer), both now and in the past. The predator in these tales—at least in this study's setting—has become generic and rationalized. He is a profiteer, has many underground connections, and is invisible to the above-ground world, law enforcement and civilian alike. Hence the sense that danger cannot be compartmentalized.

Victim blaming in these stories is subtle where it exists. While the snuff film and kidney theft legends display characteristics of the cautionary tale— through the narrative warning of the dangers of pornography and casual sex—they also display a certain sympathy for the victim. Blame is most pronounced where the setting of the crime is the most familiar—in the shopping mall or theme park where the distractions of these consumer arcades for a mother are many. In the face of this generalized danger, formal guardians are seen as unprepared and overwhelmed. The protection offered by patriarchal, informal social control and the chivalry system, especially for women, has eroded as women fully integrate into the public sphere.

The sense that informal social control has slackened in recent decades, producing overall more opportunities for crime, clearly has some basis in reality. Yet seeing an increased sense of threat as a predictable outcome of greater leisure, freedom of movement, and economic intensity holds little comfort for many. To this sense of lost guardianship and solidarity, debunkers can offer few counter-narratives. Treating the truth or falsity of a legend's content as the only issue worth considering means that both the reasons for believing and the diversity of forms of belief are obscured. Given that underlying fears are not very often addressed on their own terms during news group discussions, the vehemence with which debunkers approach their mission may seem, to the believer or even neutral observer, somehow out of proportion. If it is underlying fears and ideas about social reality which are really at stake in the promulgation of, and belief in, crime legends, then accusations of gullibility are not likely to make much of an impact in comparison to the needs that the crime legend fulfills.

Urban legends are practices as well as texts. Crime legends in particular can serve the purpose of destabilizing a hearer's sense of safety and thus join the promulgator in his or her anxiety; they can be offered solidaristically in the form of the warning; and they can serve as common discursive currency about the breakdown of modern societies.

The law-and-order message of the ascendant conservative parties has within it an ambivalence, between authoritarianism and *laissez-faire*, between privatization-friendly approaches and traditionally state-centered functions. The crime legend seems to manage this contradiction, being a populist as well as popular form. The crime legend gets around the risk-fear paradox because the stories are not risk-dependent; they make no claim to typicality. In fact, promulgators are often aware of the extremity and audacity within the story. The stories contain special cases for teller and hearer that confirm "what the world has come to." It seems that extremity and audacity themselves are seen to be an endemic condition. The crime legend also enables fear to be expressed indirectly, being offered as a kind of "news" which desires to be authoritative.

One of the striking aspects of the "postmodernization" of the crime legend is its disconnection from collective panic. Modern rumor research has investigated the role that rumors and legends have had to play in wartime, in civil unrest, and in scapegoating responses to traumatic events. Yet the casualization of the crime legend appears not to cause panics, yet produces or reinforces fears anyway—underscoring the increasingly private nature of fear. It also reinforces the argument I have presented throughout the study that crime legends speak to a view that the world is post-social. It can no longer produce safety in numbers, and formal guardians are seen as marginal. If anything, the "problem-solving" function that Shibutani identified has become more important, as the "official story" recedes into suspicion.

A Summary

I hope this study has begun to examine the shape that folklore can take in a new medium. The specific social life of crime legends in this setting points to broader cultural strains. In the current study, ambiguity and a sense of social breakdown characterize the talk around the text itself. The former, ambiguity, is a consistent finding throughout the history of rumor studies; the latter, social breakdown, is consistent with the small and more recent literature about informal talk about crime.

These themes are united by a loss of cultural authority that characterizes the current scene, affecting both the form and content of crime legends. Since the time of the apex of rumor studies, in the immediate post-World War II era, the object of study itself has shifted as has the atmosphere in which it has flourished. This atmosphere includes a surge in both crime rates and rapid changes in the informational ecology of Western countries, particularly the United States. Both have affected the ways in which crime folklore is defined, deployed, and debunked. This situation is likely reflective of the more general way in which the relationships made between people and information have also been drastically altered.

I hope the study herein has suggested that belief and disbelief, in interlocutory settings, are complicated by different styles of belief and skepticism. It is likely that other interlocutory settings are also so characterized; however, this has not been emphasized in existing literature.

As for the content of crime legends, they appear to fulfill a function not met by existing media treatments, although the latter, too, has expanded and diversified. This function is to tame the threat of victimization, and it does so in a number of interrelated ways. First, it depicts violent crime as more complex than it generally tends to be, and something to which arcane knowledge and hypervigilance can be successfully applied. Secondly, when the crime legend is understood as a practice, it can be seen to mediate between the solipsism of individualistic crime prevention, and social solidarity through warning. Rebuke of the less-than-hypervigilant is never far behind.

CRIME LEGENDS, MASS MEDIA, AND NEW MEDIA

Generally, the relationship between the "ordinary talk" of folklore and the "official talk" of mass media news and popular drama in the cultural diffusion process has been oversimplified. The first model was one of competition and succession. Good media, it was thought, could displace bad rumor, as policymakers and social scientists hoped. Alternatively, folklorists worried that the cultural legacy contained in folklore would be decimated by popular mass culture. Neither outcome has materialized. Instead, as trust in major social institutions, including media and government, has waned, folklore has begun to interact with the "official stories" in complex ways. The influence of an information-saturated culture, with its permeation into everyday consciousness, upon the career and influence of contemporary folklore remains unclear. Yet the rise and expansion of the mass media have neither extinguished the productivity of folklore; nor are the media directly, intentionally, and insidiously responsible for the dissemination of contemporary legends, rumors, and hoaxes, as is often alleged when a new round of legend circulation takes place. (Brunvand 1984). Nor are folklore and rumor a kind of resistant holdout pitched against the official and often partial story: false citations of news magazines, talk shows, and law enforcement bulletins sometimes accompany these legend warnings as forms of intended authoritativeness. This practice suggests that the desire for official imprimaturs of the information contained within the tale is still strong. These information and symbolization worlds mingle, and the study of word-of-mouth culture today requires that we imagine it not as a kind of romantic refuge from the sheer volume (in both senses of the word) of the information society, but a sphere of reflection of and interaction with it.

The study of the role of mass media in shaping the meaning of crime legends, surprisingly, revealed how widely it has debunked certain well-known crime legends. Major media outlets, including television news networks and daily newspapers have run, time and again, stories which explicitly debunk all three of the case study legends discussed here, as well as several others.

Crime legends have a much more florid life in television and cinema fiction, but even there an ample dose of skepticism consistently appeared. This skepticism, on the part of protagonists, was often only circumvented in the narrative by the introduction of supernatural powers or singular psychopathological delusion on the part of a perpetrator. Rarely were these legends promulgated in their "cognate" form-which stipulates that the story is "really" true as it has been told in the way that the protagonist had originally heard.

It was on-line conversations among debunkers, especially on *alt.folklore.urban* that originally suggested that media dissemination would play some role in the sustenance of crime legends. Participants in the news group often refer to "the media" contemptuously as a source of credulity among believers, and are often pleasantly surprised when a news organization runs a debunking story. However, I found such journalistic interventions to be quite common. Some group regulars are more specifically distressed with certain syndicated columnists, such as Ann Landers and Paul Harvey, who, they charge, are constantly acting as "vectors" for urban legends. It is fair to say, though, that despite the respect accorded to individual journalists for debunking efforts, debunkers regard the media as part of the problem. Believers (in general, not specifically) are referred to as "tabloid TV suckers," "vidiots," or "Jerry Springer fodder."

Displayed contempt for the gullible has also been more apparent since the concept of the "urban legend" itself has gained notoriety in the last decade. As more and more of the general public becomes accustomed to the concept of the urban legend (through the popularity of Brunvand's books, and some cinematic treatments of the topic), debunkers often wonder why broader skepticism seems to, nonetheless, be elusive.

The growth of public use of the Internet often poses a problem too, especially for once very close-knit, purposive news groups. As more and more people enter news group discussions, their original intimacy dissipates. Those who regard the group as a refuge from the outside world find the group has become attractive to new people whose expectations and assumptions are different. The character of the group often changes. It is likely that these changes will persist as the demographics of the Internet using public become more typical.

Debunkers, for all for all their increasing organization, have a difficult time challenging the social trends they find so discouraging. Believers, for their part, seem to have a veritable meaning-producing monopoly upon the crime legend, as the more critical-minded are reluctant to read into the stories because they are false. In interlocutory settings, the narrow emphasis on fact means that the meaning that believers derive from the stories cannot be addressed constructively by debunkers or hometown skeptics.

CRIME, LEGEND BELIEVERS, AND SOCIAL DISINTEGRATION

The world, as experienced by some participants in news group discussions about crime legends, is without social recourse. It is filled with trapdoors and snakepits. Advice is sought from others, informally, about the possible placement of one's steps, since no one is particularly accountable for the existence of the trapdoors or charged with getting rid of them.

The narratives of the stories themselves, as well as the partisans of their salience, indicate that eradication is not a possibility. For them, there are no police or law enforcement agencies that can challenge the harm directly. Most often in these tales, the police don't appear at all. Even when they do, they only appear to warn people that these practices are occurring. No investigation will be launched, and no arrest can be made. In some rare cases, police, criminal justice agencies, business elites are believed to be complicit in covering up incidents.

These tales suggest that most criminals who wish you harm act in concert and with impunity; that snuff film markets cannot be disrupted, or even detected; that the commerce in stolen body parts thrives at a healthy profit; that rings of child-snatchers prowl shopping mall bathrooms for new junior prostitutes. In sum, it is believed that small, *coherent* societies of criminals exist in a greater state of lawlessness and general social apathy. Throughout the research for this project, a sense of collective guardianship was absent or under serious challenge. To some extent, this sense of absence may be based in real changes taking place around the politics of crime control in the last twenty years.

Contemporary legends about crime straddle enchanted and disenchanted views of evil, in the Weberian sense. The stories lack explicitly supernatural elements, but bear resemblance to more archaic descriptions of evil in that worldly villains are perceived to be extremely powerful, untouchable, and in some cases hide in plain sight like esoteric forces or sensitive gods. On the other hand, the stories are presented as "news" and often inscribe secular authorities such as hospital, law enforcement, or media personnel as citations or "proof," which reflects a generally rationalistic, realistic view of the story.

While some believers espouse a chaotic world because it appeals to their sense of adventure, desire for stimulation, and access to rarefied knowledge, others, I believe, genuinely offer their tales as warnings to others: a gesture of protectiveness and abstract solidarity; a pro-social act in a post-social world. Non-obvious knowledge about self-protection is offered to others freely. While the tales certainly fulfill the conventional role of "cautionary tales" about dangers in the modern world, the sorts of advice implicit in the crime legend are always idiosyncratic and peculiar. It is specific sorts of advice that cannot be covered by the usual warnings and guidelines about crime, such as traveling in groups, avoiding dark places at night, and so forth. Fear is thus managed through specific, and often arcane rituals of protection rather than reversion to traditional, and very generalized, protective practices.

Debunkers, on the other hand, voice fear of a world in which real and hoax threats cannot be sorted out; where media sources become so distrusted as to be useless, and where the rise of "the rule of the mob" is always a looming possibility. Again, social entropy, and a loss of authority is perceived to be at work. While more pronounced a tendency among believers than debunkers, most interlocutors in the study consistently placed tales within the context of a crumbling social infrastructure. That is, that they were likely to say that contemporary conditions (from poor schooling to tabloid television) fostered the hunger for rampant untruths.

Devoid of accountable authorities and responsible bystanders, replete with universal distrust of one's neighbor and a striking sense of hopelessness to be heard about one's fears, the world evoked by participants is atavistic, anarchic, and Hobbesian. It is also one where information of an authoritative nature about one's society cannot necessarily be expected. Contrasting believers and debunkers, I find that different sorts of sources of information are distrusted. Yet since all participants enter the conversation, the negotiation of truth and distrust of most conventional sources of information about crime (for instance, local print media) are common denominators and "working principles" under which the veracity of sources are debated. Debunkers generally were more interested in the facts or lack of facts behind a given story than were believers. Believers generally emphasized the *value* of the story as a warning tale regardless of its basis in fact. Even where some sense of safety emerges from the debunking of crime legends in the present, the near future is regarded with great fear.

AWARENESS AS SOLIDARITY

People who warn others about threats are performing what they believe to be a helpful act. This act may take the form of a specific warning, or a testimony about how depraved the modern world can be. In either case the desire is largely to pass along information that conveys a reality, rather than to maliciously spread scary stories or to speak figuratively. The tendency for people online to forward such legends to friends, relatives, and co-workers goes beyond the mere technological ease of the action. Even before the Internet, and still now, there have been those who duplicate, distribute, and post flyers in public places warning of threats to drivers from gang initiation rituals, LSD-laced children's stickers, and Satanic corporations. That practice was much more labor-intensive, and no doubt, as on-line access becomes more and more popular, it will begin to shape the nature of dissemination practices as well. So far, it has mimicked this earlier practice: becoming embellished in certain circulated versions but retaining the essential information about the nature of the threat.

This practice of conscious embellishment (which I am differentiating from the natural tendency of dates, places, and case details to mutate in informal speech settings) causes the transmission of such tales to be referred to by some detractors as "hoaxes"—a term which implies intentional deception. Although it is impossible to tell who made up the false references, I am somewhat skeptical of the attribution of maliciousness here. It may be the salience of the story that the embellisher is likely to hold dear. I base this assessment not just on my own observations, but also on existing research which holds marginal the role of intentional hoaxing, even in the most socially conflictual circumstances like riots (Knopf, 100–101). To some extent, however, the challenge to the intentional deception or "hoax" model of rumor is implied in the anonymity of the act—what does an *anonymous* hoaxer have to gain by trying to convince someone something awful is true, when they know it isn't, especially if no action is called for other than "being aware?" As hard as it is to trace back the path of an urban legend, it is even more difficult to find the specific moment of an embellishment.

THE BODY AS CURRENCY

All three case studies that I present and analyze here have to do with crimes against the body. What these three case studies represent is the appropriation of the body, by violent or coercive means, for profit. In all three cases, criminals commit these crimes in order to sell something of high scarcity to a group of secretive buyers who disregard the value of human life. All three fulfill their traditional "horror tale" function as cautionary tales about straying into the arms of a stranger, doing (or even viewing) pornography, or shopping alone. But in addition, they address the fears that our bodies are mere currency to those more powerful than us.

While science-fiction, from Mary Shelley's *Frankenstein* and Robert Louis Stevenson's *The Strange Case of Dr. Jekyll and Mr. Hyde* to the *X-Files*, approaches the appropriation of the body as a consequence of the scientific will to power, the crime legend instead describes the appropriation of the body as a decadent market phenomenon. The market shall desire; the market shall have. Commodification knows no bounds, and no one nor any entity (government, civil society, social movements) shall stand in its way. But the market is a cipher, a soulless and mindless force. If one syndicate stopped stealing kidneys, another would start, it is assumed, since kidneys are scarce and in demand. The persistence of crime legends is owed neither to their basis in real events nor the lack of credible countervening debunkings, but in their underlying *resonance*, providing fuel for the legend to spring up anew, with a fresh set of details and locales. At the same time, the cultural work of the legend itself tames and makes less abstract these fears of physical insecurity by describing crime in a way that it can be overcome by controllable, specific personal practices. Simultaneously, this practice reinforces the idea that crime itself cannot be controlled collectively, and that it is an endemic part of the social landscape.

PRIVATE LIFE NOW AND IN THE FUTURE

For the believer, public life exposes you and your loved ones to victimization at any place or any time by rational, malevolent, and organized networks of flesh pilferers. To make things worse, no one is really planning to do anything about it. The very act of passing along a legend subtly acknowledges this; the lack of public panic accompanying these stories suggests an "idleness" to this word-of-mouth genre. Neither recourse (rescue from the threat) nor verification (to know the scope and reality of it) is sought. In some cases, further clarification is actually fought against.

For the debunker, public life is a sinking ship of irrational beliefs, tabloid sensibilities, bogeypersons of the week, gullibility, and evidence-free claims about reality—in short, a madding crowd. For some debunkers, the public life experienced by believers may come to fruition if certain "dumbing down" trends continue. Certain Internet news groups, such as *alt.folklore.urban*, offer a refuge for these skeptics where they expect to be among the similar-minded. Mostly they are. But not always.

By contrast, private life, among one's intimates and narrow-cast inter-locutors on the Internet, offers safety and the latitude to experiment with ideas about the outside world, where people will listen and respond, even if in a hostile and combative manner. On the Internet, you will be heard. It doesn't matter if you don't have proof. You can hold forth unfettered. If you manage to get thrown out of one group (an unlikelihood), there is always another.

In this sense, the "private" aspect of the increasingly "public" Internet retains its importance, in the form of a kind of "hypersubjectivity" which has been reinforced dramatically by the commercialization of the Internet. In a peculiar way, authority in both the sense of *authoritative knowledge* and in the sense of *law and order* are struggled with in this study of crime legends. That is, what is urban and contemporary about these legends is their rela-tionship to certain larger themes of hyper-individualism, which are reflected in both their content and the talk about them.

Appendix 1

Three Photocopied Warnings about the "Lights Out" menace, representing a popular means of legend dissemination before widespread Internet access. Gathered in Queens and Nassau Counties, New York, in 1993.

✳ READ ✳

SAFE SAFE SAFE SAFE

News

DATE: October 15, 1993.

FROM: Pat Duffy. Manager, Safety Department

TO: All Employees and their Families

We were made aware of the following bulletin from the Norfolk
Southern Police Department (Virginia); and have confirmed through
the New Castle County and Wilmington Police Departments that
similar events have occurred in Los Angeles. Chicago, and
Baltimore. Please take the time to read the remainder of this
memo and inform your family members and friends. This awareness
and precaution is important for both drivers and passengers,
whether at home or traveling on business or pleasure.

BULLETIN

!!! THERE IS A NEW GANG INITIATION !!!

"This new 'initiation' of 'MURDER' is brought about by Gang
members driving around with their car lights off. When you flash
your car lights to signal them that their lights are out, the
Gang members take it literally as 'LIGHTS OUT', so they follow
you to your destination and kill you!!! That's their initiation.

Two families have already fallen victim to this initiation ritual
in the St. Louis and Chicago areas.

This information should be given widespread distribution on your
respective territories and posted on all bulletin boards. Beware
and inform your families and friends.

DO NOT FLASH YOUR CAR LIGHTS FOR ANYONE

The above information was furnished by the Illinois State Police
Department".

*Beware' this random violence has got
the Queens & Bklyn of N.Y.

Management Services Corp
One Plaza
xx, NY 10421
xxx-3577

December 1, 1993

MEMO TO: ALL OFFICERS, DEPARTMENT HEADS & SUPERVISORS

SUBJECT: Random Violence Directed Against Motorists

The following bulletin circulated by the Los Angeles, Chicago & Baltimore Police Department has been forwarded to us by the Queens Borough Commander of the New York City Police Department because the problem has spread to the New York Metropolitan area. After reading this bulletin, please take the time to inform your family and friends of its content. This awareness and precaution is important for both drivers and passengers whether at home or traveling on business or pleasure.

BULLETIN

THERE IS A NEW GANG INITIATION!!! THIS NEW INITIATION OF MURDER IS BROUGHT ABOUT BY GANG MEMBERS DRIVING AROUND IN THE EVENING WITH THEIR AUTOMOBILE LIGHTS OFF. WHEN YOU FLASH YOUR CAR LIGHTS TO SIGNAL THEM THAT THEIR LIGHTS ARE OUT, THE GANG MEMBERS TAKE IT LITERALLY AS "LIGHTS OUT". THEY THEN FOLLOW YOU TO YOUR DESTINATION AND ATTEMPT TO KILL YOU. THAT'S THEIR INITIATION.

This information should be given widespread distribution. Please make as many copies as requested and post on the bulletin boards in your offices.

DO NOT FLASH YOUR CAR LIGHTS FOR ANYONE!

James J. Gannon

DATE: MARCH 11, 1994

TO: ALL EMPLOYEES AND THEIR FAMILIES

RE: "LIGHTS OUT KILLINGS" BULLETIN

FROM: JOHN CURCIO, SAFETY/PERSONNEL DIRECTOR

READ

I WAS MADE AWARE OF A PROMINENT DANGEROUS SITUATION PRESENTLY OCCURRING IN VIRGINIA, LOS ANGELES, CHICAGO, BALTIMORE AND NOW IN NEW YORK. PLEASE TAKE THE TIME TO READ THE REMAINDER OF THIS MEMO AND INFORM YOUR FAMILY MEMBERS AND FRIENDS. THIS AWARENESS AND PRECAUTION IS IMPORTANT FOR BOTH DRIVERS AND PASSENGERS, WHETHER AT HOME OR TRAVELING ON BUSINESS OR PLEASURE.

BULLETIN

THERE IS A NEW GANG INITIATION!!!!!!!!

THIS NEW INITIATION OF MURDER IS BROUGHT ABOUT BY GANG MEMBERS DRIVING AROUND WITH THEIR CAR LIGHTS OFF. WHEN YOU FLASH YOUR LIGHTS TO SIGNAL THEM THAT THEIR LIGHTS ARE OUT, THE GANG MEMBERS TAKE IT LITERALLY AS "LIGHTS OUT", SO THEY FOLLOW YOU TO YOUR DESTINATION AND KILL YOU!!! THAT'S THEIR INITIATION.

TWO FAMILIES HAVE ALREADY FALLEN VICTIM TO THIS INITIATION RITUAL IN THE ST. LOUIS AND CHICAGO AREAS.

THIS INFORMATION SHOULD BE GIVEN WIDESPREAD DISTRIBUTION ON YOUR RESPECTIVE TERRITORIES AND POSTED ON ALL BULLETIN BOARDS. BEWARE AND INFORM YOUR FAMILIES AND FRIENDS.

DO NOT FLASH YOUR CAR LIGHTS FOR ANYONE!!!!

THE ABOVE INFORMATION WAS FURNISHED BY THE ILLINOIS POLICE DEPARTMENT AND RECEIVED BY DRIVER DANIEL DUFORT.

Appendix 2

Schedule of Initial Interview Questions and Table of Interview Respondents

Choose Nickname/Confidentiality
Age
Sex
Racial/Ethnic Background
Highest Educational Degree
Occupation, including "student"
Parents' Most Recent/Last Occupation
Parents' Highest Educational Degree
Would you describe the place you live as rural, suburban, or urban?
What country do you live in?
What country were you born in?
Do you have kids? If so, ages?
Have you, or anyone close to you, ever been the victim of a violent crime?
When did you first hear (this) story?
Have you heard different versions of it?
Did (the story) frighten you when you first heard it? Does it frighten you
     now?
A number of people both on and off the Internet have disagreed about
     whether reports of (this story) are true. What do you think?
Have you changed your mind about the truth of (this story) since you first
     heard about it?
If so, what made you change your mind?
What things make you think (this story) is or is not true?
Did you find participating in (posting, responding) one or more newsgroups
     about this topic fun, informative, frustrating, mixed—how would you
     describe your reaction?

Did you find yourself upset or angry at any point during these disagreements
    and discussions about (this story)? If so, why?
Have you discussed the story with friends, family, or acquaintances in a
    setting other than the Internet? If so, how would you compare those
    discussions with ones you've had in news groups?
What, if anything, do you think the story can tell us about the society that
    we live in?

Table of Interview Respondents

Name	Country of Birth/Country of Residence	Age	Sex	Racial/Ethnic Background	Occupation	Reside in Rural, Urban, or Suburban Area
Greatbrit	UK/US	45	M	W	Computer Specialist	U
Simon	UK/UK	34	M	W	Computer Administrator	S
J. Pass	US/US	30	M	W	Director of Business Development	S
Adrian	UK/UK	27	M	W	Student	S
Henry	US/US	27	F	W	Student	S
Helge	Germany/US	40	M	W	Computer Programmer	U
BT	US/US	27	M	W	International Health Consultant	S
Vicki Lou	Australia/ Australia	43	F	W	Program Dev. Disability Services	S
Meri	US/US	21	F	W	Student	U
Louise	US/US	42	F	W	Lawyer/lobbyist	R
Jupiter	US/US	38	F	W	Computer Programmer	U
Joseph B.	US/US	23	M	W	Student	S
Mothra	US/US	51	F	W	Housewife and Mother	R
Gayle	Zambia/NZ	36	F	W	Self-Employed Nutrition Consulting	S
Stuart	UK/Finland	27	M	W	Computer Programmer	S
Skrybe	Australia/ Australia	26	M	W	Public Service Information Tech	S
Charles L.	US/US	30	M	W	Student	S
Milky Way	US/US	45	M	W	Temp Worker	U
PJ	US/US	27	M	W	Health Care Transplant Coordinator	S
David L.	US/US	38	M	A	Secretary	U

Notes

1. A news group, also sometimes referred to as a "Usenet" group, is a public forum on a given specific topic. They have existed and have been accessible to Internet users since the early 1990s. In 1995 there were about 5,000 groups; in 2000 there are over 40,000 owing to the rapid growth of the Internet itself and the easier technical access to them since the beginning of the World Wide Web in 1994–5. Frequencies for participant contributions ("posts") to each group can now be determined by archives. There are also private news groups, often run by commercial Internet service providers for their own members, but they are not considered here. "Listservs" are mass electronic mail distribution systems to which one must subscribe in order to participate. In both the listserv and the news group, participants may post and respond to each other's posts. Some are moderated by people who filter posts and curb behavior and some are not. Those groups and lists with high volume often have participants that will limit themselves to reading and posting to certain "threads" within the group, meanings specific conversations.

2. Source: Photocopied flyer, (n.d. but circa September 1994) Chicago area.

3. Derby discussed his encounter with the "Lights Out" story in an electronic posting on January 26, 1994 in the Internet group *alt.folklore.urban*. When Derby visited his own family over the holidays and asked about the story, he paradoxically found that the Tulsans had not heard it, but relatives and friends from elsewhere in Oklahoma, from Minnesota, from Seattle, and from Nashville all had, albeit with different locales and slightly different details attached.

4. The term "claims-making" is a term used in the social construction of social problems literature to describe a process by which individuals and groups define and frame distinct events and practices as social problems — their severity, their definitional parameters, social effects, culprits and victims — via organized civic activity, with the goal of influencing major influential institutions, such as governments, the news media, and large foundations, in order to produce social reform. See Spector and Kitsuse, 1977; Best, 1991.

5. This likely also means that these tales are the most interesting to skeptics, who dominate *alt.folklore.urban*. However, being interesting to skeptics, in turn, has likely led to more public (i.e. news media) debunking interest, thereby defining the tale as one with a considerable debunking history. This distinguishing characteristic is important, insofar as these stories are different than newer or less popular (or perhaps simply less standardized) tales not just in level of circulation, but in their socially negotiated "truth status." This archive

is distinct from the archiving capabilities of the former DejaNews website, now subsumed under Google.com.

6. There is also some preliminary indication that the Internet-using population in the United States is becoming more like its general population; see Maguire 1998. Web address for Cyberatlas reference, "Digital Divide Persists in U.S." July 8, is: http://cyberatlas.internet.com/big_picture/demographics/article/0, 1323, 5901_158701,00.html. Retrieved June 16, 2000. Not all interviewees in this study were from the United States, however. (See Appendix 2)

7. Eventually, too, the Internet's archiving capacities will mean that these legend cycles can be more accurately documented, although this is not yet the case. News group archives have been available since 1997, from a commercial web-site, Deja.com, in searchable form and begin with 1995. During the Spring of 2000 they have been temporarily withdrawn. However, public news groups are not otherwise archived systematically, although some individual groups may maintain "highlight" archives on their own.

8. Deja.com, a news group search engine, reported that users of its free service were "young, affluent, and college-educated" and 60 percent male. It claimed to attract 4 million unique users per month. The same service is now provided by Google.

9. Details of the search procedure can be found within specific chapters to follow.

10. Most anecdotal evidence, described by Brunvand and other debunkers, of print news media dissemination of urban legends comes from columns or syndicated talk shows such as radio's Paul Harvey and daily newspaper's Dear Abby. Unfortunately, these are not archived as articles, but they are popular and could be considered an exception to the general rule that the news media is not a primary disseminator of crime or urban legends.

11. In fact, the stability of the genre "rumor" is also questioned in this same later section.

12. Throughout the study, a distinction between rumor, legend, and hoax will be made. Rumor will be used to mean, more generally, a primarily word-of-mouth, extra-institutional bit of information (story or allegation) which has not yet demonstrated cyclicality; thus, a legend is a specific form of rumor. Both genres share the characteristic of uncertain origins. Hoaxes, on the other hand, often have traceable origins and can be shown to be born of an intentional effort to deceive. These distinctions are ideal-typical, rather than comprehensive, of all similar discursive practices.

13. The predominance of "wedge drivers" is apparently not a necessary feature of civil strife or war. Nkpa's study (1975) of rumor during the Nigerian civil war, 1967–1970, by contrast, shows the dominance of "pipe dream" rumor and relatively low levels of "wedge driving" ones.

14. These fears appeared outside folklore as well; see Benedict (1931) and Taylor (1959).

15. See <http://www.snopes.com> for *The Urban Legends Reference Pages* and a list of links to other pages concerned with urban legends.

16. It is noteworthy that Kapferer (1990) continues to use the term "rumor" for what would equivalently be termed an urban or contemporary legend in English language literature. This, and the citations that he uses, reflect a continuity between rumor and legend research in France. Kapferer (1989: 470) was also able to add questions designed to measure the prevalence of certain health-related rumors to Gallup's "standard omnibus polls" through the *Institut Français d'Opinion Publique*. To my knowledge this is the only recent incidence of national survey techniques employed in the research of rumor.

CHAPTER TWO: THE MARKET IN SNUFF FILMS

1. Institutional Presence: The practice, as both a thought-to-be-real practice and as a rumor, has been discussed in formal settings, such as newspapers, scholarly, and mass-market non-fiction works, over a considerable period of time. The presence of 'moral entrepreneurs' (see below) behind a legend is usually key in producing greater institutional presence; in the case of the snuff film the most consistent moral entrepreneurs have been prominent feminists such as Catherine Mackinnon.

2. Cognate Version: In folklore, the version which is appears to be modal or serves as a 'core' set of ideas which appear in all variations. It is a traditional categorization term in folklore discussed, for instance in the work of Dundes (1989: 64, 71). There is debate among folklorists about the necessary relationship between cognate types or versions and particular versions as told "in the field." Dundes also argues that a disciplinary over-emphasis on the search for "ur-" or cognate versions has tended to discount local contextual meanings.

3. Frederick Grittner (1990) describes this as a series of moral panics, to which rumors were often attached, which surfaced in Great Britain in the 1880s and the United States in the 1910s which concerned alleged abductions of young women (particularly white women) for the purposes of forced prostitution. These abductions often included deception and drugging. Modern versions of this legend are discussed in a later chapter of this study.

4. With regards to popular accounts of coercion and violence in the adult film industry, see, for example, Linda Lovelace (1986). For a contrasting view of the adult film industry, see Strossen, p 182—191. But for legend analysis purposes it matters less whether Lovelace's claims can be substantiated than that prominent feminists, including Gloria Steinem (1995: 239, 250) have given them widespread exposure.

5. The latter rumors were among those which hinted at victim complicity in the murders, although it should be noted that these rumors seemed to pertain only to the Polanski house victims and not to the LaBiancas.

6. Lake committed suicide in Canada before he could be extradited.

7. Svoray's 1997 book has not been widely reviewed, but most (Boxall, 1997; Preston 1997) concur with my own opinion that it is poorly sourced and that Svoray was taken in more than once by a series of consummate con artists and the usual fake films. More importantly, by the end of his journey he is left without a shred of corroboration.

8. This may be the latest incarnation of the snuff film legend—children as the primary victims rather than adult women, likely fueled by the recent accelerated campaigns against child pornography. See also Thomas (1991: 259-261), which makes passing (and unsourced) references to international traffic in children for sex rings and the snuff film trade.

9. Actually Svoray accuses various law enforcement agencies of being simultaneously indifferent and complicit in protecting the underground snuff film industry. (pgs. 80, 146–147, 161)

10. Expansive Definition: This is a term I am using to describe a definition of a poorly documented practice which includes other better documented practices as a means to enhance its likelihood of being true. This choice of definition is used exclusively by casual believers and not by fervent believers or moral entrepreneurs; the latter always use the strict or 'cognate' version. For instance, the term 'snuff film' has developed an expansive definition to include fictional representations of victims being killed on camera or footage of any death scenes

that have been widely circulated or broadcast, such as Dr. Jack Kevorkian's assisted suicide of a man in 1998.

11. Inferential Belief or Version: The process by which the likelihood of a practice being real rather than merely rumored is defended by reference to other practices which are 'real' (conventionally documented) and which are represent similar qualities of human behavior, usually that of depravity. For instance, inferential belief of the snuff film may involve the reiteration of really existing practices, such as widespread violence against women or the prurient, voyeuristic interest in scenes of destruction, to infer the 'realistic' probability of snuff film markets.

12. Groups devoted to folklore, *alt.folklore.urban* being the largest, can be found in Usenet at *alt.folklore.** when using an on-line search engine. The number of individual posts were calculated by selecting, with a commercial news group search engine, *Deja.com*, posts picked up by the search term "snuff film*" where the asterisk serves as a wild card as in conventional library boolean searches.

13. The following exchange appeared in a message posted by David. David's message reproduced an earlier exchange between himself and Carol. For convenience I have inserted their names above their contributions.

14. Author: "Is it your opinion that snuff films exist? How would you define a snuff film?"

15. When questioned by skeptics about whether the films he saw might have been fakes, Svoray gently dismisses his critics by speculating that they are unwilling to accept that there is real evil in the world. When skeptics persisted, he reminded them of how evil Nazis are and asserted that he intuitively "felt" the films to be real. (Svoray, p. 74–76)

16. The "western" angle is intriguing. Is Zodiac referring to JMcClennan's use of his own non-experience of snuff films as excessively logocentric? Or of his reference to the "lack of evidence," exposing him as someone who relies excessively upon modernist sources of authority? Does he think that JMcClennan is failing to acknowledge the unreason present in human society? Is Japan meant as a counter-example, i.e. not "western?"

17. "A Pinch of Snuff," Urban Legends Reference Pages, http://www.snopes.com/horrors/madmen/snuff.htm

18. Notice the high variation in the price of snuff film access suggested by various people. The cost of access to the snuff film varies depending upon one's theories about who makes them and distributes them. Organized crime and international actors expect $50,000 to $100,000 for viewings or copies, whereas in other scenarios the tapes are exchanged for very little profit and for sick thrill alone.

19. The search term "snuff w/2 film!" was used where w/2 specifies that "snuff" and "film" are to be found within two words of proximity and where ! serves as a wildcard permitting "films, filming, film maker" etc. to be included. Newspapers included in the index but published outside the countries listed were excluded. Headlines and first lead paragraphs of articles were searched.

20. Search terms were "snuff NEAR film!" where both words were required to appear in the same sentence and where ! serves as a wildcard code.

21. As with newspaper reports on investigations into alleged snuff films associated with actual violent crimes, no follow-up broadcast stories appeared in the index.

22. Perhaps the imputed location was chosen for its remoteness, or possibly because of the initial association of the birth of the snuff film legend with Manson family home in Death Valley, probably still fresh enough to Angelenos in 1977.

23. This series, now canceled, thematically, if somewhat inscrutably, linked serial and ritual murder in the present day with the oncoming ides of the change in millennium.

24. Visually, this "mikado" scene resembles a famous fake snuff film series called "Guinea Pig" which was made in Japan, and also the snuff film screened for the protagonist searching for his wayward daughter in Paul Schrader's film "Hard Core." In other words, the writers were clearly familiar with the genre. "Guinea Pig" films have more than once been mistaken for real snuff films by viewers, including actor Charlie Sheen, who contacted the FBI about it in 1991. (McDowell, 1994)

CHAPTER THREE: STOLEN BODY PARTS

1. One variation, though, has children victims that live to tell. In Brazil, *sacaojo* stories circulate where it is alleged that homeless children are kidnapped and their eyes stolen, after which they are released back to the streets (Scheper-Hughes, 1998: 50).

2. The common denominator in producing these allegation cycles, may not be developing countries but ones with considerable political or economic upheaval—recently, the theft of organs from children was similarly alleged in Tirana, Albania. (H. Smith, 1998)

3. On rumors associated with previous epidemics see Fee and Fox (1988).

4. This version (with two stories and commentary added) has circulated in a number of places, in formal news groups and informal e-mail chains. This particular one was sent to me by an employee of a large telecommunications firm, where it had been bouncing around between other employees with personalized warnings. Brunvand (1999: 398–401) documents the same New Orleans section of the text nearly verbatim to the one presented here.

5. Campion-Vincent (1997: 3) traces the first world, seduced businessman version in Europe back to 1990; Brunvand (1993) notes its appearance in the United States in 1991.

6. Turner's "Topsy/Eva" metaphor is taken from a two-sided doll popular in the late antebellum south. One side was a white, blonde, blue-eyed little girl, dressed up and combed, and the other a black girl, in shabby clothes, with unkempt hair.

7. In my study the Topsy/Eva element is strongest in the stolen-body parts case study, but echoes of it appear in the snuff film legend (traders in snuff are either above or below normal middle-class existence, elites or lowlifes) and the shopping mall abductions (in its connection to white slavery legends).

8. The free market in health care also means that the United States' social inequalities are starkly represented in organ *recipient* queue composition, as well. See, for instance, Mark D. Somerson, (1998) "Race, Sex, Income of Recipients Play Role in Kidney Transplants." *The Columbus (Ohio) Dispatch*, October 7, 1C. As to how such inequalities may be perceived by those considering signing organ donor cards, see Barry D. Kahan, "Organ Donation and Transplantation: A Surgeon's View," in Youngner, p. 135. Scheper-Hughes (1998: 51) reports that similar, albeit more dramatic recipient-queue inequalities in South Africa have dramatically affected willingness to donate organs, aided by the revival of traditional *muti* scares, in which it is alleged that people are eviscerated and organs are stolen for ritual practices by witches.

9. Using the commercial search engine *Deja.com*, the following search protocols were employed. Search terms were "kidney + (theft|thie*)" and "organ + (theft|thie*)+! kidney" where the asterisk serves as a wildcard, picking up

words such as "thieves" "thievery" and where "+!" means "and not" and "|" mean "or."

10. See "Viewpoint: " *Daily Texan*, December 1, 1996. http://tspweb02.tsp.utexas. edu/Interconnect/INDEX/STAUFFER-GOLD. INTERCONNECT$STORY

11. Author's Milky Way interview, 10/27/98. Milky Way refers to Freemantle, 1995.

12. "bit.listserv.transplant FAQ": Mike H. refers to a permanent on-line archive which answers frequently asked questions about transplantation. Originally it was developed by medical students at Yale, but it is now on health and medical servers around the country. According to the United Network on Organ Sharing, however, organ donation participation is fairly steady and has not fluctuated greatly. Yet they too worry about the potential effect of this rumor. (See http://www.unos.org)

13. The search term "(steal or stolen) w/sentence (kidney or organ)" was used where "w/sentence" specifies that terms from the first parenthetical set are to be found within the same sentence as those from the second. Newspapers included in the index but published outside the countries listed were excluded. Headlines and first lead paragraphs of articles were searched. A total of 89 articles were retrieved initially under this search protocol and 35 of these found to be unrelated to the topic, leaving 54 in remainder to be considered. (For example, one headline from an excluded article read, "Stolen Drug May Harm Kidneys")

14. Using the *Reader's Guide to Periodical Literature*, for the years 1989 through 1999, the words "stolen, steal, stealing, theft, and thief" were matched against "kidney or organ."

15. Search terms "(steal or stolen) w/sentence (kidney or organ)" were used.

16. See the website of the National Kidney Foundation (eleckid/myths.shtml); or that of the United Network on Organ Sharing (http://www.unos.org/newsroom, "Myths")

17. Although the victim is black and the perpetrators white, little is made of the racial angle in the story, other than to hint that the doctor more easily regarded him as prey and the family thought he might be more amenable to a pay off, in the form of an educational trust fund for his children.

18. United Network on Organ Sharing, Position Statement, February 13, 1997. Available on their website. Refers to Lloyd Grove, "The Kidney that Got Away," Washington Post, April 2, 1991, E01

19. "Official Statement from New Orleans Police Department Concerning Rumors of Crime Ring Involved in Kidney Stealing, Lt. M. Defillo, 1/30/97" posted on the department website. I confirmed this desire of the NOPD to hold people criminally accountable for the rumor with a phone call (12/30/98). Under the guise of being a businessman nervous to travel to New Orleans after hearing kidney theft rumors from co-workers in his Wall Street office, the author's husband Gregg Wirth called the Public Affairs office and was reassured that no such threat existed, and further that the department was deluged about two years ago with fearful callers, prompting the Official Statement. The department would still like to find out who "started" this unflattering rumor about the Big Easy.

Chapter Four: Shopping Mall and Theme Park Abduction Legends

1. http://www.snopes.com/horrors/parental/kidnap.htm

2. National Film Registry, Library of Congress: (http://lcweb.loc.gov/film/nrfser1. html)

3. It is very likely that these numbers are underestimates, as the exact wording for keyword search terms is more elusive than as with the previous two case studies. Using Deja.com, search terms were "mall + (abduct*| kidnap*) + !alien" and "disney + (abduct*|kidnap*)" where "*" serves as a wildcard and "|" means "or" and "+! alien" excludes all entries with the word "alien" appearing in the text.

4. Rosalie's post is no longer on the group's archive; Google search used.

5. The program is described in more detail at: http://www.walmartfoundation.org, under the page on children and "Code Adam"

6. Of course, it is impossible to know definitively that the legend was more coherent, generally speaking, in most tellings in previous decades or in exclusively off-line circles. What we can say, however, is that they are not currently seen together much in Internet news group settings.

7. The only reference found to an "American Press" wire is a newspaper by the same name in Lake Charles, Louisiana. A search of the paper's on-line archive (http://www.americanpress.com), between 1995 and 2000, shows no such stories. Even assuming that the intended reference was the Associated Press, no such stories appeared in that online archive either, which runs from July 1997 to the present (http://wire.ap.org). A general search for crime stories about Woodbury Common mall drew none. Search terms in addition to the mall name include "security" "Woodbury" "parent" and "mall." However in 1993, a five year old girl was abducted from Woodfield Mall in Illinois, possibly by a man dressed as a woman. (O'Connor, 1993: 19) The incident bore no resemblance to the story, however.

8. One list member noted that the mall in question, near Newburgh, New York is in fact a group of stores surrounding an outdoor plaza which in fact has no "doors" out of which to slip.

9. Morin, p. 118, 142. From an "action" or practical viewpoint, the denunciation of the rumor as an anti-Semitic canard made sense since the scapegoating version was creating real threats of incipient panic. However, a standardization of the text in its most egregious form resulted from the process of official debunking. The same seems to be true in this case study, as well, although debunking has taken place mainly in informal media settings like news groups, rather than from official sources.

10. See the Urban Legends Reference Page: (http://www.snopes.com/horrors/madmen/mallgrab.htm) for more details on the Inside Edition episode.

11. This easy cross-monitoring of news groups was made much easier by the web-based news group services, beginning in 1995.

12. Interview, exchange via email, April 1999

13. Of further interest is the fact that this large number of references refers to a diverse array of crimes across the United States and Canada. The Susan Smith case in South Carolina (October 1994) and the JonBenet Ramsey case in Colorado (December 1996) account for only 7 of these 1,238 references.

14. This database indexes articles from the 50 U.S. newspapers with the highest circulation as well as major dailies from Canada, Australia and New Zealand, and Great Britain and Ireland. The search term "mall and (abduct! or kidnap!)" was used to retrieve the initial 725 newspaper articles, where "!" serves as a wildcard to retrieve "abductions, abductors" etc.

15. No doubt in certain circles, abduction for the purpose of satanic ritual abuse might be a popular attribution for the problem. No evidence was found in the present study that this was a favored explanation by believers. Alien abduction was not, either, and fervent believers in either of these groups of abductors do form specific subcultures somewhat separate from the mainstream of U.S. soci-

ety. Nonetheless, satanic ritual abuse had a much lower public profile at the time of the study than did alien abduction, perhaps due to a significant amount of press criticism of day-care sex abuse trials by the late 1990s.

16. See Saul S. Friedman, (1978) *Incident at Massena* (New York: Stein and Day). The book concerns an incident in the 1920s in Massena, NY where a child disappeared and local Orthodox Jewish shopkeepers were suspected when a "ritual murder" rumor spread, with their stores searched and their Saturday services surrounded by an unruly mob. No violence ever did take place and the girl, having wandered away, was returned safely. Friedman examines the social dynamics in the town that led to the incident (and conflicts among national Jewish organizations in response), in the process pointing out how rare such occurrences were, even then, such that it attracted national attention and embarrassed town administrators into public denials (p. 98–99, 160–161). Large, anonymous or urban shopping districts seem to attract such rumors and scarelore more often.

17. Barbara and David Mikkelson, *Urban Legends Reference Pages*.

CHAPTER FIVE: DEBUNKERS AND THEIR ORBIT

1. For definitions of these terms, see Chapter One: Introduction

2. Again, it is impossible to know with any certainty whether the volume of legend circulation has really increased with the emergence of the Internet, and what the relative balance of word-of-mouth to electronic transmission is, short of a General Social Survey-level inquiry.

3. For instance, a small number of writers who are fervent believers in the existence of a market in snuff films, whose work is described in the previous case study chapter on snuff films, all cite one another's work, but this situation is likely the exception that proves the rule.

4. The journal is published by the Committee for the Scientific Investigation of Claims of the Paranormal, as a print journal and a web magazine that claimed 259,160 visits between March 1998 and October 1999.

5. Based on the total number of posts to the group between October 1, 1995 through December 31,1995, which according to Deja.com archives, was 5,745. It is likely that the yearly total is much lower than 23,000 if it is assumed that news group usage increased throughout the year with the fourth quarter representing peak usage for the year.

6. 1995 is the year that Deja.com began keeping public news groups archived, thus enabling the gathering of data on the volume of usage. The group *alt.folklore.urban* has existed since 1991, however. As with all public news groups, the number of messages posted is an ineffective measure of the number of people reading the news group regularly. Many and perhaps most readers "lurk" rather than "post" and many of the people who do post are "regulars" who may post several times a day.

7. Furr uses the term "old hat" member for long-term, seasoned, active members, but that term is not commonly seen.

8. Posting in all capital letters is broadly taken as "yelling" in the system of netiquette, even if the poster had no such intention.

9. "Message boards" are set up on many websites, run by entities both large and small, commercial and otherwise. These message boards enable anyone who visits a web page to post comments on a section of it. These comments are generally open to anyone and are not uniformly, or even commonly, archived. There is often a "free-for-all" quality to the message boards; they are not as

heavily peer-policed as news groups are. Nor are there any standards of argument or evidence. So, it is not surprising that long-term public news group users see the message boards as an instructive negative example of what the news groups could become.

10. The contrast here with the polarized situation that has emerged between UFO enthusiasts and debunkers is again noteworthy. UFO enthusiasts are socially organized, rely upon a unified set of facts and texts, and are *primarily* concerned with the perceived facts of UFO contact. Indeed, as both Dean (1997) and Saler (1998) report, the meaning of the thought-to-be-factual contact with aliens is highly diverse, ranging from joyous cosmic epiphanies to tales of exploitation, torture, and terror.

11. Nearly every news group grapples with the problem of placing boundaries on appropriate discussion. Most regular participants in a news group mainly object to "static": jokes, digressions on religion and politics, and advertisements, for instance.

12. The issue of civility is not peculiar to this news group; many good discussion groups and listservs have been killed off by sniping fights even when these arguments stay on point. Other group members drift away since they are bored by the conversation, those who do stay and try to tell the parties to "take it offline" often find recalcitrance in response. As a result, another tier of members will sign off after tiring of reading arguments about having arguments. This is the way in which groups can collapse or "empty out."

13. The group's archive has a cultural life of its own, attracting attention from *Harper's* Readings section (Chan, 1994) and the *New York Times* (n.b.,1994). As for newcomers who wander in to these debunkers' places, they do so briefly, often approaching with a "sharing" orientation, similar to the way in which might approach a storytelling group or a campfire with a horror tale, or especially lately, with inspirational narratives. The debunkers, though, generally do not examine the poster's motives, but rather go forward with a dissecting analysis.

14. Matthew Cecchi, 9, had died in just such a manner a few days before the posting appeared in the group. Brandon Wilson, 20, killed Cecchi with a knife in an Oceanside Harbor, California, beach restroom on November 14, 1998 while the child's aunt waited outside. Wilson was apprehended in Los Angeles. (Monteagudo and Dalton, 1998)

15. Excerpts presented here; expurgations mine.

16. Colloquially denounced as "bandwidth static" or "bandwidth hogging" the volume of mass e-mail distributed in chain letter fashion can rapidly develop a formidable effect. According to the U.S. Department of Energy's Computer Incident Advisory Capability Website (http://hoaxbusters.ciac.org) "If each of the so-called good Samaritans sends the letter on to only 10 other people (most send to huge mailing lists), the ninth resending results in a billion e-mail messages, thereby clogging the network and interfering with the receiving of legitimate e-mail."

CHAPTER SIX: CRIME LEGENDS AND THE ROLE OF BELIEF

1. That fervent believers in this study were unlikely to use this "expansive definition" strategy in the snuff film case is of some curiosity, considering that, as Best (1990: 66) shows, in more well-constructed campaigns, such as that of "missing children" the use of "domain expansion" is common. In the latter more events are redefined to fit the definition of the problem; in this way the

scope of the originally defined problem is appears to be amplified. In the case of the missing children panic, runaways and children taken in custodial interference cases were pulled into the existing category which was initially designed to describe the much rarer instance of stranger abduction.

2. Brawley, who is black, is accused of fabricating a 1988 gang-rape assault upon her by four white police officers in a bias attack in Wappingers Falls, New York; Bernall died in the gunfire at Columbine High School, Littleton, Colorado, in 1999 and subsequently an inspirational rumor circulated that she had been martyred for her Christian beliefs. In each case, challenges to the veracity of the associated narratives were defended against by using the "symbolic truth" or "greater truth" claim.

3. Some versions account for the trade in snuff films with less social distance between traders and buyers involved. (Lovelace 1986: 41; Lederer 1980: 67, 272; Kappeler 1992, 97; Morgan 1992: 87). All of these authors appeal to a feminist audience and, nonetheless, preserve the "unknown quantity of trade" attribute also seen in the "elite-conspiracy" account of snuff film production.

4. This is not to say that real crimes do not generate narrative evolutions, but rather that "affirmative unknowns" are easier to generate in the presence of an authorless text than with one that has an "official" life in the formal mass media or law enforcement records, with the exception of cases where media and/or government conspiracy are alleged—a situation that proved rare in the current study.

5. Arendt notes: "[Masses accustomed to propaganda] are predisposed to all ideologies because they explain facts as mere examples of laws and eliminate coincidences by inventing an all-embracing omnipotence which is supposed to be at the root of every accident." (p. 352) Thus the "world-view" is held to be more factual than individual facts, and such facts only are useful to the extent that they reflect back upon the "reality" depicted by the ideology.

6. Dworkin did use insider knowledge claims about the snuff film market in her Congressional testimony, but this seemed either a part of a traditional journalistic claim to be protecting sources, or more cynically to dodge a set of skeptical demands for evidence.

7. This can be achieved by using a widely available filtering technique called "killfile" in which the news group reader can designate certain authors or subjects to be filtered out of view. Many news groups routinely post directions for newcomers on how to use this command to foil known trolls and offensive posters.

8. MUD, or multi-user dimension and MOO, multi-user dimension, object-oriented. These both enable synchronous gatherings of people on-line, the latter enabling the use of graphics rather than only text. News groups, message boards, and listservs are asynchronous and thus have been in the past aptly termed "bulletin boards." Those who have written extensively about Internet culture have tended to focus upon synchronous, real time virtual environments (MUDs and MOOs) rather than the asynchronous, and much more widely used, news group format. Part of the explanation for this overemphasis is that "real-time" sites have a greater role in cybersex and fantasy games, although they are much more diverse than that.

9. This is not to say that the popularization of post-structural ideas is easily shown to be a corruption of major philosophical interventions. Both Michel Foucault (1970: p 389+) and Jacques Derrida (1981: 20, 24, 35) for instance, at times have made statements which are logically (and more to the point, widely understood) as completely idealist, where meaning is an effect of the power to define, distinguish, and categorize.

10. Kaminer's goal is to link these styles of interpretation and self-presentation with the larger disavowal of rationality throughout a number of cultural sites in the contemporary U.S.. "[TV talk shows] are emblematic of a widespread preference for feelings over ideas that is celebrated by recovery and other personal development movements."(p. 38) The current discussion, however, will draw more upon the aspect of therapeutic culture that continues to make claims upon the world of ideas, however unintentionally or hypocritically. Engagements in news groups about crime legends did not manifest a wholesale disavowal of "the head" in favor of "the heart" but rather in some cases interlocutors wished to redefine claims to objective truth in terms of patently subjective evidence.

11. The "all suffering is relative" ethos present in self-help and twelve-step groups, emerged initially with the positive intention of maximal inclusion of those who might be inclined to deny their own difficulties using altruism: one really hasn't got it so bad in life as some others have, so perhaps a stoic attitude would do. However, as Kaminer notes (p. 26), exaggerated claims quickly emerged among self-help writers, particularly those addressing unhappy childhoods, and what Kaminer regards as manifestations of the personality or the human condition became redefined as addictions.

CHAPTER SEVEN: CRIME LEGENDS, PROTECTION, AND FEAR

1. There are some crime legends that present the predator as more expressive, such as those involving "madmen" who cleverly make sure to leave a witness to their murders, thus exercising restraint. See Brunvand (1999: 58, 89–97) Here still, however, little is known in modern crime legends about the predator—in contrast to exhaustive media treatments of serial killers like Richard "Night Stalker" Ramirez or Jeffrey Dahmer.

2. It might be argued that the predators in a snuff film scenario aren't limited to those who make and sell them, but also include those consumers who seek them out. In this more extensive view of predation, the expressive element clearly dominates: viewers have no motives except their own depraved gratification.

3. The latter is associated with analyses of the Third-World versions of the stolen body parts legends; see Campion-Vincent (1997) and Scheper-Hughes, (1998).

4. Schools represent a somewhat ambiguous case here. They have been the subject of a series of more organized moral panics (e.g., the day care sex abuse scandals, and more recently, the perils of youth Internet access) as well as highly-publicized mass shootings between 1996 and 1999. Nonetheless they do not figure prominently in crime legends.

5. According to Cohen and Felson's summary of Uniform Crime Reports data, robbery increased 263 percent, aggravated assault 164 percent, rape 174 percent, and homicide 188 percent.

6. Propensity to commit crime cannot alone explain the rise in crime during the period 1960–1974 as the population aged 16–24 increased only by 31 percent and unemployment and poverty-levels decreased. (Cohen and Felson, 598–604)

7. While films such as *8mm* and *Hard Core* reinforce this sense that no one will observe or intervene besides the independent thinking protagonist, television crime drama, such as NBC's *Law and Order* and *NYPD Blue* is still "modern" rather than "post-" in its depiction of a functioning set of law enforcement and civil society institutions which intervene in crime, and individuals within these institutions are portrayed as competent and caring, at least in relation to their

jobs. If any postmodern themes emerge in these tales, they usually involve personal foibles of officers such as alcoholism, promiscuity, or family dysfunctionality. Showalter (1997: 12) argues that the appeal of the "superhero" fantasy-genres speaks more directly to disappointment in modern crime control institutions.

8. "Devolved" in the sense that a *gesellschaft,* characterized by increasing centralization, is being eroded towards a more decentralized, particularistic, and privatized world.

9. Ambitions for these syndicates do not seem to exceed that of profits, and even seem to be less politically ambitious than various real-world, ethnic or regional "mafias."

10. Altheide (1997) measured the frequency of the use of the term 'fear' in texts and headlines in the Los Angeles Times and ABC News transcripts in the comparison years 1985 and 1994. In-text references increased 64 percent while those in headlines increased 161 percent. Overwhelmingly this increase was attributable to crime and violence stories rather than AIDS, cancer, the environment or drugs. Altheide remarks that while it is generally agreed that the mass media, in both news and fiction formats, inundates audiences with fear-provoking material, especially that relating to crime and violence, and that audience research seems to confirm the fearfulness of the polled population, the mechanism defining this relationship remains unclear. (Altheide 1997: 648)

11. Aside from the instrumental gains seen by the British government, other historical and cultural forces were implicated: racism and xenophobia against Caribbean and South Asian immigrants and the sense of besieged "English identity," the collapse of the industrial sector and resulting in reignited labor militancy and class conflict, along with the emergence of new social movements.

12. This review of empirical studies conducted from 1981 to 1992 found that neighborhood watch programs may produce a protective buffer between an individual's fear of crime and general psychological stress, likely through the latent effect of increased neighborhood level social interaction. Nonetheless there is no strong evidence (from self-reports of victimization and fear of it) that these approaches are effective in reducing crime or the fear of it. Norris and Kaniasty's study, as well as most others measuring fear and victimization, control for several variables including a variety of measures of statistical risk.

13. A number of criminologists in recent years have tried to refine the process by which the fear of crime is understood in a social context. Reid et al (1998) as well as Rountree and Land (1996) have emphasized the distinctiveness of the constructs of perceived risk and emotion-based fear. Both lead to inconsistent outcomes in terms of self-protective activities, actual victimization, and the influence of fear upon overall social anxiety. Thus a number of criminologists have called for more qualitative research to increase the clarity around these categories.

14. As such, women and the aged might engage in conjecture that even a relatively minor property crime could result in injury, or that an injury resulting from a quick and limited assault could nonetheless be a serious one, or that burglary or robbery could escalate to sexual assault (Warr, 1984; Gordon and Riger, 1988).

15. Stanko (1995: 53) and O'Malley (1992: 61) have suggested that in the respective cases of Britain and Australia, the insistence upon a risk-fear paradox and none too subtle victim blaming by various official assessments is typical. Perhaps in the case of the United States, this is less common, or simply more subtle. In the latter case, it seems the risk-fear paradox enjoys little official imprimatur although victim-blaming is far from absent, the promotion of pri-

vate gun ownership as a means of crime control complicates the matter of victim-blame.

16. Glassner relies heavily upon Gerbner and Gross' (1976) "mean world syndrome" research, which links television viewing rates to feelings of living in an unsafe neighborhood, to beliefs that crime is rising, and to overestimations of one's chances of victimization. However, the direction of causation in these matters, as some critics (Hughes, 1980; Wober and Gunter 1982) have noted, is unclear.

17. Showalter (1997) makes similar arguments about recent moral panics, although with a relatively greater emphasis upon psychoanalytic underpinnings of contemporary fears, particularly those having to do with the transformation of gender roles.

18. In an interview on February 9, 2000 with New York public radio talk show host Brian Lehrer, Glassner repeats the fact that crime has declined significantly in the 1990s no less than four times in an interview lasting approximately twenty minutes. ("On the Line," 2000)

19. In particular, the role of demographics is often underestimated. Some have suggested that the maturation of the various illicit drug markets into stable turfs partially explains the decline in gun homicide, while others point to community policing, the incapacitative effects of incarceration itself, and a decline in unemployment as factors.

20. Certainly the pro-gun lobby in the US has portrayed the issue of self-protection in similar dichotomous terms—where the collective risks and costs presented by individual gun ownership is routinely ignored in favor of the rare occasion in which gun ownership for the purposes of self-protection is actually successfully utilized for such a purpose. (For a contrasting view see Kleck, 1997) While the actual figures around legitimate defensive gun use are highly disputed, gun-lobby interests interpret and present for public forums all available data to mean that defensive gun use by private individuals is a legitimate crime control strategy that displaces law enforcement and saves tax dollars.(Duncan, 2000)

21. The problem of poverty is an instructive but perhaps ominous example: proposals to dismantle Social Security in the United States not only re-individualizes the problem of old age income supports but at the same time undermines the limited degree of social solidarity between the generations and classes that it engendered. It is equally plausible that this erosion of social solidarity was a precipitator of this laissez-faire ascendancy, rather than its outcome.

22. For a contrasting view emphasizing the expansion of state-directed social control, see Nils Christie (1993), *Crime Control as Industry*, London: Routledge

23. In the case of drug interdiction, ideological loyalty to federalist principles were jettisoned. The document recommends the launch of an official War on Drugs at the federal level. Here too, it was first proposed that military deployment had a potential role to play in drug trade interdiction.

24. In an uncharacteristic concern, the potential negative impact upon civil liberties posed by the incursion of federal level agencies and/or coordination with regards to violent crime is cited, while civil liberties are described as an impediment to drug interdiction. (U.S. Department of Justice, 2) Perhaps in the former case the specter of gun control animates this concern, but neither gun ownership nor the Second Amendment are mentioned directly.

25. To some extent, the press began to echo this pessimism as well. See, for instance, *Newsweek*'s cover story, "The Plague of Violent Crime," by Aric Press and Staff, March 23, 1981, 46–54, which emphasizes crime control failures and the virtues of self-policing.

26. The experiment in the 1990s in New York City, under the auspices of the Giu-
     liani Administration, to engage in policing-based "front-end" crime control
     through an aggressive "quality of life" approach was a notable exception to the
     conservative laissez-faire rule. For the most part the strategy has been politically
     expedient, and has coincided with decreases in street crime that outpace
     declines across the nation during the 1990s, for which the Giuliani Administra-
     tion was happy to take credit. It remains to be seen whether other urban centers
     will use the same approach and what the long-term outcome will be. However
     Matthews (1992) sees the adoption of the "broken windows" (after the ideas of
     Kelling, 1996), approach by conservative urban governments as consistent with
     the ongoing sense of exhaustion and complacency regarding crime, accepting
     the criminogenic qualities of post-industrial free market economies as a perma-
     nent feature of urban landscapes. (Matthews, 1992: 44–45)

Bibliography

Aderman, David, Sharon Brehm, and Lawrence Katz. 1974. "Empathetic Observation of an Innocent Victim: the Just World Revisited." *Journal of Personality and Social Psychology* 29, 342–347.

Allport, Floyd and Milton Lepkin. 1945. "Wartime Rumors of Waste and Special Privilege: Why Some People Believe Them." *Journal of Abnormal and Social Psychology* 40, 3–36.

Allport, Gordon and Leo Postman. 1947. *The Psychology of Rumor.* New York: Henry Holt.

Altheide, David. 1997. "The News Media, the Problem Frame, and the Production of Fear." *Sociological Quarterly* 38: 4, 647–668.

Arendt, Hannah. 1973. *The Origins of Totalitarianism.* New York: Harcourt Brace.

Associated Press. 1976. "Morganthau finds Film Dismembering a Hoax." *New York Times*, March 10, p. A1.

Associated Press. 1999a. "Serial Killer Sentenced to Death for Crime Spree." June 30.

Associated Press. 1999b. "UC Berkeley Researchers Human Organs Center Will Act as Organ Police." November 7.

Baer, Will Christopher. 1998. *Kiss Me, Judas.* New York: Viking.

Bailey, Ronald. 1990. "Behind the Baby Parts Story." *Forbes*, v. 145, May 28, p. 372.

Barlay, Stephan. 1977. *Sexual Slavery.* New York: Ballantine.

Barraclough, Jenny. 1996. "Whose Pound of Flesh?" *The Observer (London)*, May 19, R8.

Barry, John. 1995. "Too Good to Check." *Newsweek* v 125, June 26, p 33.

Barry, Kathleen. 1979. *Female Sexual Slavery.* Englewood Cliffs, NJ: Prentice Hall.

Bayley, David H. and Clifford D. Shearing. 1996. "The Future of Policing." *Law and Society Review.* 30: 3, 585—606.

Beck, Ulrich. 1992. *The Risk Society: Towards a New Modernity.* London: SAGE.

Becker, Howard. 1973 [1963]. *Outsiders: Studies in the Sociology of Deviance.* New York: Free Press

Ben-Amos, Dan. 1976. *Folklore Genres.* Austin: University of Texas Press.

Benedict, Ruth. 1931. "Folklore." *Encyclopedia of the Social Sciences* 6.

Bennett, Gillian E.A. and Paul Smith. 1984. *Perspectives on Contemporary Legend.* Sheffield: Sheffield University Press.

Best, Joel. 1988. "Dark Figures and Child Victims: Statistical Claims About Missing Children." in Joel Best, ed., *Images of Issues: Typifying Social Problems*. New York: Aldine de Gruyter.

Best, Joel. 1990. *Threatened Children: Rhetoric and Concern about Child-Victims*. Chicago: University of Chicago Press.

Best, Joel. 1991. "Road Warriors on Hair Trigger Highways: Cultural Resources and the Media Construction of the 1987 Freeway Shootings Problem." *Sociological Inquiry*. 61:3, 327–345.

Best, Joel and Gerald Horiuchi. 1985. "The Razor Blade in the Apple: The Social Construction of Urban Legends." *Social Problems* 32:2, 488–497.

Best, Steven and Douglas Kellner. 1997. *The Postmodern Turn: Critical Perspectives*. Guilford, CT: Guilford Publishers.

Billington-Grieg, Teresa. 1913. "The Truth About White Slavery." *English Review*, June, 435–446.

Boxall, Michael. 1997. "Review: Gods of Death by Yaron Svoray." *Salon.com*, (http://www.salon.com/books/sneaks/1997/10/16review) October 16. Retrieved May 15, 2000.

Brightman, Joan. 1995. "Mystery Guests." *American Demographics* 17, August: 14–16.

Brunvand, Jan Harold. 1981. *The Vanishing Hitchhiker: American Urban Legends and Their Meaning*. New York: W.W. Norton.

Brunvand, Jan Harold. 1984. *The Choking Doberman and Other 'New' Urban Legends*. New York: W.W. Norton.

Brunvand, Jan Harold. 1986. *The Mexican Pet: More New Urban Legends and Some Old Favorites*. New York: W.W. Norton.

Brunvand, Jan Harold. 1993. *The Baby Train and Other Lusty Urban Legends*. New York: W.W. Norton.

Brunvand, Jan Harold. 1999. *Too Good to be True: The Colossal Book of Urban Legends*. New York: W.W. Norton.

Buckner, H.Taylor. 1965. "A Theory of Rumor Transmission." *Public Opinion Quarterly* 29: 54–70.

Bugliosi, Vincent with Curt Gentry. 1974. *Helter Skelter: the True Story of the Manson Murders*. New York: W.W. Norton.

Bureau of Justice Statistics, United States. 1988. *Report to the Nation on Crime and Justice*. Washington. DC: GPO.

Campion-Vincent, Véronique. 1990. "The Baby-Parts Story: A New Latin American Legend." *Western Folklore* 49, January.

Campion-Vincent, Véronique. 1997. "Organ Theft Narratives." *Western Folklore* 56, 1- 37.

Caplow, Theodore. 1947. "Rumors in War." *Social Forces* 25, 298–302.

Caputi, Jane. 1987. *The Age of Sex Crime*. Bowling Green, OH: Bowling Green State University.

Caro, Mark. 1999. "Legend Lives On, Despite No Proof that Snuff Films Exist." *Chicago Tribune*, February 26.

Chan, Terry. 1994. "Readings: Urban Legends—The Internet's Believe it or Not." *Harper's,* October, p. 25, 28.

Chelminski, Rudolph. 1996. "A Lie That Won't go Away. Rumor that Third World Children are Being Abducted for Their Organs." *Reader's Digest* v. 148, June, p. 188–92.

Chorus, A. 1953. "The Basic Law of Rumor." *Journal of Abnormal and Social Psychology* 48, 313–314.

Chancer, Lynn S. and Pamela Donovan. 1994. "The Mass Psychology of Punishment." *Social Justice* 21:3, Fall, 50–72.

Christie, Nils. 1993. *Crime Control as Industry.* London: Routledge.

Cohen, Lawrence E. and Marcus Felson. 1979. "Social Change and Crime Rate Trends: A Routine Activities Approach." *American Sociological Review* 44:4, August, 588–608.

Cohn, J.S. 1998. "Snuff Film." *New Republic* 219, December 14, p. 6.

Cohen, Stanley. 1972. *Folk Devils and Moral Panics: The Creation of Mods and Rockers.* London: MacGibbon and Kee.

Cook, Robin. 1977. *Coma: A Novel.* Boston: Little, Brown.

Currie, Elliott. 1985. *Confronting Crime: An American Challenge.* New York: Pantheon.

Curtis, Pavel. 1996. "Mudding: Social Phenomena in Text-Based Virtual Realities." in Peter Ludlow, *High Noon on the Electronic Frontier: Conceptual Issues in Cyberspace.* Cambridge: MIT Press, 347–373.

Cyberatlas.com. 1999a. "Gender Split Nearly Even by 2001." (http://www.cyber-atlas.com) May 27. Retrieved May 15, 2000.

Cyberatlas.com. 1999b. "38 Million Americans Getting Wired." (http://www.cyber-atlas.com) May 27. Retrieved May 15, 2000.

Darnton, Robert. 1983. *The Great Cat Massacre and Other Episodes in French Cultural History.* New York: Basic Books.

Dean, Jodi. 1997. *Aliens in America: Conspiracy Cultures from Outerspace to Cyberspace.* Ithaca, NY: Cornell University Press.

De Becker, Gavin. 1999. *Protecting the Gift: Keeping Children and Teenagers Safe.* New York: Dial Press.

Dégh, Linda. 1971. "Comments for Richard Dorson: Is there a Folk in the City?" in Americo Paredes and Ellen J. Stekert. eds., *The Urban Experience and Folk Tradition.* Austin: University of Texas Press.

Dégh, Linda. 1994. *American Folklore and the Mass Media.* Bloomington: Indiana University Press.

Derrida, Jacques. 1981. *Positions.* Chicago: University of Chicago Press.

Dibbell, Julian. 1996. "A Rape in Cyberspace." in Peter Ludlow. *High Noon on the Electronic Frontier: Conceptual Issues in Cyberspace.* Cambridge: MIT Press, 389–400.

Donnerstein, Edward and Neil Malamuth. 1984. *Pornography and Sexual Aggression.* NY: Academic Press.

Donnerstein, Edward, David Linz, and Steven Penrod. 1987. *The Question of Pornography: research findings and implications*. New York: Free Press.

Donash, Judith. 1999. "Identity and Deception in the Virtual Community." in Marc A. Smith and Peter Kollock, *Communities in Cyberspace*. New York: Routledge.

Donovan, Pamela.1998. "Armed with the Power of Television: Reality Crime Programming and the Reconstruction of Law and Order in the United States." in Mark Fishman and Gray Cavender, eds., *Entertaining Crime: Television Reality Programs*. New York: Aldine de Gruyter.

Duncan, Otis D. 2000. "Gun Use Surveys: In Numbers We Trust?" *The Criminologist: Official Newsletter of the American Society of Criminology* 25: 1, January-February, 1–7.

Duncan, Martha Grace. 1997. *Romantic Outlaws. Beloved Prisons: The Unconscious Meanings of Crime and Punishment*. New York: New York University Press.

Dundes, Alan. 1980. *Interpreting Folklore*. Bloomington: Indiana University Press.

Dundes, Alan. 1989. *Folklore Matters*. Knoxville: University of Tennessee Press.

Dworkin, Andrea. 1979. *Pornography: Men Possessing Women*. Toronto: G.P. Putnam.

Dworkin, Andrea. 1986. *Testimony to United States Attorney General's Commission on Pornography*. Washington. DC: GPO.

Eckholm, Erik.1998. "Arrests Put Focus on Human Organs from China." *New York Times*. February 25.

Edmondson, Brad. 1992. "Demographic Legends: Editor's Note." *American Demographics,* April.

Emery, David. 1997. "The Kidney Snatchers." *Urban Legends and Folklore. About.com.* (http:// www.urbanlegends.about.com), Retrieved July 3, 2000.

Eyewitness News. 1996. "Baby Stolen From Womb, Mother Killed." Television News Broadcast, WAGA-TV (Atlanta), 5 p.m.

Fee, Elizabeth and Daniel M. Fox. 1988. *AIDS: The Burdens of History*. Berkeley: University of California Press.

Fine, Gary Alan. 1987. "Welcome to the World of AIDS." *Western Folklore* 46: 192–197.

Fine, Gary Alan. 1992. *Manufacturing Tales: Sex and Money in Contemporary Legends*. Knoxville: University of Tennessee Press.

Fishman, Mark. 1980. *Manufacturing the News*. Austin: University of Texas Press.

Foucault, Michel. 1970. *The Order of Things*. London: Tavistock.

Fox, Renee C., Laurence J. O'Connell, and Stuart J. Youngner. 1996. "Introduction" in Stuart J. Youngner, Renee C. Fox, Laurence J. O'Connell, *Organ Transplantation: Meanings and Realities*. Madison: University of Wisconsin.

Freemantle, Brian. 1995. *The Octopus : Europe in the Grip of Organized Crime*. London: Orion

Friedman, Saul. 1978. *Incident at Massena*. New York: Stein and Day.

Furr, Joel. 1995. "Chicken Little: Myth, Reality, and Absurdity in Alt.folklore." *Internet World*, February, 87–89.

Gans, Herbert. 1979. *Deciding What's News: A Study of CBS Evening News, NBC Nightly News, Newsweek, and Time*. New York: Pantheon.

Garland, David. 1996. "The Limits of the Sovereign State: Strategies of Crime Control in Contemporary Societies." *British Journal of Criminology* 36: 4, Autumn, 445–471.

Garland, David and Richard Sparks. 2000. "Criminology, Social Theory, and the Challenge of Our Times." in David Garland and Richard Sparks, eds., *Criminology and Social Theory*. Oxford: Oxford University Press.

Genge, N.E. 2000. *Urban Legends: The As-Complete-As-One-Could-Be Guide to Modern Myths*. New York: Three Rivers Press.

Gerbner, George and Larry Gross. 1976. "Living With Television: The Violence Profile." *Journal of Communication* 26, Spring, 173–199.

Giddens, Anthony. 1990. *The Consequences of Modernity*. Stanford: Stanford University Press.

Giddens, Anthony. 1991. *Modernity and Self-Identity: Self and Society in the Late Modern Age*. Stanford: Stanford University Press.

Glassner, Barry. 1999. *The Culture of Fear: Why Americans Are Afraid of the Wrong Things*. New York: Basic Books.

Gleick, Elizabeth. 1994. "Rumor and Rage. Stories That Foreigners are Stealing Babies Lead to Acts of Violence Against Americans." *People Weekly* v. 41, April 25, p. 78–80.

Goldstein, Amy. 1997. "Woman Alleges Fiancé Stole Her Heart, Brother's Kidney: Lawsuit Highlights Ethical Complications of Organ Donation." *Washington Post*. October 21, A1.

Gordon, Margaret T. and Stephanie Riger. 1988. *The Female Fear*. New York: Free Press.

Gorman, Tom and Kate Folmar. 1999. "O.C. College Triggers New Willed-Body Investigation." *Los Angeles Times*. Orange County Edition, October 16, p. A1.

Gorphe, François. 1927. *La Critique du Témoinage*. Paris: Donnoz Libraire.

Goska, Danusha. 1997. "Waking Up Less Than Whole: The Female Perpetrator in Male-Victim Kidney Theft Legends." *Southern Folklore* 54:3, 196–210.

Griego, Diana and Louis Kilzer. 1985. "Truth About Missing Kids: Exaggerated Statistics Stir National Paranoia." *Denver Post*, May 12, p. 1A+.

Grittner, Frederick. 1990. *White Slavery: Myth, Ideology, and American Law*. New York: Garland Publishing.

Grossman, Wendy M. 1997. *Net Wars*. New York: New York University Press.

Gurr, Ted. 1977. "Crime Trends in Modern Democracies since 1945." *International Annals of Criminology* 16, 41–85.

Gusfield, Joseph. 1955. "Social Structure and Moral Reform: A Study of the Women's Christian Temperance Union," *American Journal of Sociology*, LXI, November.

Gusfield, Joseph. 1963. *Symbolic Crusade: Status Politics and the American Temperance Movement*. Urbana: University of Illinois Press.

Hale, Chris. 1996. "Fear of Crime: A Review of the Literature." *International Review of Victimology* 4, 79–150.

Hall, Stuart, Chas Critcher, Tony Jefferson, John Clarke, and Brian Roberts. 1978. *Policing the Crisis: Mugging, the State, Law and Order*. London: Macmillan.

Hart, Bernard. [1916] 1927. "The Psychology of Rumor." in *Psychopathology: Its Development and Its Place in Medicine*. New York: Macmillan, 94–124.

Hebdige, Dick. 1979. *Subculture: the Meaning of Style*. London: Routledge.

Hertsgaard, Mark. 1988. *On Bended Knee: The Press and the Reagan Presidency*. New York: Farrar, Straus, Giroux.

Hilgartner, Stephen and Charles Bosk. 1988. "The Rise and Fall of Social Problems: A Public Arenas Model." *American Journal of Sociology* 94, July, 53–78.

Hösch-Ernst, Lucy. 1915. "Die Psychologie der Aussage." *Internationale Rundschau* 1: 15–33.

Hughes, M. 1980. "The Fruits of Cultivation Analysis: A Reexamination of Some Effects of Television Watching." *Public Opinion Quarterly* 44, 287–302.

Human Rights Watch—Asia. 1995. *Rape for Profit: Trafficking of Nepali Girls and Women to India's Brothels*. New York: Human Rights Watch.

1994. "List: Internet Hot Spots." *New York Times Magazine*, January 30, p. 8.

Jacoby, Jacob. 1984. "Perspectives on Information Overload." *Journal of Consumer Research*. v. 10, March, 432–435.

Janofsky, Michael. 1999. "Far Beyond Columbine. Rancor and Tension." *New York Times*, October 4.

Jones, Cathaleene and Elliot Aronson .1973. "Attribution of Fault to a Rape Victim as a Function of the Respectability of the Victim." *Journal of Personality and Social Psychology* 26, 415–419.

Johnson, Eithne and Eric Schaeffer. 1993. "Soft Core/Hard Gore: *Snuff* as a Crisis in Meaning" *Journal of Film and Video*, Summer-Fall, 40–59.

Kadetsky, Elizabeth. 1994. "Guatemala Enflamed." *Village Voice*, v39 no. 22, May 31, p. 25–29.

Kaminer, Wendy. 1992. *I'm Dysfunctional, You're Dysfunctional*. New York: Vintage.

Kapferer, Jean-Noël. 1989. "A Mass Poisoning Rumor in Europe." *Public Opinion Quarterly* 53, Winter, 467–481.

Kapferer, Jean-Noël. 1990. *Rumors: Uses, Interpretations, and Images*. New Brunswick, NJ: Transaction Books.

Kappeler, Suzanne. 1992. "Pornography: the Representation of Power" in Catherine Itzin, ed., *Pornography: Women, Violence, and Civil Liberties*. London: Routledge.

Kelling, George. 1996. *Fixing Broken Windows: Restoring Order and Reducing Crime in Our Communities*. New York: Martin Kessler Books.

Kerekes, David and David Slater. 1994. *Killing for Culture: An Illustrated History of Death Film, from Mondo to Snuff*. London: Creation Books.

Klapp, Orrin. 1972. *Currents of Unrest: an Introduction to Collective Behavior*. New York: Holt, Rinehart, and Winston.

Kleck, Gary. 1997. *Targeting Guns: Firearms and Their Control*. New York: Aldine de Gruyter

Knapp, Robert. 1944. "A Psychology of Rumor." *Public Opinion Quarterly* 8: 22–37.

Knopf, Terry Ann. 1975. *Rumors, Race, and Riots*. New Brunswick. NJ: Transaction Books.

Koenig, Fredrick. 1985. *Rumor in the Marketplace: The Social Psychology of Commercial Hearsay*. Dover, MA: Auburn House.

Koenig, Fredrick. 1992. "Comment. On J. Kapferer and T.W. Smith." *Public Opinion Quarterly* 56, Summer, 234.

Lacitis, Erik.1999. "Shock Absorption: In this Information Age, We've Become Blase." *Seattle Times*, February 7.

Landler, Mark. 1991. "What Happened to Advertising?" *Business Week*, September 23, 66–72.

Lanning, Kenneth. 1992. "Investigator's Guide to Allegations of 'Ritual' Child Abuse." Quantico, VA: Behavioral Science Unit. National Center for the Analysis of Violent Crime. Federal Bureau of Investigation.

LaPierre, Richard T. 1938. *Collective Behavior*. New York: McGraw-Hill, 177–178.

Lea, John and Jock Young. 1984. *What is to be Done about Law and Order?* Harmondsworth: Penguin.

Lederer, Laura. 1980. *Take Back the Night: Women on Pornography*. New York: William Morrow.

Lerner, Melvin and Dale Miller. 1978. "Just World Research and the Attribution Process: Looking Back and Ahead." *Psychological Bulletin* 85: 1030–1051.

Leventhal, Todd. 1994. "The Child Organ Trafficking Rumor: A Modern Urban Legend'." *USIA Report to the United Nations Special Rapporteur*, December, Washington. DC: GPO. 1–44

Lianos, Michalis with Mary Douglas. 2000. "Dangerization and the End of Deviance." in David Garland and Richard Sparks, eds., *Criminology and Social Theory*. Oxford: Oxford University Press.

Linz, Daniel, Edward Donnerstein, and Steven Penrod. 1987. "The Findings and Recommendations of the Attorney General's Commission on Pornography: do the psychological 'facts' fit the political fury?" *American Psychologist* 42, 946–953.

Lipowski, Z.J. 1970. "The Conflict of Buridan's Ass, or Some Dilemmas of Affluence." *American Journal of Psychiatry* 127, September, 273–279.

Loader, Ian. 1997. "Policing the Social: Questions of Symbolic Power." *British Journal of Sociology* 48:1, March, 1–18.

Lopez, Laura. 1994. "Dangerous rumors. Story that children are being stolen and killed by Americans for organ transplants." *Time* v. 143, April 18, p. 48.

Lovelace, Linda with Mike McGready. 1986. *Out of Bondage*. Secaucus: Lyle Stuart.

Ludlow, Peter. 1996. "Self and Community On-Line." in Peter Ludlow, *High Noon on the Electronic Frontier: Conceptual Issues in Cyberspace*. Cambridge: MIT Press, 313–316.

Lyotard, Jean-François. 1985. *The Postmodern Condition: A Report on Knowledge*. Minneapolis: University of Minnesota Press.

Macdonald, Andrew. 1978. *The Turner Diaries*. Hillsboro, WV: National Alliance Books.

Mackinnon, Catherine. 1993. *Only Words*. Cambridge: Harvard University Press.

Maguire, Tom. 1998. "Top Lines: Web Nets the Masses." *American Demographics*. December.

Malthotra, Naresh K. 1984. "Reflections on the Information Overload Paradigm in Consumer Decision Making." *Journal of Consumer Research* 10, March, 436–440.

Matthews, Roger. 1992. A Replacing Broken Windows: Crime, Incivilities, and Urban Change." in Roger Matthews and Jock Young. *Issues in Realist Criminology*. London: SAGE, p 1–50.

Mays, Alan. 1994. "Lights Out/Blood Initiation Rumors." *FOAF Tale News: the Newsletter of the International Society for Contemporary Legend Research* (Heindel Library, Pennsylvania State University, Harrisburg). November.

McDonald, A.P. 1972. "More on the Protestant Ethic." *Journal of Consulting and Clinical Psychology* 39, 116–122.

McDowell, Rider. 1994. "Movies to Die For." *San Francisco Chronicle*. August 7.

Mikkelson, Barbara and David. n.d. *The Urban Legend Reference Pages*. (http://www.snopes.com) Retrieved May 15, 2000.

Millea, Holly. 1999. "Voyeurs, Guns, and Money." *Premiere Magazine*, v. 12. no. 7. March.

Miller, Leslie. 1995. "A Net Gain: 24 Million Users Are Logging On." *USA Today*. October 31, 8D.

Miller, Martin. 1994. "Disney's Lost and Found: Tales of Missing Children have Happy Endings at Park." *Los Angeles Times*, Orange County Edition, June 12, M3.

Monteagudo, Luis, Jr. and Rex Dalton. 1998. "Parents' Worst Nightmare: Boy's Throat is Slashed in Restroom as Aunt Waits." *San Diego Union-Tribune*. November 16, p. A1.

Morgan, Robin. 1992. *The Word of a Woman: Feminist Dispatches. 1968—1992*. New York: W.W. Norton.

Morin, Edgar. 1970. *Rumor in Orleans*. London: Heinemann.

Murphy, William. 1993. "It's Lights Out for Hoax." *Newsday*, December 11, p. 13.

Nkpa, Nwokocha K. 1975. "Rumor Mongering in War Time." *Journal of Social Psychology* 96: 27–35.

Norris, Fran and Krzysztof Kaniasty. 1992. "A Longitudinal Study of the Effects of Various Crime Prevention Strategies on Criminal Victimization, Fear of Crime, and Psychological Distress." *American Journal of Community Psychology* 20: 625—48.

O'Connor, Phillip. 1993. "Link Seen in Ohio, Woodfield Abductions." *Chicago Sun-Times.* July 2, p. 19.

O'Malley, Pat. 1992. "Risk, Power, and Crime Prevention." *Economy and Society* 21: 3, August, 252—275.

"On The Line with Brian Lehrer." 2000. WNYC-AM (New York), radio broadcast, February 9.

Ove, Torsten. 1999. "Nabbing Children for Sex a Rarity." *Pittsburgh Post-Gazette,* February 28.

Peterson, Warren and Noel P. Gist. 1951. "Rumor and Public Opinion." *American Journal of Sociology* 57: 159–167.

Pilat, Oliver Ramsay. 1965. "Anatomy of a Rumor." *The Realist,* April.

Preston, Gregor. 1997. A Book Review: Gods of Death" *Library Journal* 122, July, p. 106.

Radford, Benjamin. 1999. "Bitter Harvest: The Organ-Snatching Urban Legends." *Skeptical Inquirer,* May-June, 34–39.

Reid, Lesley, J. Timmons Roberts, and Heather Hilliard. 1998. "Fear of Crime and Collective Action: An Analysis of Coping Strategies." *Sociological Inquiry* 68:3, 312–328.

Ridley, Florence. 1967. "A Tale Told Too Often." *Western Folklore* 26:2, 153–156.

Richardson, Ruth. 1996. "Fearful Symmetry: Corpses for Anatomy, Organs for Transplantation?" in Stuart J. Youngner, Renee C. Fox, and Laurence J. O'Connell, *Organ Transplantation: Meanings and Realities.* Madison: University of Wisconsin.

Roeper, Richard. 1999. "S'nuff already: Do the films exist or are they just another urban legend?" *Chicago Sun-Times,* Late Sports Edition, March 21, p. 402.

von Roretz, Karl. 1915. "Zur Psychologie des Gerüchtes." *Österreichische Rundschau* 44: 205–12.

Rosenbaum, Dennis P. 1987. "The Theory and Research behind Neighborhood Watch: Is It a Sound Fear and Crime Reduction Strategy?" *Crime and Delinquency* 33, January, 103–134.

Rosnow, Ralph and Gary Alan Fine. 1976. *Rumor and Gossip: the Social Psychology of Hearsay.* New York: Elsevier.

Rothman, David. 1998. "The International Organ Traffic." *New York Review of Books.* March 26.

Rountree, Pamela Wilcox and Kenneth C. Land. 1996. "Perceived Risk versus Fear of Crime: Empirical Evidence of Conceptually Distinct Reactions in Survey Data." *Social Forces* 74: 1353—1376.

Rubin, Beth. 1996. *Shifts in the Social Contract: Understanding Change in American Society.* Thousand Oaks, CA: Pine Forge Press.

Russell, Diana E.H. 1993. *Making Violence Sexy.* New York: Teacher's College Press.

Sagan, Carl. 1996. *The Demon-Haunted World.* New York: Random House.

Saler, Benson, Charles Ziegler, and Charles Moore. 1997. *UFO Crash at Roswell: the Genesis of a Modern Myth*. Washington, DC: Smithsonian Institution Press.

Salzman, Rachelle. 1995. "This Buzz is for you: popular responses to the Ted Bundy execution." *Journal of Folklore Research* 32: 2, 1995, May-August.

Samon, Katherine Anne. 1993. "The 8 Most Incredible Stories You've Ever Heard." *McCall's*, September, p. 120+

Sanders, Ed. 1971. *The Family: The Story of Charles Manson's Dune Buggy Attack Battalion*. New York: Dutton.

Sasson, Theodore. 1995. *Crime Talk*. New York: Aldine de Gruyter.

Savage, Dan. 1998. "Savage Love." *Village Voice*. December 17.

Scanlan, David. 1994. "Stolen Children? Foreigners Under Suspicion." *Macleans*, v107, April 18, p. 36.

Scheper-Hughes, Nancy. 1992. *Death Without Weeping: the Violence of Everyday Life in Brazil*. University of California Press

Scheper-Hughes, Nancy. 1998. "Truth and Rumor on the Organ Trail." *Natural History*, October, 48—56.

Schrieberg, David. 1990. "Mexican disinformation campaign accuses U.S. of Child-snatching for organ harvesting." *New Republic*, v203, December 24, 12–13.

Schroeder, Barbara. 1996. "Animal Sacrifice." Fox Morning News, KTTV-Los Angeles, Television Broadcast, July 17.

Shenk, David. 1998. *Data Smog: Surviving the Information Glut*. San Francisco: Harper Edge.

Shibutani, Tamotsu. 1966. *Improvised News: A Sociological Study of Rumor*. Indianapolis: Bobbs-Merrill.

Showalter, Elaine. 1997. *Hystories: Hysterical Epidemics and Modern Media*. New York: Columbia University Press.

Skogan, Wesley and Michael Maxfield. 1981. *Coping with Crime*. Newbury Park, CA: Sage.

Smith, Helena. 1998. "Trade in Children's Organs Alleged." *Chicago Sun-Times*, October 28, p. 40.

Smith, R. 2000. "Snuff Films Mayhem ho-hum?" *Toronto Globe and Mail*, February 5, p. B2.

Smith, Susan. 1986. *Crime, Space, and Society*. Cambridge: Cambridge University Press.

Smith, Tom. 1990. "Comment." *Public Opinion Quarterly* 54, Fall, 436

Somerson, Mark D. (1998) "Race, Sex, Income of Recipients Play Role in Kidney Transplants." *The Columbus (Ohio) Dispatch*, October 7, 1C.

Souster, Mark. 1990. "Rumors Abound but Proof of UK Dimension is Elusive." *The Times (London)*, July 28.

Sparks, Richard. 1992. "Reason and Unreason in Left Realism.'" in Roger Matthews and Jock Young, *Issues in Realist Criminology*. London: SAGE, 119–140.

Spector, Malcolm and John I. Kitsuse. 1977. *Constructing Social Problems*. Menlo Park, CA: Cummings.

Spitznagel, Eric. 1994. "Are Today's Actors Up to Snuff?" *Harper's*, August, p. 20+

Stanko, Elizabeth. 1995. "Women, Crime, and Fear." *Annals of the American Academy of Political and Social Science* 539: 46—58.

Stanko, Elizabeth. 1997. "Safety Talk: Conceptualizing Women's Risk Assessment as a 'Technology of the Soul' " *Theoretical Criminology* 1: 4, 479—499.

Steinem, Gloria. 1995. *Outrageous Acts and Everyday Rebellions*. New York: Henry Holt.

Stine, Scott. 1999. "The Snuff Film: The Making of an Urban Legend." *Skeptical Inquirer* 23:3, May-June, 29–33.

Stookey, Laurena L. 1996. *Robin Cook: A Critical Companion*. Westport: Greenwood Press.

Strossen, Nadine. 1995. *Defending Pornography*. New York: Scribner.

Suczek, Barbara. 1972. "The Curious Case of the 'Death' of Paul McCartney." *Urban Life and Culture* 1: 61–76.

Svoray, Yaron with Nick Taylor. 1994. *In Hitler's Shadow: An Israeli's Amazing Journey Inside Germany's Neo-Nazi Movement*. New York: Nan A. Talese.

Svoray, Yaron with Thomas Hughes. 1997. *Gods of Death: Around the World, Behind Closed Doors, Operates an Ultra-Secret Business of Sex and Death: One Man Hunts the Truth About Snuff Films*. New York: Simon and Schuster.

"Snuff Films Just Another Handy Myth to Exploit." 1999. *The Toronto Star*. March 5.

Taylor, Ian and Ruth Jamieson. 1998. "Fear of Crime and Fear of Falling: English Anxieties Approaching the Millennium." *Archives Européenes de Sociologie* 39:1, May, 149–175.

Taylor, Mark. 1959. "Television is Ruining Our Folktales." *Library Journal*, December 16.

Terry, Maury. 1987. *The Ultimate Evil: an Investigation into America's Most Dangerous Satanic Cult*. Garden City, NY: Doubleday.

Theodorson, George and Achilles Theodorson. 1969. *A Modern Dictionary of Sociology*. New York: Thomas Crowell Company.

Thomas, Gordon. 1991. *Enslaved*. New York: Pharos Books.

Torgerson, Dial. 1969. "Ritualistic Slayings. Sharon Tate, Four Others Murdered." *Los Angeles Times*, August 10, p. A1.

Tuchman, Gaye. 1978. *Making News: A Study in the Construction of Reality*. New York: Free Press.

Turner, Patricia A. 1993. *I Heard It Through The Grapevine: Rumor in African-American Culture*. Berkeley: University of California Press.

United States Department of Justice. 1981. *Attorney General's Task Force on Violent Crime: Final Report*. August 17.

U.S. House of Representatives. 1984. *National Organ Transplant Act*. 98th Congress. Public Law 98–507.

U.S. House of Representative. 1981. "Hearing: Missing Children's Act." Subcommittee on Civil and Constitutional Rights. Committee on the Judiciary. November 18.

Wachs, Eleanor. 1988. *Crime Victim Stories: New York City's Urban Folklore.* Bloomington: Indiana University Press.

Walkowitz, Judith. 1992. *City of Dreadful Delight: Narratives of Sexual Danger in Late Victorian England.* Chicago: University of Chicago Press.

Wallace, Susan Besze. 1999. "Val Schnurr Knows What She Said on that Horrifying Day." *Denver Post,* September 28.

Wambaugh, Joseph. 1987. *Echoes in the Darkness.* New York: William Morrow.

Warr, Mark. 1984. "Fear of Victimization: Why are Women and the Elderly More Afraid?" *Social Science Quarterly* 65: 681–702.

Wellman, Barry and Milena Gulia. 1999. "Virtual Communities as Communities: Net Surfers Don't Ride Alone." in Marc A. Smith and Peter Kollock, eds., *Communities in Cyberspace.* New York: Routledge, 167–194.

Wendling, Ted. 1998. "FBI Raids Hollywood Office of So-Called Organ Broker." *Cleveland Plain Dealer.* November 11, A1.

Wireman, Peggy. 1984. *Urban Neighborhoods, Networks and Families.* Lexington, MA: Lexington Books.

Wober, Mallory and Barrie Gunter. 1982. "Television and Personal Threat: Fact or Artifact? A British Survey." *British Journal of Social Psychology* 21: 3, September, 239—247.

Wright, Peter L. 1974. "The Harassed Decision Maker: Time Pressure, Distractions, and the Use of Evidence." *Journal of Applied Psychology* 59, October, 555–561.

Youngner, Stuart J. 1996. "Some Must Die" in Stuart J. Youngner, Renee C. Fox, Laurence J. O'Connell. *Organ Transplantation: Meanings and Realities.* Madison: University of Wisconsin.

Zimring, Franklin and Gordon Hawkins. 1997. *Crime is Not the Problem: Lethal Violence in America.* New York: Oxford University Press.

Zipes, Jack. 1980. "The Instrumentalization of Fantasy: Fairy Tales and the Mass Media." in Kathleen Woodward, ed., *The Myths of Information: Technology and Post-Industrial Culture.* Madison, WI: Coda Press.

Zurcher, Louis A. and R. George Kirkpatrick. 1976. *Citizens for Decency: Antipornography Crusades as Status Defense.* Austin: University of Texas Press.

Index